Nine Worlds of Seid

CW00832563

Shamanistic practices known as *seidr*, often involving interactions with the spirit world and states of altered consciousness, lie at the heart of the pagan religions of Northern Europe. This accessible study explores the ways in which *seidr*, a key element of ancient Scandinavian belief systems described in the Icelandic Sagas and Eddas, is now being rediscovered and redeveloped by people around the world. The book draws on a wealth of research and experience to analyse the phenomenon and place it in context.

Written by someone who is a practitioner as well as a scholar, this is a unique exploration of what Northern 'shamans' do, and how they speak of the spirits they meet. It is set within discussions of shamanism, identity, insider ethnography and new directions in the anthropology of religion. It will fascinate all those with an interest in the possibilities for alternative spirituality in today's world.

Jenny Blain is a senior lecturer in the School of Social Science and Law at Sheffield Hallam University, where she is route leader for the MA in Social Research Methods.

Nine Worlds of Seid-Magic

Ecstasy and neo-shamanism
in North European paganism

Jenny Blain

London and New York

First published 2002
by Routledge
11 New Fetter Lane, London EC4P 4EE

Simultaneously published in the USA and Canada
by Routledge
29 West 35th Street, New York, NY 10001

Routledge is an imprint of the Taylor & Francis Group

Typeset in Times NR MT by Exe Valley Dataset Ltd
Printed and bound in Great Britain by Biddles Ltd, Guildford and King's Lynn

British Library Cataloguing in Publication Data
A catalogue record for this book is available from the British Library

Library of Congress Cataloging in Publication Data
Blain, Jenny.
    Nine worlds of seid-magic: ecstasy and neo-shamanism in northern
    European paganism / Jenny Blain.
        p.   cm.
    Includes bibliographical references.
    1. Shamanism–Scandinavia–Miscellanea.   I. Title.

BF1622.S34 B57 2001
293–dc21   2001041828

ISBN 0-415-25650-X (hbk)
ISBN 0-415-25651-8 (pbk)

To Marion,
who is the future,
and to all my Dísir,
women of the past

Contents

Preface

It's customary to say something about how one comes to write a book. I do that, in part, in the introductory chapter: it is part of the story. Here, though, I wish to say something about 'location': mine, as author. This is not only a book about a loosely defined spiritual community and its practices, but a product of that community. As researcher/practitioner I occupy one those 'strange positions' that Marcus (1999: 3) indicates: even more strange because the experiential communities that I explore are at once 'exotic' and personal; strange and familiar; with roots deep in Western society, and yet – because they draw directly on those roots, different, 'irrational' and in many people's eyes 'weird'. Or Wyrd. The word is the same, and implies fate, that which follows, active construction of obligation and meaning.

Next, I am located as a practitioner within the communities I study. I am neither an 'objective' ethnographer, nor a representative member. I belong to some organisations, not others; I run workshops and participate in e-mail groups; I hold opinions and include on my website(s) 'rants' about the politics of practice; I am implicated in the construction of seiðr.

A word about what I am not. I am neither a linguist or an archaeologist, but I draw on both disciplines in what follows. I do so both as practitioner and ethnographer. This book is not only 'about' seiðworkers, it is for seiðworkers (among others), and it is my hope that it may be as valuable (though, doubtless, as disputed) within this community of study as it may be within religious studies, anthropology, or sociology.

Finally, a note about some of the words found here: today's seið-folk draw on the Icelandic literature, and words from that literature find their way into their discourse — like 'seiðr'. I have been in something of a quandary about transliterating these. The Icelandic characters ð and þ (eth and thorn, pronounced as 'th' in 'there' and 'thin', respectively) feature in a number of these words. In the end I have adopted the following rule: when the word is used in an Icelandic context, I retain the character. When it is used in an English context, I transliterate using 'd' for ð, 'th' for Þ. Thus I describe Þorgeirr the Lawspeaker of the Alþing, but my friend's name is Thorgerd, and a seeress from the old literature may be referred to as Thurid or Þuriðr, depending on the context. Exceptions are made where today's practitioners often retain the letter — most notably in the word 'seiðr' itself, and often the god-name 'Óðinn'. Seiðr, by the way, is pronounced approximately 'say-th', with the 'r' coming from the Icelandic nominative case (you can say 'say-thur', if you prefer) — alternative versions being noted in chapter 3.

With this short note (and with an apology to Icelandic-speakers for any liberties I take with their language, and especially for any mis-spellings or inaccuracies that my inexpert eye and my language-challenged Mac's spelling checker have not caught) I welcome you to a small exploration of the Nine Worlds.

Acknowledgements

Many people have contributed to my construction of this book, in multiple ways. Not all can be named here. Those to whom I am indebted include the seiðworkers that I have seen, and the many other practitioners of 'shamanisms', whether 'neo-' or 'traditional', with whose work I have engaged.

In particular, they include those who gave their stories, their time, their own analysis, trusting me with their experiences. I give grateful thanks to Winifred, the first person I saw enter the seiðworker's deep trance, when I felt called to follow; to Diana and the members of Hrafnar; to Karter and Jordsvin and those others whom I have seen sit in the 'High Seat' or engage with other uses of seiðr. Particular mention must be made of Rauðhildr, for her 'seeing' and for her friendship, in addition to her narratives of seiðr-initiation, her understandings of the ethical issues inherent in performing seiðr within a community, and her continued discussions of situations and happenings. Similarly I thank Bil, for sharing his insights. Thanks are due also to those in Nova Scotia, notably Amber, Thorgerd, Erin, Silværina, and Shane; 'Bride' who sat in the High Seat when I needed someone to 'see' for me; and all those who participated in our rituals, each of whose questions led me further along my own path. I mention also those for whom I have 'seen', or guided in Britain, and the members of the 'seidrland' email list. All experiences and discussions with participants, seiðworkers, shamans both 'traditional' and 'neo-', have furthered my understanding. I thank also Jörmundur and other members of Iceland's Ásatrúarfélagið, who made me welcome and shared their insights.

Special thanks go to those who shared their interpretations of 'ergi' as it applies to their practice: notably Jordsvin, Malcolm, Bil and 'James', who gave their narratives to the 'gender paper';

Ybjrteir who has added his voice to theirs in this book, and Rod, Gus, Andy, Sifsson, 'Badger' and numerous others. In this context and that of a general sharing of perspectives, and comparison of approaches, I owe sincere thanks to Annette Høst, Dave Scott and Karen Kelly. To all who have contributed, your words and experiences mean much to me, and I hope I have represented them fairly and in the spirit in which they were given. To all those others implicit in the construction of those experiences, this book is an offering.

For comments and feedback on chapters, I thank Patrick Buck, Katy Jordan, Karen Kelly, Annette Høst, M.J. Patterson, and Robert Wallis. For permission to quote from material used in seiðrtraining and from her own account of 'initiation' experiences, and for her support for my work (not least in reading a 'post-modernist' paper on seidr at the Viking Millennium Symposium when the authors could not attend) I thank Diana Paxson. A special 'thank you' is due, also, to the people at http://www.snerpa.is/net/netut-e.htm who have created and maintain the 'Netutgafan' website, with Icelandic texts of a wide range of sagas and other literature: an invaluable resource to all who are interested in this material. Not least, I acknowledge the financial support of the Canadian Social Science and Humanities Research Council, whose research grant enabled travel and interviewing.

Within academia, Graham Harvey has been a constant source of support and encouragement. Many others who have encouraged my work and supported my analysing seiðr as 'shamanistic' include Galina Lindquist, Ronald Hutton, Marion Bowman, and Michael York; Fritz Muntean, Shelley Rabinovitch and others of the Nature Religion Scholars' Network; Robert Adlam, Hope McLean, and others from the Canadian Anthropology Society; members of the Society for the Anthropology of Consciousness; and those at numerous conferences who contributed their questions and their insights. Stephan Grundy's analysis gave me a beginning, and I thank him and many other specialists, including Britt-Mari Näsström, Neil Price, Ingegerd Holland, and Christie Ward, who answered my emailed questions.

A particular acknowledgement is due to my friend, collaborator and co-author on various papers, Robert Wallis, with whom the decision to 'go public' as an 'insider' engaged in experiential ethnography was debated extensively, whom I thank for insights, theoretical discussion and sharing of experience and analysis begun during the writing of 'the gender paper' and continuing since, and for permission to quote from his own forthcoming material. In this book, I walk a strange path of transformation that winds between academia and the Nine Worlds, through post-modern politics of neo-shamanic experience. It is good to know that others walk there also. To other good friends who have provided encouragement during this endeavour, Arlea and Stormerne, Bill, Cara, Julia, Katy, Ken, MJ, Malcolm, Patrick, members of The Troth, co-workers in Canada and in Britain, and not least to my family in Canada, I say again a heartfelt 'thank you'.

Finally, to Roger Thorp and the Routledge editorial staff, thank you for giving me this opportunity to expand my understandings of seidr, shamanisms, and multi-sited ethnography in book form, and for your support and enthusiasm for the project.

Jenny Blain
Hathersage, January 2001

how will my journey change me? I asked
the seeress, and she replied,
seated on Hlidskjalf:
'I cannot see beyond the trees
but they are calling you,
only the trees.'

Chapter I

Introducing shamanism, seiðr and self

On a day at the end of April 1999, I journeyed by plane from Nova Scotia to Boston, Massachusetts, on my way further west to Illinois. In Boston I had to perform a particular ritual of transition, challenge and answer, one familiar to many people in today's Western world: going through customs. Why was I entering the United States? asked the official, and I replied, 'I'm an anthropologist. One of the people I'm studying is getting married. I'm going to dance at her wedding!'.

He laughed and waved me on. I walked, musing on the meanings of the words I'd said, for myself and for the recipient. On the plane I'd been scribbling notes for a paper I had to write, and a future research proposal, and thinking about George Marcus' discussions of 'multi-sited ethnography' (Marcus 1998). Now here was I, caught in a maze of meanings, on my way to a wedding, and it was Walpurgisnacht: Beltane Eve, May Eve.

Some years before, I had met Winifred. She was the first seiðworker – she prefers the term 'spae-woman', one who sees what is to come – that I ever saw in action, and I'd greatly enjoyed the discussions, in person or email, with her since, as we struggled to work out the disputed territory of seiðr, sets of shamanistic practice of pre-Christian Northern Europe. She had talked of her friendship with another Heathen, and then the wedding invitation had arrived and I made the long trip from Nova Scotia to, indeed, dance at the wedding. But neither the 'wedding' nor the 'dancing' were likely to be quite as the customs officer envisaged. The wedding – indeed an exchange of marriage vows – was part of a weekend celebration of spring, with rituals and a maypole, and the dancing I had in mind would be that very night, before rather than after the exchange of vows. There would be drumming, and guests were encouraged to dance around the bonfire, to – in the words of Winifred's invitation – 'leap, spring and bound', in honour of the festival: and if they so chose, to dance to honour their animal spirits, taking on the movements of the animal, in a sense becoming the animal, strengthening spiritual links between the worlds, between human-kind and animal-kind, masked or unmasked, veiled or unveiled, drawing on and adding to the energies of the night and the fire.

Winifred and others like her live between worlds – both the everyday and shamanic worlds, here the Nine Worlds on the tree Yggdrasill. Even within the 'everyday' worlds of people, they meet a range of discursive constructions from the rationalism of (much) scientific/discourse to the rationalist tolerance of 'liberal' mainstream religion or agnosticism, and from the human-privileging, God-centred discourse of (much) Christian fundamentalism to the Earth-centred focus of (some) Aboriginal groups and the 'Earth is the Goddess' approach of (some) goddess spirituality. Winifred, and others like her, are emphatically part of Western, society, with its tensions and contradictions. She is therefore making her way, living her life, within sets of relations and modes of consciousness that link her to all these groups and more, at work, in community endeavours, in attempting to create alliances that further her goals and those of the Earth that she is, personally, sworn to protect.

Less than a month later, I described the incident of the customs officer, at a conference on folklore with the topic of 'Going Native' (Blain 2000). Ethnography is changing and the 'insider's' view is no longer debarred. I was exploring ways to express my experiences, linking the communities of shamanists and seiðworkers, and academics. Two months later I was in Britain, talking with neo-shamanic practitioners there about seiðr and debating theories of what was 'shamanism'. So many understandings, so many relationships – and I saw myself within the web of practitioners, connected to all by strands of Wyrd, fate, history or social construction, positioned in such a way that I could write about these experiences for a wider audience. The result is before you now.

This book presents an ethnographic exploration of Northern European shamanistic practice called seiðr, within a framework of recent theorising of shamanisms and neo-shamanism. Its purposes are those of advancing thinking on neo-shamanisms and their increasing relevance within social relations of post-modernity; broadening knowledge of seiðr while examining the present-day construction of this specific 'neo-shamanism'; and dispelling misconceptions about neo-shamanisms in general (e.g. that they are 'all the same') and seiðr and Northern European 'reconstructed-indigenous' religious practices in particular. Additionally, the book examines the use of experiential anthropology in understanding and theorising phenomena of altered consciousness and the interactions of seiðworker or 'shaman' with their spirit worlds.

This therefore is an ethnography of seiðr, as it is presently being rediscovered, even 'reinvented', by groups in Europe and North America. As such, the book not only describes seiðr, its construction and 'performance' – a term disputed within practice and theory – and its sources, but engages with debates within and about ethnography and experiential anthropology.

Focusing chiefly on 'oracular' or divinatory seiðr reconstructed from instances in the Icelandic sagas, I locate seiðr as ecstatic practice within specific cultural contexts: Northern Europe of 1,000 years ago, though with roots deep in the past, and the Western Earth-religions revival of the present day. I examine the extent to which seiðr can be said to be either 'shamanistic', or 'shamanic', understanding the latter term to imply community sanction and structuring of ecstatic/magical practice (Blain and Wallis 2000). My work here is aligned, therefore, with new research within anthropology and religious studies that understands shamanisms, whether 'traditional', 'neo-' or 'urban', as historically and culturally specific, at once transforming and themselves in process of transformation, within contexts which are economic, socio-political and spiritual.

In chapter 2 I introduce seiðr, within a framework of North European 'Heathenry', and some of the debates surrounding it. Chapter 3 is an exploration of the (re-)construction of oracular, 'high-seat' or divinatory seiðr, the rituals most likely to be met with by observers. Chapter 4 explores issues of trance states, 'shamanisms' and 'the spirits'. Chapter 5 is an experiential narrative of my introduction to, and exploration of, these relationships. In chapters 6 and 7, questions of ambiguity, ambivalence, gender, sexuality and the 'otherness' of seiðworkers – then and now – are explored, and the final chapter examines some challenges and questions of magic, neo-shamanisms, rationality, and the location of myself as ethnographer.

Within Western 'post-modern' society an increasing number of people are turning to construct their own spiritual relationships with the earth, other people, and those with whom we share the earth: plants, animals, and various spirit-beings found in the mythologies of the world. For many, this goes hand-in-hand with a search for 'roots', authenticity, a quest for meaning that seekers do not find in the hustle and pressures of their fragmented everyday lives. If as Bauman (1997) has suggested 'post-modern society' is about 'choice', one of the most obvious examples lies in this quest for located spiritual meaning.

There are several ways in which this quest has become manifest: religions, traditions or 'paths' often confused by researchers, but distinct in the discourse of their followers. The 'new age' (not dealt with in this book) focuses, in the main, on self-development, while borrowing from a number of spiritual traditions including Christianity, Hinduism, Buddhism and various indigenous practices from around the world. Numerous 'neo-paganisms' look to a remembered, or invented, past, often romanticised, although an increasing number of today's Western Pagans emphasise their deliberate construction of religion for today. A third strand is 'neo-shamanism', also romanticised, which draws heavily on constructions of 'indigenous' or 'traditional' (world-wide) shamanic practice in the Western literature from the eighteenth century onwards. Seiðr can be envisaged as a point of intersection of these second and third strands.

These ways of relating spiritually to the world have been too often dismissed by anthropology, sociology or religious studies as irrelevant, either small-scale manifestations of dissatisfaction, or even adolescent rebellion, teenagers' attempts to distance themselves from 'establishment' of church, state and parents. However, viewed from an approach that sees wealth in diversity, and contestation as creation of meaning, they become part of the patchwork of post-modernity, processes of dynamic construction of present-day Western society. Followers of these new/old religious traditions may be computer programmers, cleaners or clerks, graduates of seminary education, bartenders or barristers, accountants, archaeologists, teachers, students or systems managers, or even anthropologists – engaging with social life in many ways, and attempting to blend their spiritual practices with everyday life.

My interest in writing this book lies in the intersection of reconstructed European pre-Christian religion with 'shamanisms' described from elsewhere, indeed in the overlap or interweaving of the second and thirds strand of spiritual thought described above: 'reconstructed' Paganism, and neo-shamanism. Many descriptions of neo-shamanisms are available, the most familiar of which is probably Michael Harner's (1980) *The Way of the Shaman*, which has become a basic 'text' for many practitioners. (For other accounts see e.g. Wallis, forthcoming, a.) Constructions of 'Celtic Shamanism' and 'Norse Shamanism', as magical practice for today, are increasingly appearing within pagan communities in Europe and North America. A number of popular books and magazine articles dealing with 'Celtic Shamanism' (e.g. J. Matthews 1991; C. Matthews 1995; Cowan 1995) have whetted appetites for more, and while 'Norse Shamanism' or 'Saxon Shamanism' – either of which might conceivably be called seiðr – have received less attention, these too are now attracting notice, particularly through the world wide web and through Jan Fries' book *Seidways* (Fries 1996). Groundwork was laid by Brian Bates' novel *The Way of Wyrd* (Bates 1983), which deals with some of the Old English healing 'charms' within the context of a shaman training an assistant, and his later non-fiction account *The Wisdom of the Wyrd* (1996) which gives as background for shamanistic practice (and for the derivation of his novel) both Old Norse and Old English material.

This leads therefore to the 'North European Paganism' of the subtitle (a term which its practitioners are rather unlikely to use, but which may make some sense to academics). Under various names, this can be regarded today as a set of linked religious and spiritual 'traditions' that are being derived by their practitioners from various source texts and archaeological finds. Notably, these sources are the Eddas and sagas – the great mediaeval literature of North Europe, much of it written in Iceland, popularised/romanticised during the nineteenth century and subsequently as 'Norse Mythology', and most familiar to English-speaking readers in the form of children's stories. The Eddas and sagas have been fruitful fields of study for scholars of mediaeval literature, anthropology, history, religious studies, and folklore. They are also assiduously scanned (together with Old English texts and other pieces which might give clues to pre-Christian spirituality) by practitioners. These latter have a number of names for themselves and what they do: *Ásatrú* is the name used in Iceland (see Strmiska 2000) and common in North America: other Scandinavian formations of this term – literally 'faith in the gods', coined as part of the nineteenth century romantic movement – include *Åsatro, Åsatrú, Asatro*. The adoption of this term in Iceland was for present-day political reasons, and many practitioners, there and elsewhere, prefer the terms *forn siðr* or *forn sed*, simply 'the old way'. However, the term preferred by many practitioners in Britain, gaining popularity in North America and used by people elsewhere as a descriptor, is simply 'Heathen' (heiðinn, hedensk), initially used by those who followed the 'new' religion of Christianity to describe the followers of the 'old ways', later becoming a term of abuse, now being reclaimed by those who have read the mediaeval literature, and those who refer to the 'people of the heath' (Thompson 1998; Cope 1998) – suitably for those who would follow the spirits of the land, wherever they may be.

So, here, I explore the construction and experience of today's seiðr, as shamanistic practice derived from accounts in the Icelandic sagas. Seiðr has a basis within reconstructionist Northern European spiritual communities, and shamanistic groups who adopt methods and principles derived from shamanisms elsewhere and from core-shamanism (Harner 1980). For an ethnographer of post-modern society it is a rich field of study. Its construction is somewhat problematic, with terms and practices disputed in past and present, and gendered political aspects of its implementation that rapidly become apparent where discourses of seiðr and seiðworkers conflict with discourses hegemonic in Western societies. In particular, there are issues around gender and sexuality, and practitioners use the terms of the past within today's narrative constructions, to recreate or subvert hegemonic practice and to shape new meanings for themselves and directions for their communities. As culturally specific shamanistic, possibly shamanic, practice, seiðr positions its practitioners within the cosmology of the North and North-West of Europe – the Well of Wyrd and the great tree Yggdrasill – as seekers move within the Nine Worlds in quest of knowledge from deities and ancestors.

I write as an anthropologist and as a practitioner. I follow the strands of seiðr practice from present to past, across an ocean and through the Nine Worlds of Norse, Northern, or more generally, 'Heathen' cosmology. In this, what I produce here is a multi-sited ethnography (Marcus 1998), as I explore processes of seiðr, from practitioner to practitioner, community to community, time to time; from spatially located ritual practice and my ethnographer's taped interviews to worldwide email-discussion lists, and through my own, as well as others', experiences. I write, then, in quest of my own knowledges, situated by my relation to the practices I discuss: like a seer or shaman, and indeed at time *as* a seer, I go out into a world of many levels that is only partly known, and return with experiences to share. My journey has taken me into possible, disputed, past understandings of being and consciousness, linguistics and comparative religion, mediaeval literature and archaeology, queer theory and understandings of 'self' and 'meaning' that slip away, change even as they are examined, as the vision changes when the seeress tries to probe further. On many levels, therefore, this is a work of experiential anthropology (Goulet 1994): observation is not enough to understand relations between seiðworkers and the spirit world. My own experiences form part of what I analyse, and inevitably position me within the layers of meaning that are constructed within the seiðr seance and within the communities of those who engage with it. Insights within this book have been developed in dialogue with many beings. As practitioner and as writer, I engage with worlds and meanings, exploring ways to relate these within the discourses of academia and everyday writing, and by stepping outside these into the language of poetry and imagery. I deal here with current debates within academia and anthropology, on disputed 'realities', metaphor and representation, ethnographic theory and methods, 'shamanism' as a Western construction of assumed primordial, primaeval, and 'primitive' religion versus 'shamanisms' as creative, contested political and spiritual invention, as well as the multiple realities of the seiðworkers.

So, like the shaman, I journey out and back, within the cultural contexts of the discourses of academia and those of seiðworkers, and I am transformed by the experience.

Chapter 2

The saying of the Norns

The Welling of Wyrd

They sit, three raised above all others in the room, hands joined: Urðr, who knows all past, and who has direction of this ritual; Werðende who holds the strands that make the present, and tells their weaving; centrally Skuld, *obligation*, asking: 'do you understand me?' Before them stands Jordsvin, the guide for this spae-working, who asks 'is there one here who has a question for the Norns?' And one after another, we step forth.

We have come here by means of a journey beginning in the barn at Martha's Orchard, which serves for the great hall of our feasting and assembly at Trothmoot,[1] June 1997. We have seen the three women move to the high seats, we have heard the song which, in this spae-working, attunes our consciousnesses to the cosmology of the North, the high clear voice of Werðende, the present, the now, singing:

> Make plain the path to where we are
> A horn calls clear from o'er the mountain
> The gods do gladden from afar
> And mist rises on the meadow ...
>
> The hounds and eight-legged horse we hear
> A horn calls clear from o'er the mountain
> The heart beats quick as Yggr draws near
> And mist rises on the meadow ...

Diana has called for guardianship to Norðri, Suðri, Austri, Vestri, the dwarves of the quarters: for inspiration, assistance and blessing to those of the Elder Kin who do this work, Freyja and Óðinn. Then she has called for energy and guiding on the power

animals, the spirit guides or guardians of the three seeresses to
come to them, dancing and drumming before she became Urðr in
the high seat, and we have descended to the great plain of Miðgarð,
to the tree Yggdrasill itself, and beneath its roots to the place where
Wyrd, 'weird', fate, wells before us and the Norns sit, waiting. I
realise, with shock, that quite how we came here I do not know: at
some point the familiar meditation became unfamiliar, and so I
have travelled here by unknown roads. The air is charged with
potential, with waiting, with anticipation and with magic. Now, led
by Jordsvin, we sing the song which gives the seeresses access to
knowledge that is otherwise hidden: each has trained herself to
respond to it by a shift in awareness, and their words, coming from
beyond themselves, are charged with meaning.

The guide, Jordsvin, lit by flickering torchlight, asks:

> *The spell is spoken, the Norns wait.*
> *Is there one here who would ask a question?*

And one after another, at Jordsvin's beck, we step forward, each
to ask of what is near to our hearts and our minds: thoughts
that preoccupy us; problems, spiritual or physical, to be faced;
partners; health; occupations; future plans. It is my turn. *I have a*
question for the Norns. It seems likely that my academic career is
nearing an end, due to job shortages, and I describe this, asking
what waits for me, what path I should take. Then I stand in this
half-world, feeling my body swaying slightly, concentrating
intently on the replies as the seeing passes from one to another to
another, and back again, and Skuld, in the centre, jolts, as the
energy passes through her.

Two paths lie before me now, they say, together with the one I have
travelled upon to reach this place, the path straight ahead which is
short and ends soon. They resemble the rune elhaz. I stand at the point
of division. Do not choose too soon: do not choose until the last
moment. One path is easier, one carries more of sacrifice. Yet the
paths bend around, so that both lead in the end to the same place: I
know where I will go in the end, I know where my home is. The
guardian stands by the way ...

I stand in two worlds balancing their demands. Do I understand? I
must not choose too soon ... I stand balanced on a knife edge, I walk a
knife edge ...

'Do you understand this?' says Skuld.

Ritual and community

Anthropologically, this is indeed an extra-ordinary experience,[2] and part of my mind is taking notes, comparing this with other seiðrs that I have participated in, as attendee, guide or seeress, noting the similarities, the regularities, the pattern of the ritual. First there is scene-setting, calling for protection by Landspirits and other entities, or, as in the first session I observed, chanting the runes of the elder futhark, followed by invocation of those deities who themselves perform spae-working: Freyja Vanadis, and Óðinn. These preliminaries over, the leaders create, through singing, drumming and guided meditation, a state in which those present enter a light trance. The seeress however goes further, entering realms where the others do not follow, in order to seek answers to their questions. The questioning takes a form derived from the Eddic poems *Baldrsdraumar* and *Völuspá*.

> *...through worlds have I wandered,*
> *seeking the seeress whom now I summon...*
> *Cease not seeress, 'till said thou hast,*
> *answer the asker 'till all (s)he knows...*

Within this highly charged setting, the seer or seeress indeed produces answers, which do make sense to the questioners. According to experienced spae-workers, the accuracy or precision of the answer is directly proportional to the emotional involvement of the one who asks a question. Experienced workers stress the difficulties of interpreting seiðr imagery – answers are often complex and may be misleading – and emphasise obtaining a 'second opinion' before committing oneself to a course of action based on seiðr knowledge, for instance through rune divination, seen as another way to dip into the Well of Wyrd in quest of knowledge.

I note also the differences between this public working, with its many questioners, and the private 'journey' sessions in which people seek their own answers, perhaps without knowing what it is they seek. The small group with whom I had been working structure their rituals according to whether the rite is private or public: private journeyings require less scene-setting, as the group members know where they are going, and do not always have the pattern of question and answer, question and answer. At times, all journey together to a known point, the great tree Yggdrasill, the centre of all the worlds, and then diverge to pursue their own visions. Other spae-workers, in interviews, report similar circumstances. Winifred – Werðende of the Three Norns ritual – speaks of a far less elaborate setting when she does spae for a friend, or for herself. Jordsvin, himself a *spámaðr*, a man who speaks prophesy, modifies and omits part of the ritual when performing spae for his kindred. The seeker can be solitary, 'sitting out' to seek guidance.

Yet however simple or elaborate the format of the ritual, those who do this work report on the intensity of the experience and its centrality as a focus of identity construction. Winifred describes the first time she did spae-working:

> the moment when I stepped up to the high seat for the first time and sat down in it and put the veil over my head and they started singing for me, what I felt then was that I had been walking my entire life to reach that one moment. So it was like, it's really like a vocation for me, that's calling me. And all the different paths have come together in that.

It is her contribution to the Heathen community, a way that she can assist her deities and her people. Jordsvin points out that 'people love it. My kindred loves it. When I do this some other people from among the pagan community show up also.' He says that compared to Winifred, he is only beginning to 'scratch the surface'. He has learned from her, and from receiving materials from the group known as *Hrafnar* in California, and attending their workshops. Winifred in turn says:

> I had been taking trance journeys myself for about five years before having Diana's training...And I, for that I used, I've read lots and lots of books on shamanism and you know, picked and chose what seemed to make sense to me, in terms of ways, but it came very easily to me.

If answers are produced, where do they come from: Gods, spirits, those who have gone before, the seeker's subconscious? Rational-liberal anthropology, of course, says the latter. Jungian psychology would suggest a collective-unconscious origin. The answers do not always have meaning for the speaker, but they do seem to for the questioner. Practitioners have their own answers. 'It's not archetypes and the collective unconscious, or at least it's more than that as well,' says Jordsvin. 'I expect most of this is coming from the dead people, because that's where I go.' He journeys within Hel's realm: in Norse tradition, wisdom comes from the dead, from the mound. Others may focus on deities as the source of the answers, depending on what is asked: rituals may involve deity-possession (described by Wallis 1999b: chapter 2).

Cosmology, deities and 'lore'

We are dealing, here, with people who have immersed themselves in the mythology, literature and folklore of the North: the poetry and prose of the Eddas and Icelandic sagas, together with Old English poetry, and folktales and folklore from Scotland, England, Scandinavia and much of Europe. From this, and drawing on the work of scholars such as Hilda Ellis Davidson (e.g. 1964) or Kevin Crossley-Holland (e.g. 1980), practitioners have put together what is today called Heathenism or Ásatrú, which they perceive as a religion for today, based on pre-Christian beliefs and traditions.

Why do people come to this? Their stories vary considerably. Some, particularly in Europe but occasionally as part of an emigrant family, grew up with the mythology and the folklore. Others feel a connection to land, and the spirits of the land. Many followers in Europe or North America seek a form of connection with ancestors, either physical or spiritual. Some approach from a dissatisfaction with 'established' religion, others from atheism or agnosticism, often experimenting first with other 'Earth-religions', particularly Wicca. Often the search has taken some time. 'I hunted for this religion, since youth,' one North American Heathen says. In one way or other, they have formed personal connections with the mythology, imagery, or philosophy. Thus, the spae-woman Winifred tells her story. During her not inconsiderable quest for spiritual meaning:

> I realised that all the images I had and that I related to were of Northern Europe, of monasteries and traditions and customs and everything, and that the more I looked into all of those things the more I realised that they had Heathen roots.

But an even stronger strand came from philosophical approaches, and own quest within religious studies. She describes her search, including:

the wish to move into a polytheistic religion, because I have always had trouble with the idea of a monotheistic religion. I think polytheistic is much closer to reality as I see it anyway, and then of course that made room for the feminine principle that I was looking for, also. I was able to find some of these books that came out in the late 80s and early 90s, and was very impressed and was definitely seriously considering it, but what finally tipped the balance was reading Bauschatz' *The Well and the Tree*, and his explication of the philosophy with Wyrd, you know, coming out of the layers of the well, coming up into the tree, dripping down after life, life had formed the deeds ... I mean I've studied I think all of the major religious and philosophical systems with, with great interest and having learned and gained from doing so, but none of them did I feel really described reality the way I see it. And this did.

A practitioner in England experimented first with Wicca and 'Celtic' mythology, before turning to Heathenry after connecting with 'the runes', the Northern writing systems used (at least today) for magic or divination.

How did I get into this?...always had a feel for nature, and decided, having not stuck with Wicca, Hermetic magic, etc, to get into my own land. But the 'Celts' didn't work – too many romantic images and too complex (enigmatic) a mythology. Then came the runes. I was home.

In Britain, Harvey (1997) has described Heathen beliefs and cosmology, focused on the tree Yggdrasill and the Nine Worlds, and the deities and other spirits described in Norse mythology: the Æsir and Vanir, and the Norns who spin Wyrd below the tree, together with *jotnar* or giants, *álfar* or elves, and Landwights. There are numerous ways in which Heathens relate to this cosmology, including seiðr and rune-use in addition to formal (non-ecstatic) ritual practice. Within North American practice, I earlier investigated public narratives that prevail in the Heathen community, as they are indexed in the discourse of practitioners. These include (derived from Blain 1997, 1998a and forthcoming, b):

1   References to myths and stories of the Æsir and Vanir, for instance to explain characteristics or personalities of the gods.

Followers of Ásatrú index specific pieces of what is referred to as 'the lore'. Knowledge of this material forms a backdrop to ritual and discussion. Many Heathens consider that people do experience the deities in their own ways, and personal revelations (point 4, below) are known on one email list as Unusual Personal Gnoses (UPGs), which can be checked against, and remain secondary to, 'the lore'.

2   A concept of polytheism (as distinct from monotheism or duotheism, or a Jungian discussion of 'archetypes'). The gods are spoken of as real entities, separate and distinct, with rounded personalities and *different* from, for instance, Celtic or Greek or Native American beings or deities.[3]

3   Along with this goes a sense of *cultural specificity*. Blót and Sumbel, the ritual forms of Ásatrú, are spoken of as distinct in kind from, e.g., a Wiccan circle. Again, they are drawn from 'the lore'.

4   The possibility of direct communication with these beings, to speak with them and gain various forms of knowledge. In interviews with Heathen practitioners and theologians, this narrative of communication appears as an explanation of how they 'know' about their deities and why these deities appear so 'real' to them. Direct communication is a means of achieving personal gnosis (UPG). With this discourse of direct communication may go:

5   The manipulation of consciousness or 'reality' by them or through magic inspired by them: including *galdr* (chanted magic), runic magic, and spae-working or *seiðr*. Not all Heathens practice seiðr or attend sessions. More, probably the majority, engage in rune-divination or rune-magic, often including galdr. However, not all practitioners of Ásatrú engage in, or give credence to, magic as something they can perform.

6   A sense that spirituality is not separate from everyday life, but informs it. Many Heathens place a high value on skills of daily living known from 'lore', archaeology or later folk-practices – woodcraft, fibre-crafts, smith-crafts, brewing, etc. A craft-fair is an important part of an Ásatrú gathering. Part of this is the relation of Heathens with Earth: focused on by some more than others, though all see Earth as living, or personified by a deity.

7   A sense of individual merit and responsibility, combined with community worth. Some Heathens list 'Nine Noble Virtues',

moral values or strictures. Others talk about individual
responsibility and 'being true' in more general terms: people
have a choice in what they do on a daily basis, and need to
accept responsibility for their choice.

8 This sense of responsibility goes hand in hand with an
elaborate concept of 'soul' and 'self', which is currently being
explored by some Heathen researchers – with reference, once
again, to 'the lore'. With this goes a concept of personal or
family fate or *ørlög*, and overall 'Wyrd', which people, and the
Norns, weave.

9 The Elder Kin (deities) also are subject to the workings of
Wyrd.

Not all Heathens, then, are involved with seiðr practices. Those
who are, combine 'lore' with their personal experiences of deity and
cosmology. They seek answers, for not only their own questions, but
those of the community, concerning direction, relations between
deities and people, environment and the spirits of the earth. Their
descriptions of where the answers come from make reference to
cosmology, the Norns, the Well of Wyrd, and the tree Yggdrasill,
which seiðworkers see as the centre of the Nine Worlds and the link
between them, signified in the Common Germanic futhark (24-stave
rune-set) by the rune *Eihwaz, the Yew Tree. This concept of Wyrd
is one that is being developed within the community. Though often
translated as 'fate' and sometimes equated to 'karma', it has a more
dynamic sense. People are active agents in the creation of their own
personal wyrd, or *ørlög*. Their deeds and vows, strands of *ørlög*,
become part of the fabric of Wyrd. Seiðworkers may be
conceptualised as 'reading' Wyrd, seeing along the threads of the
fabric to possible outcomes. Others within the community consider
that seiðr in the past involved active interception of the fabric,
'tugging' at the threads, and this concept will be investigated in
further chapters.

Seiðr or spae? What's in a name...

Within the seiðr séance, the answers are only part of the experience.
For the participants, there is a journey of discovery, a quest to obtain
the answers, assisted or accompanied by spirit-helpers, as already
outlined. This is soul work: the seeress sends out part of her spirit,
faring forth through the worlds to seek knowledge. There are different

ways in which the search for answers is described, experienced, or accomplished. It may indeed be a 'journey', the seer may be 'transported' to a place where answers are, or at times answers may be brought by other beings. Practitioners develop their own techniques.

Winifred calls her technique 'spae', from *spá*, speaking or foretelling. She is *spákona*, a spae-woman: the word is akin to the Scottish 'spaewife'. Others use the term 'oracular seiðr' for these forms of divination, and seiðr comes also in other, non-oracular forms, reflecting a wide range of practices associated with healing, protection, transition. According to Jordsvin:

> There are other forms of seiðr being done, and there are other uses besides what I was taught...I've also found, uh, that I can use this to basically unhaunt houses.

'De-ghosting' is his term for this. He could also point to the use of seiðr for warding people against harm, particularly psychic or psychological danger, although physical danger may be warded also. Seiðr may require a more active or deliberate participation than spae, involving as it does journeying to speak with other beings – spirits – to find that which is unknown, or invoke their aid towards some stated end.[4] Seiðr was brought first to the Æsir by Freyja (according to Snorri[5]), and apparently learned by Óðinn who could use it not only to forecast future possibilities but (again according to Snorri) to manipulate them. This includes the possibility of use for protection, and also for what Jordsvin calls 'a kind of psychic attack, as messing with people's minds'. He emphasises that this is not what he does:

> You have to have a pretty damn good reason before you go playing games like that. I've had some pathworking where I've been shown how to do that, and it would be for self-defence in emergency purposes only. Uh you don't do this because you're pissed at somebody, because they were snide to you, you do this because they're a threat to your life or health or somebody in your family. So I stress I do oracular seiðr, I also stress that what I have done so far has been Diana Paxson's and Hrafnar's version of oracular seiðr. People develop their own varieties but mine is definitely a variety of that.

Those who have derived the modern practice of spae-working – or oracular seiðr – have drawn on accounts from the sagas, most notably the scene in the *Saga of Eirík the Red* where a *spákona*, a spae-woman or prophetess, is asked to come to a Greenland community which has been undergoing hard times. Her costume – gloves, hood, staff, belt and talisman pouch, the stones that decorate her blue cloak – is described in some detail. Even her eating utensils are described. She is asked to predict the progress of the community, but to do so requires her to engage in an elaborate ritual. She eats a meal of the hearts of all the kinds of animals kept on the farmstead, and the next day at nightfall she prepares to do seiðr, which requires a special song[6] to be sung to 'the powers'. In this case the song is sung so well that she is able to learn more information than ever before, as many spirits, or powers, are said to be satisfied by its singing.

This and other accounts of seiðr and/or spae-working have been examined in detail by those who are reconstructing the rituals within the North American Ásatrú community: most notably Diana Paxson and other members of her group Hrafnar (as Jordsvin's account makes plain), who in the article 'The Return of the Völva' (Paxson n.d.) and other materials produced for circulation within the Heathen community indicate the derivation of their practices. From the old material it is unclear where the boundaries of 'seiðr' and 'spae' lie and whether these were distinct, though overlapping magical techniques. Was the Greenland völva, Þorbjörg, a seiðr-worker who included spae, foretelling, as part of her seiðr-practice, or was she primarily a prophetess who drew upon seiðr techniques to enhance her spae-work? She is addressed with respect, and always as a spae-woman (*spákona*), whereas some others given the term *seiðkona* are portrayed in a negative light.

For instance: one source readily available[7] to Heathens and others attempting to reconstitute Northern religious practices is the thirteenth-century *History of the Kings of Norway*, written by the Icelander Snorri Sturluson, usually known as *Heimskringla* from its first words relating to the circle of the earth. The opening section is *Ynglingasaga*, the story of the Yngling dynasty. Initial chapters trace descent from the deities, euhemerised as kings, priestesses and priests. Chapter 7, dealing with Óðinn's practice of seiðr, journeying and transformatory magic, indicates a very negative approach to seiðr and other forms of what is usually translated 'witchcraft'. In particular, Snorri says that men performing seiðr were *ergi* – a highly insulting word at the time – so that it was taught instead to gyðjar, priestesses. The negative associations may occur in older material, such as the verse which deals with the coming of Heiðr in *Völuspá*, the Speaking of the Seeress, the first poem found in the Poetic Edda. Common translations give something approximating: 'She practised seiðr where she could...playing with soul, she was ever dear to evil women.' (This glossing is disputed, and is examined in chapter 6, and 'ergi' in chapter 7.)

In accounting for the 'evil magic' of seiðr, historian Jenny Jochens (1996) suggests that it was magic practised initially by women, with its practice by men seen as problematic, effeminising or *ergi* (even for Óðinn), possibly because it may (in her view) have included female 'receptive' sexual activities. Though Jochens' characterisation of *ergi* as necessarily sexual is not shared by all who analyse the material within academia or within Northern spiritual practice, the term has become part of the vocabulary of today's practitioners, as I examine in chapter 7. Further, and related to this as part of the context of today's practice, ambiguity and ambivalence about seiðr and its implications for gender and sexuality are not all related to interpretation of the old material. These are those who still fear 'women's power', and for whom rituals performed mostly or exclusively by women are suspect: many practitioners of spae and seiðr today are women, or gay men – marginalised by today's society – and for some few this is sufficient to render the practice of either seiðr or spae (or any ritual form in which clearly defined gender categories and gendered dominance is challenged) doubtful at best, evil at worst. The discourses of mainstream twentieth/twenty-first-century categorisations are hard to overturn, and it must be admitted that some of those who profess to be 'Ásatrú' or 'Odinist' are seeking confirmation, not challenge, to their dearly held beliefs of superiority.[8] Knowledge and power are linked, and in the poem *Völuspá* the Völva's power is clearly demonstrated: Óðinn will know only as much as she tells him, while she knows all.

> Alone she sat out when the Old One came,
> the terrible Ás, and looked into her eyes:
> Why question me? Why test you me?
> All I know, Óðinn, where you left your eye
> Within the wondrous well of Mímir.
> Mímir each morning drinks his mead
> from Valfather's pledge. Would you yet know more?
>
> (*Völuspá* 28, my trans.)

Throughout the anthropological literature, there are indications of magic-workers being viewed ambivalently within their cultures, with this ambivalence easily transformed to negativity. Suspicion of sorcery is evident in the classical studies of African 'witchcraft' (notably Evans-Pritchard 1937), and in later material such as Crawford (1967).[9] In her anthropological novel *Return to Laughter*, Bohannan (1964) produces a narrative of how a magic-worker becomes a highly threatening figure. Turning attention nearer home, accounts from the Scottish witch-hunts of the early modern period show that a 'good witch' was considered by the church to be at least as problematic as one who used her (usual) talents for 'evil' (Larner 1981). When this material is viewed within an analytical framework supplied by anthropological considerations of gender, magic and social power, the negativity becomes more comprehensible, especially if dominant Western discourses of gender and dualism are considered as part of the equation – under development during the 'witch-craze', shaping the anthropological accounts of twentieth-century African magical practice, and informing consciousness and practice of present-day Heathens. The embedding of 'witches', 'victims', 'unwitchers' – and ethnographer – in ambiguities of politics and discourse is made evident in Favret-Saada's (1980) *Deadly Words: Witchcraft in the Bocage*. More recent accounts of specific 'shamanisms' within changing socio-political contexts point to the re-emergence of 'shamans' as something that is not unproblematic. Thus, King (1999) discusses the re-emergence of 'vampiric shamans' in Kamchatka. In a situation of change, one who is seen as responsible may be viewed with suspicion, and the ally may easily become the one most feared.

Seiðr and shamanism

It seems possible that both seiðr and spae-working may form part of the rather scattered remnants of shamanic techniques in Norse culture, and have been related to the shamanic practices of other cultures (Dubois 1999; Hultkrantz 1992). Writ large, Norse culture of the Viking age viewed through the (later) saga accounts does not strike the reader as *shamanic* as such: this would have required the shaman to be a central figure within society, even while being viewed ambiguously, whereas seiðworkers appear in the sagas as marginalised figures, and spae-workers, though respected, are rare. Yet, seeresses and other practitioners apparently did work in ways describable as 'shamanistic' – and often it is said that they were trained by 'the Finns', referring probably to the nomadic Sámi, a people who were truly 'shamanic' (see e.g. Pentikäinnen 1984, and Hultkrantz 1994). Today's seiðworkers are drawing on the shamanic practices of various indigenous religions, and the work of those who have studied these cultures and religions. Like other neo-shamans they have read *The Way of the Shaman* (Harner 1980) and Eliade's *Shamanism* (1964), and some have read recent ethnographies. Winifred draws also on her training within Christian spirituality. However practitioners point to a need to keep the cosmological focus, maintain the journeying within a multi-dimensional 'map' of the Nine Worlds. They engage, therefore, with a debate over 'authenticity'. When sources are sparse, how 'authentic', how close to an original, can today's practices approach? Rather than attempting perfect reconstruction, at least some practitioners focus on the cultural and cosmological framework. Techniques may be transferable – drumming, chanting, singing to achieve ecstatic communication with 'spirits' – but the experience of the journey or the spirit contact, its focus and its outcome for self or community, is specific. As Heathen *seiðman* Bil Linzie says (in an interview for the magazine *Idunna*):

> First off, I am faithful to the Northern Gods – in other words, Ásatrú – and have been for almost twenty years. Everything that I do, think, say, perceive, or whatever is passed through that belief system. And because it is filtered through that system, everything I practice is authentic.
>
> (Linzie 1995: 17)

This sense of 'authenticity' is rather far from that of practitioners who consider that whatever they do must be a direct reflection of past practices. In Bil's case the present day is experienced through a cosmological filter. Indeed, if seiðr experiences are 'shamanic' they must be constructed in dialogue with whatever helping spirits are present, and therefore each seiðr experience is unique, newly negotiated: never simply replication. Bil makes plain that he is a 'shaman' for today (he prefers the term 'seiðman'), a North American working within a living landscape specific to his area of the United States. He is neither a Viking nor an ancient Saxon nor a Germanic tribesperson. What he constructs is for today, as a community practitioner dealing with a multi-cultural, multireligious community, mediating between folk, land and spirits.

One point that many seiðr practitioners make is that learning to do seiðr is taught through doing it, and that the 'teachers' are not so much other practitioners as those met within the journey: which again fits with traditional shamanic, and present-day neo-shamanistic accounts. Teachers may be ancestors, animal 'allies', spirits of the land or of plants, the Norns, deities including Óðinn himself. Highly intense experiences can be involved with finding a teacher or communicating with ancestors or land spirits. Initiation or other trance-journeys may be experienced as terrifying, as revealing, as wondrously beautiful, as all of these, resulting in major changes in how the person interprets their 'self' and other relationships in which they are involved.

The most common questions about seiðr, however, regard *what* occurs or *where* the seer/ess journeys. Writer Diana Paxson, who has done considerable work in this area and derived much of the form most often used for oracular seiðr, recommends preparatory activities including breathing exercises, and guided meditations within a Norse cosmological framework, including those in which the purpose is to meet a spirit ally or guardian, a 'power animal'. The one who journeys to seek answers should be able to deal with transfers of energy and to have a source – from drumming, from a power animal, from a personal reservoir – to provide this energy. A necessary part of the experience is to be able to describe it. Here – in the start of an initiation story, which led to her initial construction of oracular seiðr – Diana Paxson has described a key event, occurring within non-ordinary reality, during a neo-shamanic workshop run by Michael Harner.[10]

> *I am walking through a grey land ... a world of grey mist that swirls among mighty stones. The raven flies ahead of me, not clear... but brilliant as the image of the sun against closed eyelids, bright/dark/bright wings against the shadowed stones.*
> *Where are you taking me?' I ask, and try to go faster.*[11]

I was aware of faint sounds from the world that I had left behind me, but wrapped in my grey cloak, I was insulated from both the noises and the chill of the building where the workshop was being held. Long practice helped me control my breathing and sink back into trance, to trust myself to Michael Harner's steady drumming and let it thrust me into the vision again.

The stones stand like pylons to either side, their rough surfaces inscribed with scratches whose meaning has been worn away by the winds of countless years. The raven alights on one of them, wings twitching impatiently. Clearly, she considers me rather stupid, but so far she has always waited for me to catch up again.

'You asked for a teacher – ' she tells me. 'That's where I'm taking you.'

I don't argue. I would never have dared to claim a raven as an ally. Especially not this one, this Grandmother of ravens, whose tongue is as sharp as her pointed beak.

But I thought that she was going to teach me what I want to know...

Ms Paxson adds, in her commentary, that she analysed the process even as she experienced this shamanic 'journey'. As a Westerner, she had learned to separate personal experience from scientific 'textbook knowledge', and to discount the former. She was suspicious also, because of her knowledge of ravens in both Native and European mythology, and what they implied.

...When I sought a power animal in the Underworld, I understood the significance of the raven who came to me. But just because I recognised her, it was easy to suspect myself of wishful thinking. ... If I had been inventing an ally for a character in one of my novels, I might have chosen a raven. That too, was a reason to doubt what I was hearing. I know that I can make up stories. Was I inventing this one now?

Her vision thus included, and was almost interrupted by, her commentary, stopped by the exasperated raven who told her:

'Did anybody ever tell you that you think too much? Shut up and come along!'

The process of initiation, by spirits or deities, not people, can be quite terrifying. The experience of the seeress Rauðhildr is a case in point. This is how it appears in my field notes, written after she had told me the story in a coffee-shop in Berkeley, California.

She made a journey to visit the Maurnir, who (according to her and Diana) are female giants. The Maurnir dwell in a cave, and she went there, naively she says, because she thought it would be interesting. She was attempting to journey to all of the denizens of the Nine Worlds.

They were there, and saw her, and asked why she was there. The Maurnir have much wisdom, and she asked (again naively, she says) if they would teach her, if she could learn from them, share in their wisdom. They said no, they couldn't teach her, but if she wished she could become part of the wisdom. She agreed that this would be a good thing.

So they ate her.

They threw aside the bones, as they ate. Her bones were lying on the cavern floor, when Loki appeared and started dancing and singing, calling to the goddesses and gods to put her back together, which they eventually did. So Loki was dancing a shaman dance. When she was together again, she thanked him and asked him why he'd done this. He said 'once, you gave me a drink' (as an offering in a ritual).

This account is also discussed by Wallis (1999b: 87) as involving the 'death and dismemberment' experiences of traditional shamanic initiations. I give another 'initiation' account, that of Bil, in chapter 7. Such accounts are difficult to deal with, for many anthropologists, and lead to questions about how to regard and treat such data as part of the construction of meaning and expertise of practitioners. Part of the work I am turning to within experiential anthropology involves finding ways to convey these meanings, in poetry or prose.

Performance or accomplishment?

Within studies of shamanisms today, a word much in use is 'performance'. Seiðr as I have described it here can indeed be seen as 'performance': the scene is set, those working within it act to change the awareness of their 'audience', and there is a script, an outline which the production will take, even though the details of it emerge from the interaction of all those present. Seiðr can be analysed with the same tools used to evaluate a stage production; and from the point of those observing, either the performance 'works' (in its effect on the audience), or it does not. From the point of view of the 'performer', things are rather different. Galina Lindquist (1997) has discussed the use of this term and the theoretical perspectives associated with it, in entitling her book on neo-shamanic seiðr in Sweden, *Shamanic Performances on the Urban*

Scene. As my own orientation to the material is that of both seiðworker and theoretical analyst, I will give several sides to this argument in stating my own position.

Several seiðworkers and other neo-shamanic practitioners have expressed opposition. The popular view of 'performance' is of something that is a scripted role ('playing a part'), unreal, fictional, 'made up', fake, put on for effect, or all of these at once. 'What a performance!' we say when a child throws a temper-tantrum: or with very different emphasis, when the singer who has transported us to another realm bows, smiles and becomes – we consider – like everyone else: despite the glorious voice, to the audience she was not 'really' Brunnhild, she neither truly loved, nor truly died.

So, for Jonathan Horwitz, shamanic practitioner and teacher, whose essay on the internet (Horwitz n.d.) addresses problems of viewing shamanism as 'performance' or 'role analysis': in his shamanic work there is nothing that is 'fake', he engages with real worlds and real spirits. Lindquist explains that for her also, as participant/ethnographer within Horwitz' seance, the moment was clearly real. Yet within anthropology 'performance' has distinct meanings, as outlined by Csordas (1996) and Schieffelin (1996), which Lindquist examines, and which I turn to, below.

First though, for me the word holds another meaning, from early training as a dancer, where 'performance' was contrasted with 'rehearsal' and so implied total involvement, focused appreciation of what one was doing, and a sense that meaning cannot be separated from doing: seiðr (or dance) is process, not 'thing' or definition. The performance, as 'doing', as 'creating', engages the 'performer', absorbs her, demands fullest attention, to be successful in likewise involving its audience. This meaning resonates with attempts to connect experience with 'what is done', perception with action, and hence performance with event, within a cultural interpretative frame, as persuasive act which creates conditions for change in both audience and performer (to use Csordas' 1996 definition).

Seiðworkers like other neo-shamans – and traditional shamans – are sensitive to the charge that their 'performance' is not 'real'. Yet indeed where traditional shamanisms are fuelled by community energy (Turner, pers. com.) part of the process may be construed as 'performance' within the popular discursive sense, in its scene-setting, and the need to put on a 'show' that is sufficiently engaging to draw in the (human and spirit) bystanders so that that interaction of shaman and spirit can become increasingly 'real' or vivid to all concerned. Shamans may be judged by their 'performance', therefore: is it sufficiently convincing? Schieffelin (1996) gives an example of rival practitioners, in a New Guinea mediumistic séance, where the performance of one *or of his spirit-helper* is not successful: it is rejected by the audience/participants. In oracular seiðr there may be audience members for whom the 'performance' is not effective and questions are asked about the validity of this seiðr: which relates not only to whether a particular seeress did 'actually' engage with spirits or 'see' as claimed, but to the use-value of information received and reliability of the spirits the seer contacts. Is a particular spirit trustworthy? Each audience member evaluates the séance through their own past experiences and engagement with discourses of spirit beings.

Csordas indicates that the 'performance' concept is often applied to 'a ritual' as a whole, without attention to the details within it as also, anthropologically, 'performances', and explains further:

> Here is what I mean: The shaman's formal narration of his journey to the realm of spirits is taken as data by anthropologists, but he is rarely questioned about the qualities of that realm and what it is like to move about in it. The shaman's narrative is treated as an element within the ritual performance – is it not the case, however, that the experience he narrates has the structure of performance in itself, prior to narratization?
>
> (Csordas 1996: 94–5)

Csordas refers here to what he calls the 'imaginal performances' of the shaman's engagement with spirits, clients, or others, details of which do not necessarily appear within whatever narrative is produced in the course of the event observed. He calls, therefore, for attention to those invisible details: 'experiential specificity'. Those details, for me, form the central experience of the shaman or seiðworker – which I am trying to display in this book – but it is here that the concept of performance (particularly 'imaginal performance') becomes most problematic, because here the shaman is most open to the (outsider's) charge of invention. Schieffelin's point that for the New Guinea Kaluli it is the spirit (not the medium) whose performance is judged raises the question of how, anthropologically, we can approach questions of evaluating the

construction of meaning within seiðr or shamanism. Rather than
'performance', therefore, my preference is for a phrase which is
more cumbersome but avoids the concept of 'fake' or 'role': what
the seiðworker does can be addressed as negotiation within a
cultural framework, interaction with spirits, and through this, *active
accomplishment of meaning*.

Seiðr and the anthropologist

Within today's anthropology, therefore, there are attempts being
made to find ways to discuss such experiences, dealing with
concepts such as the reality of the experience to the participant, and
within it (or its narration) the use of what is seen by outside
observers as symbol and metaphor. Goulet and Young (1994) speak
of such 'extraordinary experiences' in terms of multiple realities.
Within one reality mode, so to speak, we construct experience and
meaning by attending to sets of symbols and sensations that within
another reality mode would go unchecked. As we shift mode, new
possibilities become apparent, and old ones disappear. Ms Paxson's
commentary on her experience illustrates this point. By her
account, she had to work rather hard to prevent her rationalist
preconceptions from disrupting her journey; and the subsequent
events involving finding her teacher led her to consider that she was
not simply inventing a scenario. *I know that I can make up stories,*
Diana said. *Was I inventing this one now?*

Other seiðworkers have likewise answered: No. Jordsvin points
out that his physical experiences after doing oracular seiðr tally with
those of others: a feeling of cold, hunger, and a need to replenish
energy, often followed by a 'second wind' he calls 'seiðr rush'. His
answers, even those which make no sense to him, do so to the
questioner.

> I don't think I'm crazy. I get people coming up to me after these
> seiðr sessions when I'm stuffing my face, and resting, and they'll
> say, oh you said this that and the other. And you know I'll say,
> yeah, I wonder what the Hel that meant. And they'll say, well it
> meant this this this, that was right on the money. And I did not
> know it, this is things for people I did not know.

But can I, as an anthropologist, tell his experiences in this way?
As a fieldworker, I collect descriptions of seiðwork, from Jordsvin

and others. His experiences are direct, compelling. As an experiential ethnographer, I also record my own impressions, images, experiences. The description with which this chapter commenced was of my experience as an audience member: later chapters will indicate how I, as well as others, experience the High Seat of oracular seiðr. A large part of my work is in discovery or invention of ways to relate these experiences, so that the audience for my telling – conference attendees, readers of this book – does not dismiss them as 'fantasy', 'imaginary', or by asking 'what were these people *on*?'

In relating participants' accounts, I treat them as description of processes which are occurring. I do not, however, seek to test the 'objective reality' or otherwise of the processes or the events. Here I look to the work being done by others such as Goulet and Young who emphasise the need to take seriously the accounts of informants, as perception, description informed by world-view, experience constructed within shamanistic framework, situated knowledge. In order to describe processes of identity construction, as I am attempting to do, this is essential. It does not mean presenting emic or subjective-insider accounts and theorising as a single, literal truth. As research fieldworker, I become a broker, attempting to create understandings between cultures or sub-cultures. This task of brokering is a necessary component in attempting to represent 'insider' meanings, and translate these into a discourse that 'outsiders' will find acceptable or comprehensible: and hence a concomitant to making a contribution to any theoretical discussion of identity formation.

It is becoming more acceptable to present aspects of the world – or worlds – in ways that do not lay claim to total 'Truth' or ultimate 'Reality'. Post-modernist rejection of metanarrative opens possibilities for multiple analyses, in which contradiction does not invalidate insight. Put more simply, the ethnographer need not, in my view should not, attempt to force observation into a single, scientific, explanatory framework. Seiðr is experienced by participants from within their own spiritual world-views, as partial truths, as community construction where 'community' includes more than the visible human participants. I do not attempt to 'rationalise' the experience or its narrative. I examine its discursive construction, its specificity, its embeddedness and its political dimensions, and pose questions about how seið-processes structure identity, in the knowledge that participants themselves view 'identity' as a complex matter, and 'self' as requiring both spiritual and socio/psychological theorising. How do these participants, in this setting, at this time, accomplish meaning? The tradition of rejecting definitions of ultimate 'Truth' is an honourable, though minority, one within the social sciences: from the interpretative/hermeneutic approaches of (e.g.) Winch (1958) or Taylor (1971), to later social constructionist and narrative approaches, to Smith's (1987) bifurcated consciousness or Haraway's (1988) situated knowledges or Marcus' (1998) multiple meanings and multi-sited ethnography. I draw on discourse theory, and speak of competing discourses, in order to attempt my own understanding not only of individuals' construction of meaning and identity, but of the social natures of self-perception and self-construction, and how these in turn form part of the constitution of social relations within today's multi-cultural, multi-ethnic and multi-faith societies: including social relations of shamanisms.

I stand between worlds, as broker – between liberal-humanism, constructed from academic scepticism and the need for knowledge, and Heathen understanding of the Nine Worlds. Further, I stand between present and past. I move from one to the other, in my words and my sentences, drawing on first one narrative, then another, examining likewise my own. I draw on those ethnographers who maintain the necessity of an anthropologist experiencing and positioned within what she is attempting to understand (Favret-Saada 1980), and speak of the need to enter 'the realm of spiritual experience', and treat one's own experiences as analysable (Turner 1994: 72).

Yet I continue to write academic papers where I use other folk's words to describe what I myself know, in part because doing it this way is more readily *acceptable*. And I do this in the knowledge – which I in turn present likewise – that my experiences of doubt, of attempting to rationalise, of attempting to 'switch off' my academically trained mind – are not unique but shared with those whom I study, and that they too theorise their practice of tenth-century skills within a twenty-first-century milieu. After writing an article in which I looked at paradoxes inherent in presenting seiðr for an academic audience – prepared for a book on fieldwork research – I discussed my account with Winifred, who balances her work as a spae-worker with that of a government research ecologist. This is part of her comment.

Scientific/ rationalist thinking has a knowledge-domain – a large one – where it is an eminently suitable tool for the tasks within that domain. But as you pointed out in your paper, any conceptual approach comes with its own built-in blind spots, and science is certainly no exception. There remains a large – I would say infinitely large – domain where science/rationality is in many ways one of the more inferior tools which could be applied to acquire knowledge about it...One of the things one must know as a craftsman is 'which tool is right for the job?'

Her spae-working does a different job. As a way of knowing the world its possibilities are currently limited by its lack of validation, of the sort a twenty-first-century scientist can accept. Yet it has its own means of testing.

Spae-working is another, different route to knowledge; another tool for the toolbox of the knowledge-craftswoman, which I aspire to call myself. In the same way that I seek to acquire, interpret, and use knowledge about the world we live in through the tool of science/rationality (and I am perfectly competent to use this tool, and respect it as far as it goes), I also seek to acquire, interpret and use other forms of knowledge, outside the domain of science, using very different tools. These other tools have gone through their own very rigorous process of technical evolution, testing, validation and interpretation, through many generations of many different cultures, religions and world-views. They are not foolproof, not perfect, not yet fully developed – just as can be said with respect to science and rational thinking – and even more, it is hard to acquire good training and 'professional' validation in these areas, at least in our own society.

Her task now is to combine her realms of knowledge, and use one means within the area of the other. My description of it – in terms of multiple competing discourses – is somewhat different, because my starting knowledge-domains are different, but I feel also the need to defragment the whole, and agree with her sentiment that:

None of this is easy, either intellectually or psychologically, but you know how it is: one feels the irresistible urge toward whole-ness, and must heed the call no matter how difficult the path.

So now I conclude this chapter, with the words that came to me as I first wrote of the experience of the Three Norns' seiðr. I write as a scholar, seiðworker, an academic, storyteller, skald: my life fragmented yet feeling that urge towards wholeness, which aligns me with what seiðworker Bil Linzie terms *wholemaking*. The chapters that follow will include my own perceptions of experience, along with those of the people who have helped my study, as I follow the search for a poetics of daily life and ask my own questions of the Norns to guide my steps.

Writing these words, I see myself, again, standing on that knife-edge. I walk the knife edge, and I balance the demands of my worlds. Two paths stretch before me, in addition to the one that I have been on, and that ends. They stretch before, and wind around, and I cannot see the ends, though I know where my home is ... And I must not make my choice too soon.

Chapter 3

The Greenland Seeress

Seiðr as shamanistic practice

Þorbjörg the Seeress

The *Saga of Eirík the Red* describes the visit of a *spákona*, a seeress, to a Greenland farm, one thousand years ago. Her clothing and shoes, her staff and cloak, are detailed. She is asked to predict the progress of the community; she eats a meal of the hearts of the farm animals, and the next day a 'high seat' is made ready for her, where she will sit to foretell. She engages in ritual practices known as seiðr, which requires a special song to be sung to 'the powers' in order that she may gain their knowledge, in what appears to be ecstatic trance.

Today, people are making attempts to reclaim practices of seiðr. The previous chapter described a specific seiðr ritual: later chapters will relate more of what people do, and meanings they inscribe in/from their practices, meanings which are not always simple or uncontested. They rely on accounts from the sagas and Eddas, scholars' analyses of this literature, and parallels with shamanic practices elsewhere, using these within a framework of Norse cosmology and beliefs about soul, afterlife, and the Nine Worlds. Seiðworkers engage in faring-forth, trance-journeying, for a variety of ends, including healing and divination.

In this book I am attempting to discuss seiðr as sets of practice informed by shamanisms (traditional and 'neo-') within a largely non-shamanic community, today and in the past. I hope to indicate some of the ambiguities inherent in early descriptions and implications for present-day understandings and contestations of seiðr and its practitioners, and to examine how today's workers are reconstructing seiðr along with its dilemmas and contradictions, as shamanistic practice, which may possibly at times be described as shamanic, within spiritual and religious movements around the turn of the millennium: 1,000 years after the Viking voyages to Vinland.

Many diverse interpretations of seiðr are possible, and the term does not imply the same practices to all people. Within North America and elsewhere, groups such as Hrafnar, mentioned in the previous chapter, are developing 'high-seat' or 'oracular' seiðr within a context of present-day Heathenism: they are also experimenting with 'god-possessory seiðr' as described by Wallis (1999b and forthcoming, a). Within Scandinavia, neo-shamanic groups are reconstructing oracular seiðr in somewhat different ways, described by Lindquist (1997) and Jakobsen (1999). I make no claim to have uncovered the ultimate or only meaning of the term; nor is this claim made by any of the groups that I know. It seems likely that meaning and implication varied across time and even from one community to another and between individuals during the period from which we have stories of seiðr practice. It may have been that, at times, groups of individuals were interested in meeting and sharing techniques and practices; certainly this is the case today, as an issue of the neo-shamanic newsletter *Spirit Talk* (Kelly 1999a) makes plain, by offering a platform to shamanistic and Heathen practitioners, myself included. The diversity of articles in this issue, and in a 1998 issue of the Heathen journal *Idunna*, indicates a wide variety of meanings persist for the term *seiðr*.

I will begin with the sources from which reconstructions commence, and some of the debates, ambiguities or arguments around seiðr practice and meaning, today or in the past. As today's Heathens are well aware, the past shapes the present, with actions or thoughts long within Wyrd's Well forming part of the weaving of present-day Earth-religion. And so I begin where everyone begins, Heathen, neo-shamanist, or academic, with the narrative from the *Saga of Eirík the Red*.

A *spákona*, Þorbjörg, is invited to that Greenland farm. She wears a hood of lambskin lined with catskin, and has white catskin gloves. Her gown is girdled with a belt of touchwood, from which hangs a bag to hold magical items. Her cloak is blue, fastened with straps and adorned with stones, and stones stud the head of her staff, which is topped with a large brass knob. Her calfskin shoes are tied with thick laces, with tin buttons on their ends. On arrival, she does not foretell, but eats the meal described before. The next day she sits in the high seat, on a cushion stuffed with hens' feathers, to make her predictions.

The description continues:

A high-seat was prepared for her and a cushion laid under her; ... at sunset, she made the preparations which she needed to have to carry out seiðr. She also asked for those women who knew the wisdom (chant) which was necessary for seiðr and was called *Varðlokur*. But those women could not be found. Then the folk dwelling there were asked if anyone knew it. Then Guðríðr said, 'I am neither magically skilled nor a wise-woman, but Halldís, my foster-mother, taught me that chant in Iceland which she called Varðlokur'...The women made a ring around the seat, and Þorbjörg sat up on it. Then Guðríðr recited the chant so fairly and well, that it seemed to no one that they had heard the chant spoken with a fairer voice than was here. The spae-wife thanked her for the recital and said (that) many of the powers were now satisfied and thought it fair to hear when the chant was recited so well... 'And now many of those things are shown to me which I was denied before, and many others'.

> (*Eiríks saga rauða, 4*, trans. Gundarsson 1994: 33)

The song Guðríðr sang is, unfortunately, not given us.

The account of Þorbjörg the Seeress is the basis for today's practice of *oracular* seiðr, also known as *high-seat* seiðr or spae-working, which I examine in this chapter.

Seiðr in today's Heathen practice

Hrafnar and other groups, beginning their reconstructions with the story of Þorbjörg, look for details emerging from the account. The Greenland Seeress needed first to familiarise herself with the community and its energies, she then sat on a high seat and a special song was sung to 'the powers' that enabled her to gain her knowledge – or 'the powers' to give it to her. The word 'powers' (*náttúrur*, from Latin *natura*, nature, in plural meaning spirits, and therefore an adopted rather than native Old Icelandic word) is uncertain: it may refer to ancestral spirits, elves (*álfar*), guardian or animal spirits or other wights or beings, or deities. Siikala, drawing a parallel with descriptions of the Finnish *tietäjä*, suggests that 'the vardlo(k)kur song invokes the companions guarding the witch, her guardian spirits, and at the same time conducts him [*sic*] to a state of altered consciousness' (1992: 72).The mechanisms of how the seeress entered the trance in which she was able to acquire knowledge and the process of questioning her are not evident in the account. Hrafnar have therefore gone to other sources to find details of how a seiðr seance might be conducted.

Their main resources have been the Eddic poems *Völuspá*, *Baldrsdraumr*, and *Völuspá in skamma* (the '*Shorter Völuspá*', forming a part of the poem *Hyndluljöð*). Each of these appears to show part of a question-and-answer process, in which one who knows, a seeress, a *völva*, is asked to reveal her knowledge. In *Völuspá* the seeress speaks in answer to Óðinn, the god/magician; in *Baldrsdraumr* Óðinn travels to a grave-mound, just outside Hel's realm, and there raises the dead völva to answer his questions. In *Hyndluljöð*, the giantess/seeress Hyndla is speaking to Freyja and her follower Óttar about Óttar's ancestry, when (in the *Shorter Völuspá*) she starts to foretell the coming of Ragnarok and the fates of the Gods. From *Baldrsdraumr* Hrafnar have taken the calling of the seeress:

> Way-tame is my name, the son of Slaughter-tame,
> tell me the news from Hel – I know what's happening in the world:
> for whom are the benches decked with arm-rings,
> the dais so fairly strewn with gold?
> (Baldrsdraumar, 6; Larrington 1996: 244)[1]

From *Völuspá* and the *Shorter Völuspá* comes the pattern of question and seeress' answer.

> Much we have told you, we will tell you more,
> It's important that you know it, do you want to know more?
> (Song of Hyndla; Larrington 1996: 258)[2]

or the briefer version of *Völuspá*:

> Do you understand yet, or what?
> (Larrington 1996: 7)[3]

Diana Paxson (n.d.) has described the construction of the high-seat seiðr ritual *in The Return of the Völva*, written initially for *Mountain Thunder*, a Heathen journal. I begin here, though, with a different narrative – what the anthropologist, observing, sees and hears, what she is told is happening. It is therefore the account of a sympathetic 'outsider'.

The ethnographer's narrative

A room is prepared, with a 'high seat' or seiðhjallr. The seiðr leader may use various ways of 'warding' this space, by singing a runerow or calling to the dwarf-guardians of the directions. She or he calls to the deities who themselves do seiðr, Freyja and Óðinn. A song referring to various spirits or wights, and to Freyja and Óðinn, evokes an atmosphere in which people align their awareness with the cosmology of northern Europe: alternatively one could say that the song summons the spirits, and people become aware of them. Those who will 'seið' (the word is a verb as well as a noun) ask their spirit or animal allies to assist or lead them. Drumming and singing accompany and facilitate the induction of the ecstatic state. The guide narrates a meditative journey whereby all present, seers and questioners alike, travel down from an initial 'safe place', through a tunnel of trees, to the plain of Midgard and the great tree Yggdrasill, then below one of the roots of the World Tree past Urd's well and through caverns of Earth, or spiralling through various of the Nine Worlds, and finally across the echoing bridge with its guardian maiden Módgudr to the gates of Hel's realm, the abode of the dead, for in Old Norse tradition wisdom comes from the dead, the ancestors. Audience members are expected to engage with the meditation through visualisation, so that they are conceptually in the other world, or worlds, described. The 'audience' are told that they now sit outside the gates: only the seeress or seer will enter Hel's realm, urged on by further singing and drumming, 'journeying' to seek answers to participants' questions. The audience participants remain, in a light trance state, while the seiðworker enters deep trance and journeys on her or his own, assisted by spirit allies or 'power animals'. The seiðr-guide sings the seeress through Hel's gates, and invites other participants to ask their questions, for the seeress to answer.

Questioners step forward, and the seeress speaks to them. Usually she sits still, with a veil over her face. Sometimes she may sway; one, Rauðhildr, leans forward, unveiled, and may take the querant's hands. When she tires, or when there are no more questions, the guide 'calls' her back from the ancestors' world, and she steps down from the high seat, often moving stiffly, cramped and dazed: another may take her place.

Questions are asked with emotional intensity, and indeed experienced seiðworkers say that the degree of emotion, or meaning, which the question has for the asker is an important part of how 'truly' it is answered. The experience of being an audience member at a large seiðr is quite intense. There may be forty or fifty people in the room, focused on the seeresses or seers, and each inscribing her or his own meaning on the events. Many audience participants are themselves seiðworkers, sharing understanding of what it is to sit in the 'high seat'.

Finally the guide narrates the return journey meditation, so that all, seers, guide and audience/participants, return together to 'ordinary consciousness'.

The seiðman's narrative

From the high seat, the experience is more profound. A *seiðmaðr,* Jordsvin, describes the journey and what he finds there.

...there's a guided journey down to Helheim. The people that are doing the public oracular seiðr go with me, they stop at the gate. We stress stay with the group, don't go runnin' off and stirring up the jotnar [giants, etins], you can mess yourself up. This is real stuff, you're dealing with real beings, it can have real results.... I go down, I go through Hela's gate... I always nod respectfully to Hela, I'm in her living room. I see, other people see different things, I see a lake, an island and a torch burning on it. It lights up, the torch and the lake light up the area enough to actually see the dead people. And I walk down there and they tend to gather round, and I'll say, would those who need to speak with me or speak with the people I'm here representing please come forward. ...I've never seen anything scary, they look like people, the ones that have been there are passing on I guess to another life or whatever they're going to do, sometimes they're just like shadows, some look like living men and women, some are somewhere in between. Of course there's many, many many of them. They ask me questions, sometimes they'll speak ... Sometimes I hear voices, sometimes I see pictures, impressions, feelings, I have my eyes closed physically, and I'm in a trance, and I got a shawl over my head, sometimes it's almost like pictures on the back of my eyelids...

Multiplicity of narratives

Not all seiðworkers see what Jordsvin sees. Even within Hrafnar's scenario, each worker faces the task of seeking knowledge in their own way, within the trance. For Winifred, a large part of her work is in making contact with deities, and attempting to place other people, her seiðr clients, in a relationship with them.

> One of the reasons that I love the seiðr work is that due to people's questions I have the chance to see their relationships with the deities that are, for example Sif comes often for a friend of mine, whom I do seeings for...
> And one of the most interesting seeings that I had was for a young man, and Heimdall came for him ... I'm trying to bring people closer to the gods and to their own souls.

Rauðhildr undertakes the journey to Hel and there speaks mainly with ancestor-spirits, often the ancestors of the querants. Canadian seiðworker Whiteraven traces his seeings to varying sources depending on the questioner: after passing Hel's gates, he often journeys on a ship, which transports him to where the answer to the question can be found. At other times he travels as a raven, seeing the countryside below him. A question may bring contact with deities, particularly Heimdallr, Freyja, or Óðinn. Chapter 5 will describe my own experiences of being in darkness within a mound, solitary, and called forth by the seiðr-guide: others have related experiences akin to this; visions, sounds, sensory experiences then arise in response to the questions that are asked, and these may involve people, animals, birds or trees, specific scenes or objects, sometimes music.

Hrafnar has now trained several people in their methods, and these people are training others, so that a fellowship of seið-people, working in similar ways and following broadly similar methods, is emerging within North America and Britain, where Hrafnar have conducted workshops. Differences are emerging, for instance in the meditation: not all groups follow the process of spiralling through different worlds on the path to Hel's realm which Hrafnar has developed. Further, not all seiðworkings are oracular: people 'make seiðr' for protection and for healing (Blain, forthcoming, a). Jordsvin finds himself called upon by people outside his religion to use his trance-journeying abilities to 'unhaunt houses'. Some have derived their practices independently of Hrafnar, such as Bil Linzie, whose work is chiefly in healing and soul-retrieval, and in dealing with death. As 'seiðman' and 'wholemaker' (Linzie n.d.) his task is to make others whole.

Some draw on Hrafnar methods together with other practices: training elsewhere, whether this be 'core-shamanism' or other neo-shamanisms, teachers from Sámi or other traditional backgrounds, observation of practices and familiarity with the anthropological literature on 'traditional' shamanisms. 'James' was used to working shamanistically within Heathen contexts but had not observed oracular seiðr before attempting it. He described his first venture to Hel's realm, and how he negotiated being in two worlds and meeting an otherworld seeress.

> I found it difficult at first, but it got easier and I think as the time went by, whatever that was, it got increasingly easier and more and more vivid.. and I was more and more *there*. And at first I had some trouble negotiating being in that world and this world, being in the room and in Hel, but I found the staff very useful, and ended up clinging onto, onto that for dear life quite a lot of the time. That was a good connection. I found myself able to sort of look both ways at once. So yeah it got increasingly vivid. And I, I heard – the seeress speak as much as I did 'see' things myself, and pick up, I don't know how else to put it, pick up and sense things from what people were asking.
>
> ...I didn't experience anything I was expecting to experience. Well that's not entirely true. I mean, I think, I understood the way to, I was going to narrate things, and the way I would experience them in terms of seeing and speaking and listening, I was expecting that to happen because that's the way I work with spirits anyway, it's often all the senses at once, and all over the place, rather than you know I just have visions or I just hear voices. So I was expecting that. But everything else, you know getting to Hel's gate ... one of the gates was made of bones, human bones... And I went through and it was just darkness everywhere. Loads of darkness. Which was actually very, very nice, because as much as it, you know, didn't feel very pleasant because it was a place of death it was also very pleasant because it *was* a place of death. Quite appealing and welcoming. And then you know the mound appeared, just this green turfed mound, very sort of – reminds me of a painting by

Rousseau, just sort of very *there* amongst this blackness and then there was a tree there, yew tree there, and then the seeress comes out...

This diversity of practice is welcomed by experienced seiðworkers. Hrafnar seiðkona Rauðhild commented that 'the more of us doing the work in different ways, the more we have to teach and benefit each other'. Here I will consider first a more detailed account of the Hrafnar journey to Hel, then compare this with seiðr-practices from other neo-shamanisms.

The road to Hel's realm

Within the Hrafnar method, the guided journey to Hel's realm has a purpose. It puts the listeners into a frame of mind where they can start to think in terms of cultural symbols from Northern European mythology. This is particularly important when the seiðr is performed for a large audience, or one including people who normally work within other systems of symbols and meanings. Diana Paxson explains the journey and its meaning and purpose, in materials she has prepared for training seiðworkers (Paxson, in prep.).

The journey begins in Midgard, described as the 'non-ordinary version of ordinary reality', a parallel to the everyday world with landscapes and creatures that are familiar. In its centre stands the tree Yggdrasill, 'the axis of all the worlds,' which Hrafnar and other practitioners see as equivalent to the World Tree of Siberian cultures. She continues:

> Its structure provides an organizing principle for the mythology and a map of the cosmos which can be used for journeying. Its form is convenient for visualization; it can be circled to explore the four elemental worlds attached to the Mid-world, climbed to reach the world of the light-elves (devic forces) and Asgard, home of the gods. Beneath its arching roots lie the entrances to the world of the Dark Elves and the road to the Underworld.

For Hrafnar, the Tree is central, and the starting point for the major journey. Those who prefer a less formal approach to the seiðr journey also use the Tree as a focal point. In training exercises designed to acquaint people with their animal allies and with journeying, the tree is emphasised: wherever you are, you can find the World Tree, and with experience journey on it. The Hrafnar journey leads now beneath one root, linking ideas gained from descriptions found in the old material. I quote part of Paxson's explanatory materials, here, to give a sense of how this is presented (note that this is not a script for the meditation journey).

The entrance to the Underworld lies to the north, where primal ice and fire met to produce the mists of Niflheim. There, beneath the level of Midgard, lies the well called Hvergelmir, the boiling cauldron, source of the river Gjöll (roaring, resounding). Here, perhaps is also where we encounter the dog Garm, who must be fed before the traveller can continue on. Below the level of Midgard we pass first through Svartalfheim, the home of the dark elves, or dwarves, which can also be interpreted as the personal unconscious, populated by the shadows of one's past. This world is also a source of knowledge, but when we are journeying for others, we seek the chthonic depths, home of the ancestors.

The river plunges downward, but the path circles to the east, passing through the Ironwood where wolves roam... Here rise the roots of the moist mountains of Jotunheim. The river Slith blocks the path, its lead colored waters rushing down to join the hidden Gjöll. Swords, spears, and all kinds of weapons are tumbled along in its torrent. Fortunately a bridge allows the traveller to cross.

...The traveller passes through the outskirts of Myrkwood, which bars the way to Muspelheim, the realm of fire. Here, perhaps, the path is crossed by the river of blood which Thomas the Rhymer encountered on his journey to Faerie, fed by all the blood shed on earth, which rises to the traveller's knee.... But still the road leads around and downward, until the thundering of another river is heard, that of the Thund Thvitr (Thunderflood), which cascades down from the heights of Asgardr. Only Thor can wade that river...

... Louder and louder resounds the roar of the river Gjöll, rushing through a deep chasm. As the path winds down, a stone building, perhaps a tower, can be seen at the edge. From its door comes a Jotun maiden, Modgudh, who bars the way with her spear. In order to pass, the traveller must state his or her purpose in travelling to the Underworld.

From the brink of the abyss a bridge arches to the other side, bright as the gleam of a sword. The air above it glitters as if it were thatched with gold. If this is indeed a sword bridge, it will grow broader if the traveller crosses without fear, but narrow to a cutting edge if he is afraid. On the other side of the river a wall surrounds Hella's realm. To the east the air seems bright; to the west, dark and gloomy.

The seeker moves around to the eastern gate, from which Odin summoned the Vœlva. Hemlock grows here, even when it is winter in the world. A slain cock thrown over the wall will fly up alive on the other side. Of the land beyond the gate we know only that it holds the Vœlva's gravemound, Hella's hall, Eljudhnir, and Na-strond, the Corpse-strand, whose walls are woven of serpents whose venom floods the floor. It is there that the oath-breakers and murderers must dwell. I suspect that Hella's hall is in the middle, and that like the goddess herself, it is half bright and fair and half in gloomy shadow. Some of the descriptions of Hel are forbidding indeed, but when Hermod sought Baldr there, he saw him feasting in splendor.

(Paxson, in prep.)

The importance of the journey to the seeress may be different. The training material suggests that by providing symbols and images that stem from the Norse literature, it increases the possibility that the 'original material' that follows, the visions of the seeress and her description of these, will be also within 'the same stratum of the collective unconscious,' the imagery of the North. The meditation, then, becomes a way in which the subsequent seeings are embedded in cultural/cosmological awareness.

The descriptions come from an assiduous search in, and familiarity with, the literature, especially the *Poetic* and *Prose Eddas*, Saxo's *Gesta Danorum*, and relevant modern commentaries such as *The Road to Hel* (Ellis 1968) and *Gods and Myths of Northern Europe* (Davidson 1964/1990). Part is from those poems of the *Poetic Edda* that give cosmological description: *Grímnismál* (the sayings of Grímnir) tells of Hvergelmír, source of all waters, of Thund, or the 'thunderflood', and of the concept of rivers flowing from Asgarð to Hel. The same poem speaks of the three roots of Yggdrasill, Hel lying under one. From *Völuspá* comes the dog Garm who guards the way to Hela's realm: Óðinn meets him also in the poem *Baldrsdraumr* (Baldr's dreams), as he rides to Hel to raise a dead Völva, to learn the meaning of the dreams of his son. The echoing bridge and the giant maiden Móðguðr come from Snorri's account (in his *Edda*) of Hermóð's ride to Hel's hall after the death of Baldr. The details of the hemlock, and the crowing cock, come from descriptions in Saxo Grammaticus' account of the visit of the hero Hadingus to the otherworld. Other details are from folklore.

This guided meditation or 'pathworking', however, has been much debated within the community of Heathen seiðworkers. To some, it appears to slant the seiðr ritual in the direction of present-day neo-pagan practice, where 'pathworkings' are more familiar: a criticism is that the audience members are not 'really' journeying, as the imagery is provided for them. One practitioner, Yngona, commented that pathworkings are training exercises connected with 'the journey within': if someone is 'really there' in the otherworld, what they will see will not be the pathworking.

> The route above seems far too circuitous. If I wish to go somewhere then I simply GO. I indeed utilize Yggdrasil as the 'ladder' it is. Descending both up & down (so to speak), but all this other rigmarole is fluff. Again, in my opinion. . . When you are really, truly in the other planes you will see things that you cannot describe. When we apply paths, tunnels and shrubs and such we are merely applying what our mind feels it needs to cope with a world not defined by time, space or events. When we break free from these restraints, for indeed they are, our Visions become more clear and our journey more profound.

The Hrafnar seeress Rauðhildr replied:

> There is a part of the human mind that from time to time needs to be distracted so it does not interfere with the work at hand. The journey 'persuades' that part of the 'busy mind' that a 'real' thing is happening and that one needs to pay attention. . . Another reason Hrafnar does the long journey is because of where we offer seið. It gives context and spirit worldview to non-Asatruar or new folk who are not as well read. Another reason to do it this way has been that some folk go into trance more slowly than others. Those who go into trance quickly tend to not recall the long version of the journey, just that they are where they need to be.
> Is this the sort of answer you wanted? Forgive the humor in this, but, would you know more?
>
> (From email discussion of seiðr, 1999)

Much of this discussion may have arisen from a perception that the pathworking is a way of inducing ecstatic trance in the seer: its primary purpose however appears to me to be for the audience, particularly where, as Rauðhild says, this audience is not familiar with the cosmology.

Neo-shamanistic practitioners, constructing the seiðr within a setting in which all present are used to working shamanically, use singing, not pathworking, as a means of allowing a more general access to an ecstatic state, as do some Heathen groups. However, among those practitioners that I have met, there is a general acceptance that people will reconstruct the seiðr in their own way, and that the Hrafnar version with its elaborate meditation performs a different function from the seiðr trances described by Lindquist (1997).

I turn, therefore, to seiðr as described by other shamanic practitioners.

Neo-shamanistic seiðr

Lindquist gives a detailed account of today's 'seid' in Sweden,[4] as conducted by the neo-shamanistic group known as 'Yggdrasil', and something of its history: beginning as an idea about 'Nordic shamanism' and resulting in research by practitioners which led them to the Greenland seeress. In her description, seid appears first as a means, for its practitioners, of focusing spirit power and influencing events, with a specific example of the rescue of the Hansta woods from developers. Several people may take their places, in turn, on the seidhjälle, each völva (female or male) stating an intention at the outset, for instance; 'I seid for all the woods on the Earth, and especially for the Hansta woods' (Lindquist 1997: 139). She or he undertakes an ecstatic journey and speaks with spirits or deities, towards the stated purpose. On return, the völva may or may not make statements about their journey. Lindquist terms this 'instrumental seid', made for a purpose.

'Research seid' is taken similarly, though in quest of information of the past rather than to effect change. Lindquist also discusses seid for divination, and for personal counselling. In all cases the outline of the ritual is the same. The seid begins with the völva seated on a high platform, the seidhjälle, holding her staff between her legs as if riding it. Others in the circle drum and sing seid songs, while the seeress journeys, with a specific question in mind or generally to seek knowledge from present, past or future. The völva raises her staff to indicate when she is ready to speak, and describes what she has seen. The others then drum her back. In counselling seid the focus is to answer the specific questions of individuals in the circle. When the seer raises his staff, members of the circle take their places before him, one after the other, each asking what has been seen for them. (It should be noted that since the time of Galina's description, practices have developed further (Høst, pers. com.)

Within Britain, some shamanistic practitioners (with initial links to Harner's 'core-shamanism') have been learning seid, under the guidance of Danish seidworker Annette Høst, who first made contact with seiðr through the Swedish 'Yggdrasil' network. A group member produces the newsletter *Spirit Talk*, of which the issue dated Early Summer 1999 (Kelly 1999a) was devoted to seid/seiðr. Here, and in a more detailed account in an academic conference volume (Høst, forthcoming) Høst describes her basic seiðr ritual: basically similar to that of Yggdrasil, but drawing on her own study of the sources in the literature.

> The volva sits on the high seat holding onto her staff, surrounded by a circle of singers. The sound carries the volva into an altered state of awareness, into the spirit world. There she meets with spirits, gods and forces, and puts forward her request for help or knowledge. When her main task is completed and the song dies out, and volva is still 'between the worlds' and in this state she can give oracular answers to questions from members of the group.
>
> (Kelly 1999b)

From this, and from a discussion with Annette Høst, David Scott and Karen Kelly, divergences between this modern European shamanism model and Hrafnar's oracular seiðr become more plainly located within the orientation of practitioners and, particularly, their sense of what the seiðr is planned to do. David and Karen participated in a demonstration of the Hrafnar version, conducted by Diana Paxson in London, which they found interesting though somewhat disorienting in its differences. Karen pointed out that for her group of 'shamanically experienced' people – in the sense that all present have quite extensive acquaintance with working shamanically – doing a guided meditation to the gates of

Hela's realm, with the expectation of gaining a light trance state but not necessarily remaining in this, was much less 'ecstatic' as an experience than being part of a singing circle accompanying the seeress into a trance state and remaining there throughout the ritual. They find the Hrafnar ritual more formal, more highly structured, but appreciate its suitability with a large group where some may have little previous experience with shamanistic technique. In the Hrafnar version, not all practitioners use the staff while in the high seat.. They found the lack of a staff strange, though David pointed out that in the Hrafnar version, a person stands behind the seeress, 'shadowing' her and giving emotional and energy 'support' (and occasionally physical support if needed). He had taken this role, and considered himself to have been acting 'like the staff', becoming a channel for the energy that carries the seeress through the ecstatic journey.

There are other differences of implication and approach, concerning the meaning of the term 'seiðr'. Whereas the Hrafnar version focuses on the cosmology of the Nine Worlds, the Well of the Norns and the tree Yggdrasill, and includes invocations to Óðinn and Freyja, other shamanistic versions have less specificity, most practitioners assuming a more general 'neo-shamanic' approach to the upper, middle and lower worlds though drawing on familiarity with Nordic mythology and cosmology. However, for those practitioners who have grown up with the mythology of the North, or who have studied the literature extensively, this may not make a difference: for many of the European practitioners, it seems that the cosmological framework is *there*, whether or not deities are invoked – a cosmology rooted in the sense of the land and its spirits, and of the tree Yggdrasill. Likewise, when Heathens work in small groups, no guided meditation may be used: the cosmological framework is simply *there*, as it is when one individual 'sees' for herself or on behalf of another. Invocations may be to landspirits and to one's fylgia or animal ally rather than to deities; indeed there may be no formal 'invocation' but simply chanting in which names from the mythology are used.

For practitioners whose consciousness is not rooted in the cosmology of the Well, the Norns and the tree Yggdrasill, though, there may be a substantial difference in meaning and implication, so that 'seiðr' (however undertaken) becomes but one more way to contact 'the spirits'.

Some shamanistic practitioners may use the term 'seid' to refer specifically to an ecstatic experience involving song, staff and high seat. Conversely, Heathens tend to use the term 'seiðr' for any shamanistic practice conducted within Heathenism, that is within the cosmology of the Norns, the Well and the Tree. Healing, seeing, or engaging with Wyrd, accomplished within an ecstatic trance is therefore 'seiðr', and outsitting or *útiseta* (described in the next chapter) is equally 'seiðr', because of the mythological embedding, the cosmological focus. For the European practitioners associated with Høst (and many Heathens practising in Britain and Europe), embedding likewise results from drawing on powers of earth and nature spirits associated with the land, and this sense of embeddedness – be it based in cosmology or nature – returns us to the words of Bil, quoted in the last chapter:

> Everything that I do, think, say, perceive, or whatever is passed through that belief system. And because it is filtered through that system, everything I practice is authentic.
>
> (Linzie 1995: 17)

In order to further appreciate these practices of seiðr, it is necessary to turn to a consideration of seiðr as shamanic or shamanistic practice, definitions of shamanism, and contested interpretations of the descriptions of the old literature; to concepts of what or who are these 'spirits'; and to the means by which people might approach them, today or in the past, and this I do in the next chapter.

Chapter 4

Approaching the spirits

The seer/ess as shamanistic practitioner

In this chapter I intend to introduce some theorising of 'shamanism' as engagement between practitioner and spirits, emphasising the 'reality' of spirits to the participant and hence the need to 'take spirits seriously'. It should be stated at once that Norse culture of 1,000 years ago was not obviously 'shamanic' in the sense in which Tungus or Sámi or Déné culture is said to be or have been shamanic: the sense in which Guédon says that 'Shamanism permeates all of Nabesna culture: the worldview, the subsistence patterns, and the life cycles' (Guédon 1994). In the saga descriptions we find neither a reliance on a shamanic worldview nor a 'shamanic complex' of activities; no 'shaman' is described as central to community life. There are kings and queens and battle-leaders, goðar associated with different deities, and in Iceland the emergence of a representative system of goðar, as regional administrators, co-ordinated by a 'lawspeaker' – and no shamans, only occasional seiðworkers and other magic practitioners. Yet there are occasions – particularly in times of trouble or famine – where these seiðworkers become important, as in the episode of the Greenland Seeress.

What does this mean for interpretation of the cultures described in the old material? Particularly, what does it imply for today's practitioners, in terms of their constructions of meaning?

A possible conclusion is that oracular seiðr and other magical practices may represent rather scattered remnants of shamanistic techniques in Norse culture, related to the shamanic practices of other cultures, notably the Sámi (e.g. Dubois 1999), though not necessarily derived from Sámi practice (Hultkrantz 1992), and indeed this is where I began my inquiry as to the existence of shamanic versus shamanistic traits in Old Norse society (Blain

1999). Grundy points out (1995: 220) that 'The only figures in Germanic culture which we can point to as bearing significant resemblance to the "professional shaman" ...are the seeresses who occupy a position of respect based on their visionary capabilities' though they do not demonstrate other shamanic techniques or activities. The seeresses often are said to have been trained by 'the Finns', which probably refers to the nomadic Sámi. Sámi shamanism has been described in Scandinavian accounts at least since the twelfth century, and up to the present day (Pentikäinen 1984).

This question of 'seiðworker' or 'shaman' connects with questions of what 'shamanism' is and how it can be used, as a concept, to explain or assist understanding of cultural manifestations such as seiðr or out-sitting: and how far the term 'shamanism' can be used of people's ecstatic practices in today's Western world. The term and its use have a history, discussed for instance by Flaherty (1992), and Pentikäinen (1998). 'Shaman' was initially specific to Tungus/Evenki speaking peoples: from explorer's accounts, 'shamanism' was constructed, generalised and universalised into a Westernism (Wallis 1999a), an abstraction coined to explain aspects of religious and spiritual practice of 'other people', in societies as different from the defining Westerners as possible. In short, the term has been a Western way of 'othering', exoticising and decontextualising specific spiritual/religious/magical practices.

Attempted precise definitions of 'shamanism' range from Eliade's (1964), of soul flight to an upper world, to Jakobsen's (1999), of mastery of spirits. These definitions, to my mind, miss essential components of what shamans do: social dimensions of practice (Oosten 1984). Shamans work within communities, and what they do, spatially, geographically and politically located, changes over time and with changing circumstances. Yet conventional views, whether within academia or the popular culture of the 'new age', are of shamanism as somehow 'timeless' or 'primordial' (as Greene (1998) points out), with the shaman as a repository of unchanging magical practice, close to 'nature' and the animals. A different kind of understanding may be gained by viewing shamans, and their shamanisms, in context, in particular times and particular (socio-spiritual, economic, geographical and climatic) landscapes, as political beings engaged in forming and maintaining relationships with other members of their specific communities, both human and non-human: with their activities supported by the community (Blain and Wallis 2000). For example, in the regeneration of Buryat shamanism, 'the determinants of locale and kinship establish the specific connection to nature and to the particular efficacious spirits' (Fridman 1999: 45). However, the reluctance of contemporary Western scholarship to take magic, or spirits, seriously (Tambiah 1990) may be reflected in what Dowson (1996) and Wallis (1999b) call 'shamanophobia' – to which Wallis adds 'neo-shamanophobia' – within academia.

In attempting to understand seiðr I prefer to approach 'shamanism' as indicating the construction of specific relations of negotiation and mediation, achieved through techniques of trance – ecstasy attained by otherworldly experience – embedded in specific social relations and cultural settings. Thus the trance both emerges from and partly constitutes socio-political relations within the community. A particular 'shamanism' becomes a specific expression of community and identity (see e.g. Pentikäinnen (1994), on circumpolar shamanism as identity), while simultaneously implicated in processes of cultural/political change through the agency of 'shamans' and others within the community. I take, therefore, a dynamic approach to 'shamanism', which here becomes a convenient way to describe specific ecstatic practices, supported by the community and on its behalf, together with the specific cultural support for such activities.

The Old Norse material becomes particularly interesting, however, because shamanistic activity is *not* supported by the entire community: it is contested on a number of levels (Blain and Wallis 2000). Here it may be useful to remember processes of change within the period described by the sagas: expansion of trade links, centralisation, Christianisation, the settlement of Iceland, among others. Conceivably, in some communities, in some periods a seiðworker *did* hold a position not so dissimilar to that of a Sámi shaman. Rather than saying that there was one unified 'Norse' culture, it may be more helpful to examine instances – told long after the occurrences they purport to describe – in terms of how they reflect shamanistic techniques elsewhere, how these techniques may have been embedded in community practice, and how their definition may have been contested, in past and present. That is: understandings of 'seiðr' (or for that matter of Sámi shamanism) were likely to have varied from one person to another, one community to another, one time to another, and some clues to the diversity of those understandings may be held in the stories that were told by the saga writers.

How far, therefore, do or did these seeresses, and seers, work 'shamanically', according to this more dynamic approach to 'shamanism'?

Seeresses enter again and again into the Icelandic poems and sagas. Katherine Morris (1991) has catalogued some of their activities. For instance:

> Heið, the sibyl of *Hrólfs saga Kraka* 3, was also treated hospitably and then asked to prophesy... King Frodi asked her to make use of her talents, prepared a feast for her, and set her on platform for her spell-making. She then opened her mouth, yawned, cast a spell and chanted a verse...
>
> (Morris 1991: 45)

Þórdís, the seeress of *Kormáks saga* and *Vatnsdæla saga*, was 'held in great esteem and knew many things', and the hill behind her dwelling was named after her, Spákonufell, the mountain of the seeress. These women, and others, such as Oddbjörg of *Víga-Glúms saga*, Kjannok of *Heiðarvíga saga*, Heimlaug of *Gull-Þóris saga*, are woven into the fabric of the family sagas, the stories of everyday life, written by Icelanders two or three hundred years after Christianisation to tell of the lives of their ancestors who settled the country. Some details of these women are given in chapter 6. They can be seen as semi-historic; they, and others like them, lived and had their being within a cultural framework in which trance, magic and prophesy were possibilities for women: to the extent that in the later legendary sagas and short stories (told for entertainment value), the seeing-women appear once again.

Thus, in the *Tale (þáttr) of Norna-Gest*, it is told that three wise women came to the house of Norna-Gest's parents, at his birth, and foretold his future: a lack of attention to the youngest norn caused her to attempt to countermand the great prophesies of her elders, stating that the boy's life would be no longer than that of the candle burning beside him. The eldest norn extinguished the candle and gave it to the boy's mother to preserve. Three hundred years later, so goes the story, Norna-Gest related his story to the king of Norway, accepted Christian baptism, and had the candle lit, dying as the flame expired. Arrow-Odd, the hero of *Örvar-odds saga*, likewise had an extended life, of 300 years, and both this life and the strange death that ended it were predicted by a seiðkona known as Heiðr. The implication is that the prediction of the death is in some way adverse to Arrow-Odd, and indeed it occurs through his (much earlier) attempts to circumvent it.

Seeing might be only one component of what one who was *fjölkunnigr* – possessing much knowledge – could do. The accounts refer to people who change shape, to avoid enemies, to seek knowledge, or to cause trouble. In sagas and later folktales, people would discover that their problems were associated with the appearance of a particular animal. When this animal was wounded or killed, a woman would have a similar wound. In the *Saga of Kormák the Skáld*, when Kormák and his brother set off in a ship, a walrus appears close by. Kormák aims a spear at it, striking it, and it disappears. The walrus had the eyes of the woman Þorveig, described in the saga as *fjölkunnig*. 'Þóttust menn þar kenna augu Þórveigar.'[1] Reportedly, Þorveig died from this spear-wound.

At other times the metamorphosis was made for protection, as in accounts of swan-maidens who guarded chosen warriors. The shapeshifter is *hamhleypa*, one who is *hamramr*, shape-strong. Another example from *Kormáks saga* is Vigi, who is both *fjölkunnigr* and *hamramr*; he sleeps by the door of the hall, and knows the business of everyone who enters or leaves.

In the old material there is no overall word for 'shaman', but many words for components of shamanic practice. This may indicate that by the time of the composition of the sagas, two hundred years post-Christianisation, the practices were in decline. Alternatively, it may suggest that the specific components of shamanic/ecstatic practice were widespread, general knowledge within the community, with individuals having their own specialisations of practice. What people were called depended not on the techniques they engaged in, but their relations with others in the community. If these relations were bad, a woman was *fordæða*, a word implying one who performed evil magic. Where relations were good, we have the spae-woman. (In Scotland, the term *spae-wife* is still used today.)

So, seiðr-related practices are described, in the Icelandic literature, as relating to individual skills, but their practitioners are named according to their relations with others in the community. Seiðr was not simple, and not necessarily either 'good' or 'evil', but was in some sense woven into the daily life of practitioners and those they worked for. In the stories the episodes deal mostly with individual seiðworkers and individual clients. There are, however, exceptions.

In one case we have a woman awarded a name within those communities she visited: Þurídr *sundafyllir*, 'Thurid sound-filler', who according to the *Book of Settlements* gained her name by calling fish into the sound, by means of seiðr, thereby providing prosperity for the people. Borovsky (1999) points out that this instance and that of the Greenland Seeress hold an association with fertility or prosperity, and she speculates that practitioners used seiðr techniques, calling the spirits, to actively accomplish this fertility by bringing the components of *innangarð* and *útangarð* – approximately settlement and wildness, deities and giants, knowable and unknowable – back into balance within the communities. If so, these are examples of seiðr as active magic, involving spirits and ecstatic practice for community benefit and with community support: that is, potentially 'shamanic' in the dynamic, community-based sense referred to above. Several of today's practitioners, including Rauðhildr, Jordsvin and Susan, have speculated likewise: it 'fits' with their practices today.

References to seiðr, therefore, are plentiful but fragmented. They do not form a manual for practice. Yet from this fragmentation, today's practitioners work to construct seiðr, not as an individual technique in itself, but as part of a developing complex of beliefs about soul and self, person and community, within community relationships that involve people with other beings, wights of land and sea or stream, deities known to Heathens as their 'Elder Kin'. All these beings form part of the fabric of Wyrd, the destiny which people and deities make together, woven by the Norns, Urð, Verðandi and Skuld, who are invoked within Hrafnar's seiðr ritual, as they sit by *Urðarbrunnr*, Urð's Well, at the root of the Ash Yggdrasill.

Seiðworkers have the task of contacting these beings, negotiating with them, linking together these multiple communities through the use of altered-consciousness states. How they do this, and who they meet with, we shall see.

Attaining trance

A word about ways of attaining trance or altered-consciousness states is in order. As mentioned above, Hrafnar's oracular seiðr utilises both drumming and singing, the journey meditation may also provide a way into trance states, and the repetitive nature of the pattern of question and answer may help sustain the focused trance state in the seer/ess. This is not the only mechanism for attaining trance, or the only ones used by Heathen seiðworkers. Whether for oracular seiðr or in other forms, some practitioners use forms of galdr or rune-chanting; many have their own 'shamanic songs' that they have received (or composed) in trance and use to attain, deepen, or work within ecstatic states; some use rattles or other instruments, others dance, and of course many combinations of those methods are possible, and means of attainment will bevaried to suit circumstances and surroundings. Harner-based neo-shamanism, though, tends to privilege the drum above other methods (for discussion see Wallis, forthcoming, b).

Within 'traditional' shamanisms or contexts of altering consciousness a number of other methods are described. These are not necessarily ways into the trance: in Sámi shamanism, drum and chant may be a vehicle for travel within the otherworlds. Shamanisms described within Eurasian contexts include use of a number of string and wind instruments (see e.g. Basilov 1997). Other methods of achieving or assisting trance states include use of consciousness-altering substances such as alcohol, cannabis, and ergot (*Claviceps purpurea*) in Eurasian contexts, or tobacco, peyote, psilocybin mushrooms (*Psilocybe* and *Stropharia* spp.), ayahuasca/yajé (*Banisteriopsis* spp.) and a variety of other plants in the Western hemisphere (see e.g. Ripinsky-Naxon 1993; Schultes and Hoffman 1992). Within seiðr practice whether in the past or today, a number of these may be relevant. First, however, a word about the use of entheogens within neo-shamanisms generally.

Despite Harner's early engagement with specific consciousness-altering substances, notably ayahausca and (terrifyingly, by his account on pp. 14–16) maikua, a species of datura, as described in *The Way of the Shaman* (Harner 1980), core-shamanism's methods do not usually include use of entheogens. Harner states:

> Shamans have to be able to journey back and forth between realities. To do this, in some cultures, shamans take mindaltering substances; but in many other cultures they do not. In fact, some psychoactive materials can interfere with the concentration shamanic work demands.
>
> (1980: 44)

and elsewhere comments that in his own research,

from (various North American Native groups) I learned how shamanism could be practiced successfully without the use of the *ayahuasca* or other drugs of the Conibo and the Jivaro.

(1980: 19)

Opinion on use of entheogens is divided among neo-shamanic practitioners, and may emerge, heatedly, as disagreements over what is or is not 'real' shamanism. However, a number of other writers accept that entheogens have uses, for instance practising shaman Gordon MacLellan.

The use of mind-altering, usually plant-derived, drugs has been one of the most widely promoted traditional shamanic practices and, alongside drums and rattles, seems to be an expected part of every shaman's repertoire... 'Teacher plant' is a title given in some traditional cultures to certain plants which are recognised as being especially effective agents for inducing trance and for taking a shaman on powerful journeys...The teacher plants are very powerful, and the drugs that are derived from their extracts open routes into Otherworlds that may be wildly different from those entered by other means. These worlds are full of colour and changing perspectives, deeply surreal experiences and, at times, numbing horrors... in the hands of an experienced shaman, the teacher plants themselves will meet the traveller and through their influence she will encounter spirits rarely met elsewhere and experience a world of awareness and consciousness far in excess of the basic chemical influences.

(MacLellan 1999: 45–6)

So, some of today's neo-shamans make use of 'psychoactive' substances, in addition to drumming, rattling, chanting, music, dancing, etc. Complexities arise, however, in the ways in which entheogen use, more than any other method, is politically contested within Western societies. It is noteworthy that those neo-shamanic 'best-sellers', the 'shamanovels' (I borrow the term from Noel 1997) of Casteneda, in the psychedelic 1960s described entheogen use, but by 1972 Casteneda's teachers promoted ways to get there without using 'drugs': as Wallis says, 'again nicely timed for a post-psychedelic audience' (Wallis 1999b: 35). Harner's espousal of an entheogen-free neo-shamanism seems to me likewise to relate to prevailing tendencies within the mostly US context of the Foundation for Shamanic Studies, and the time of the 'war on drugs'.

Where does this leave today's seiðr practitioners? The most relevant substance for seiðr practice in the past would appear to be *Amanita muscaria*, uses of which in Siberian shamanisms have been attested by a variety of writers (see e.g. Basilov 1997; Eliade 1964; Wasson 1971). While there can be no direct claim for use, there have been speculations that *A. muscaria*-induced trance has features similar to trance states described in sagas, notably the ability of the Lawspeaker, Thorgeir, to remain 'under the cloak' in what is apparently a trance state for a very long period of time (as described later in this chapter). The sagas, however, do not mention any entheogens in any context that I can discover: the special meal prepared for the seeress in *Eiríks saga rauða* is of the hearts of animals and is eaten the night before her seiðr is to occur. References to drinking in the Eddas (e.g. Mimir's well, the mead of poetry) are ambiguously metaphorical at best (though in a highly speculative mode, Steven Leto (2000) suggests that the use of both *A. muscaria* and *P. semilanceata* may be represented metaphorically in various poems or sagas). Archaeology, however, gives some evidence, from several hundred henbane seeds found in the pouch of a burial considered to be that of a seeress (Price, pers. com.) and a very small number of cannabis seeds present in the Oseberg burial (often considered to be that of a seeress or a priestess), carefully placed, Neil Price tells me, between the cushions and feathers piled by the bed.[2]

This should be seen in context. *A. muscaria* was (and is today) used by Siberian shamans, and a variety of other plants which are today recognised as psychoactive do and did grow in Northern Europe and may have been known and used shamanically from very long before the period of seiðr (remembering that that designation covers a wide area, and that the period of time in which seiðr might have its roots is indeed long).[3] These include the rather dangerous nightshade family members henbane (*Hyoscyamus niger*) and deadly nightshade (*Atropa belladonna*), and fungi including ergot (*Claviceps purpurea*, found apparently in the stomach of the Iron Age 'Grauballe Man' in Denmark), and 'liberty caps' (*Psilocybe semilanceata*); there may be evidence of use of hemp in the European 'Celtic' Iron Age (Green 1996); and other plants that may have mildly psychoactive effects include artemisias such as wormwood and mugwort. (While the activity of the last is very mild if indeed there at all, at least it has some claim to status as a 'sacred' herb within Anglo-Saxon magical/healing practice, for instance in the 'Nine Herbs Charm' (Rodriguez 1993: 136) and numerous commentators, notably Leary (1968; Leary, Metzner and Allpert 1964/1983) have pointed to the importance of cultural/psychological assumptions or 'set' in evaluating the effects of mind-altering substances.)

The foregoing should indicate that both psychoactivity of substances, and the concepts of what are meant by 'ecstatic' or 'trance states', are highly complex. Attempts to 'measure' the effects of different methods of trance-induction (see e.g. Dronfield 1993, 1995) may succeed in associating particular entoptic patterns with means of trance-induction, but they do not indicate what is possible for the 'shamans' to effect through the trance. Similarly (though non-entheogenically), Goodman (1990, 1999) indicates patterns and similarities in altered consciousness visions described by volunteers, facilitated by the adoption of positions indicated in statuettes, cave paintings, and other sources seen as 'shamanic', while listening to a drumbeat. Yet, while such attempts give insight into altered consciousness in Western naïve subjects, they do not indicate what a 'shaman' may do with experiences so derived or how she or he interacts with spirits. The Foundation for Shamanic Studies differentiates between an 'ordinary state of consciousness' (OSC) and 'shamanic state of consciousness' (SSC), a distinction used in turn by Achterberg (1985) and others. But (as Achterberg indeed indicates) there are many states of consciousness that each of us goes through in the course of a waking day – and in sleeping, dreaming, or 'lucid dreaming'. Privileging one state as 'shamanic' implies that this is what shamans do – but shamans may deliberately seek different states for different types of interaction with spirit and human worlds (and indeed much of their work may take place in a very clear-headed 'everyday reality'). It seems to me that what distinguishes 'shamanic' from 'shamanistic' or 'alternative' prac- tices is that the 'shaman' works with these states, and with cultural/cosmological understandings of spirits met, to achieve something – useful knowledge, diagnosis, healing, balance, a shift in perceptions of others, an alteration in Wyrd; not only a temporary alteration in the practitioner's perception.

As already stated, there seems no direct evidence for the use of any entheogens specifically in seiðr or for trance-induction during the saga period: yet it would seem highly unlikely (especially given contacts with Sámi and other practitioners, and given that seeds have been found in appropriate contexts) that *no* psychoactive substance would be used in any 'Germanic' area for trance purposes – the prime contenders, as implied above, being *Amanita muscaria*, henbane, hemp, ergot, and probably *Psilocybe semilanceata*. It is interesting to note that while at least in the UK and much of Scandinavia (Leto, pers. com.) 'toadstools' (referring to almost any wild mushroom) have been regarded with extreme suspicion, the colourful red-and-white fly agaric (*A. muscaria*) has been the subject of much ambivalence, regarded as 'poison'[4] yet in folklore associated with elves, and the subject of copious nineteenth- and twentieth-century illustrations. The small, inconspicuous *P. semilanceata* had by contrast apparently dropped out of sight and folk-memory until the middle of the twentieth century, when the discovery by Westerners of psilocybin mushrooms in Mexico led to a developing awareness of 'magic mushrooms' in Europe.

An alternative etymology for the term 'seiðr' relates it to 'seethe', and indeed one version of today's seiðr practice, in Norway and Britain, includes *tein-seid*, herb-seið. This is related more to healing herbalism than to shamanic use of entheogens, but is indicative of an association with plants, and their preparation and use, by practitioners or clients.

Of today's seið-practitioners, one describes his association with the 'Little Red Man' (*Amanita muscaria*) in the website at http://www.angelfire.com/nm/seidhman/luck.html (Linzie n.d.). More common, though, is the attitude that 'drugs' are not appropriate: particularly within a US context. Certainly in oracular seiðr sessions that I have attended, entheogens have not been in evidence (other than mead or beer used as an offering and for consumption after the ritual, not before). However, some seið-practitioners make use of entheogens in private 'journeying' or spirit contact, and for healing-seiðr and protection seiðr, often in an attempt to determine courses of action to follow, to give greater clarity to what can be seen and understood: these might be *Psilocybe* mushrooms or cannabis, artemesias such as wormwood or mugwort, or sometimes *A. muscaria*. Some say they have 'tried everything', to find what works and to explore possibilities. It should be pointed out that (as MacLellan stresses), sacramental use of entheogens is not the same as recreational use. 'It's not just dropping acid', said a practitioner.

Bil gave me a detailed account of his use: once again stressing that these are spirits that he contacts to help him 'make seiðr' and use the seiðr effectively.

I make fairly extensive use of entheogens, in particular, Fliegepilz (amanita muscaria var. muscaria), toloache (datura inoxia), Johnson grass seed (stipa robusta) and several varieties of artemisia (a. lucoviciana; a. franserioides). All of which are legal. I use them to make seidh, both healing kind and the protective kind. I don't recommend them to anyone, personally. Their ghosts are of their own mind and they will often volunteer their services. They will not be controlled, and toloache can be very dangerous although the others don't have the same personality that he does (which is fairly ruthless and occasionally bloodthirsty).

I only deal with these because they came to me during the period when the spirits had me. They showed me where they grow and how to use them (and still do). They make decisions in many cases and possess skills that I don't have. They can go places I've never heard of and can figure out things that I am unable to.

Most (or many of these plant-ghosts) can be very seductive, I suppose. I personally have never trusted any of them although I find the Fliegepilz to be friendly. All of them have a fairly ruthless side, though, including the Fliegepilz.

When I make a seið, I work with a team of ghosts; different situations call for different team makeups. Inevitably, one of the members, for me, will be one (or more) of these. They lend power, control, intelligence, or clarity. They come together with others and act through me to make changes here on this Midgard. They maintain an interest here – their physical forms are here – but they are more like ghosts than plants. They are like the blackmarketeers of the ghost world. They can make shady deals, seem to know everyone, have their hands in everyone's cookie jar and are master string-pullers and button pushers.

I've definitely gotten into tight binds because of the way that they work, but they are thorough. They are able to make long range plans far better than I. Sometimes, I'd rather not work with them, but everytime I've tried that option there were truly large messes to clean up afterwards.

I work with them because they were the ghosts who picked me up when I was dying. We have a bond, an understanding.

They may eventually initiate the end of me as well – this I don't know. But while I live they are my staunchest comrades-in-arms.

Finally, in god-possession seiðr the Hrafnar group may find alcohol consumption to be a component of the trance (Wallis 1999b), but alcohol is not generally used as a trance-producing substance, although it may be used as an offering in heathen rituals and there is acknowledgement that it has the power to alter consciousness, not merely through the usual effects of alcohol but through ritual blessing and through similarity to the 'mead of poetry' consumed by oðinn and given by him to those people selected as poets.

The description in the saga of Eirik the Red includes one sentence on the preparations the seeress needed to make. The platform is already built, with its cushion of hens' feathers in place. The seeress' costume has been described. She has yet to find the woman to sing the song. We are told:

> En um morgininn at áliðnum degi var henni veittr sá umbúningr sem hon þurfti at hafa til at fremja seiðinn.
>
> (Gordon 1957: 56)

> And the next day at sunset she made the preparations that she needed to carry out the seiðr.

What these preparations were, we do not know. Anything is possible: adding items to her dress (which is another possible reading of the sentence), lighting a smoke smudge, arranging the torches, addressing her spirit guardians or deities, dancing, or even ingesting mushrooms. Nor are we likely ever to know.

Seiðr as evil magic?

Of today's practitioners, many follow the Hrafnar group or Bil in using the word 'seiðr' for what they do, whether they work as community-diviners using oracular seiðr, 'sit out' in quest of private knowledge, work with spirits to make others 'whole', or otherwise engage with Wyrd. Some prefer to use the term *spá*, well-attested in the sagas for those who speak with foreknowledge. Thus Winifred is a *spákona*, Jordsvin a *spámaðr*. *Spá* (or *spae*, as in the Scottish 'spaewife') refers to foretelling, or prophesying. These words, *spá* and seiðr, have differing implications within the old literature – the *spákona* or *spámaðr* is spoken of with respect, for the most part, whereas the *seiðkona* or *seiðmaðr* is often regarded ambivalently. Seiðr may imply not only trance-divination, but what Jordsvin calls 'messing with people's minds' (this is not, he emphasises, what he does, whatever people call it); or using shapeshifting to journey in this world, not the spirit world, and use the knowledge gained to the detriment of others, and influencing or affecting other people's behaviour by means of the journey.

An example from the old literature is from *Egils saga Skallagrímssonar*. Egill is in the power of his enemies, in York, England, attempting to write a poem which will save his life. He cannot concentrate for the twittering of a swallow – all night long – by his window. His friend goes up onto the roof, and sees the bird flying off. The implication is that the bird is his arch-enemy Gunnhildr – Queen at York, and later of Norway – who is striving (unsuccessfully, thanks to the friend's intervention) to prevent his composition and thereby cause his death. Various interpretations of Gunnhildr, and of 'evil magic' and 'women's magic', will be further explored in chapter 6.

This leads to another important point about the old literature. It deals in seeresses and *fordæða*, female practitioners. Most accounts of seiðr are of women. Male seiðworkers of saga-times – in the late, Christian accounts that we have – were deemed to be 'ergi', un-masculine, possibly crossing gender barriers in ways not then acceptable. It is unclear at what time this negativity spread to include *seiðkonur* (seiðr-women), or how the spread of Christianity affected ways in which seiðr-workers were regarded.

Another word, though, is *útiseta*, and this is how some men – including leaders, kings – are spoken of in the sagas as gaining knowledge, *seta úti til fróðleiks* (sitting out for wisdom). A variant of this may be going 'under the cloak' as it is said did Thorgeirr the lawspeaker of the Icelandic Althing, prior to taking the decision to have Iceland formally convert to Christianity (Blain, in press). Out-sitting is used by Heathens and neo-shamanists today, and its description forms another piece of the puzzle within this chapter of how people 'make seiðr', as part of the construction of Northern ecstatic practice today.

Under the cloak

As the story is told, one thousand years ago, the Icelanders were in a quandary. Some were adherents of the old religion, *Heiðni* or

Heathenry, while others had taken up the new religion of Christianity, and there were external pressures, including economic sanctions and threats to people who were held hostage overseas, inclining the people towards the new religion. There was debate and argument before the Law Rock. In the twelfth century Ari Þorgilsson wrote a description of the 'conversion', in his *Islendingabók*.[5]

> ...the Christian people and the Heathen declared that they would not live under each other's laws, and they went away then from the law-rock.
>
> Then the Christians asked Hall of Sída to declare the laws for the Christians to follow. But he declined, making a bargain with Þorgeirr the Lawspeaker that he should declare the law, being himself still Heathen. And when the people came to the booths,[6] then Þorgeirr lay down, and spread his cloak over him, and he lay all day, and the night after, saying no word. And the next morning he sat up and called people to the law-rock.
>
> There he addressed them, when the people came, saying that this seemed to him a desperate condition, that the people and the land be not under one law; and he related to the people many things that they should not allow to come to pass, and said that such disturbances must happen, that it was to be expected that such fights would arise between people that the land would be laid waste...

To resolve the situation, therefore, Þorgeirr went 'under the cloak', and his pronouncements when he emerged were adopted by both sides. His solution was that the people and the land become officially Christian, but that some Heathen points of law should be retained and that people's religions, practised in their own houses, should be their own business.[7] The account does not reveal the sources of Þorgeir's knowledge, though it indicates that the people, of both old and new religions, were inclined to take his word for it. Þorgeirr speaks with authority and assurance, and his method of going 'under the cloak' is accepted as a valid means of pursuing knowledge: and when he emerges, he speaks as though he has seen possible futures. He appears to be engaging in a form of útiseta, 'sitting out for wisdom'. I find convincing Jón Aðalsteinsson's (1978) arguments that the account of Þorgeirr is comparable with descriptions of others who clearly go 'under the cloak', and stay there for extended times, for magical or divinatory purposes. Sometimes they are described as 'muttering', 'mumbling' or 'murmuring' into the cloak. Aðalsteinsson points out that:

> To mutter or murmur or mumble into one's cloak thus means, as far as one can tell, to rehearse some kind of soothsaying. Those who practised this seemed by their conduct to be able to see what was hidden to others and to gain information in a supernatural way. They appear to have pulled their cloaks over their heads merely to concentrate better on their task.
>
> (Aðalsteinsson 1978: 113)

Aðalsteinsson sees Þorgeir's behaviour as more intense and longer-lasting: paralleling descriptions from Ireland and Scotland of the seer who would lie wrapped in a bull's hide, for knowledge, other accounts from Iceland of those who lie still while their spirits travel and cause events to occur, and indeed the *Heimskringla* description of Óðinn who lay as if 'asleep or dead' while his spirit journeyed, discussed in more detail in chapter 7.

In the descriptions, the knowledge gained through sitting out would be used by the out-sitter, or revealed at a later stage, rather than narrated in trance. Sitting out typically involved sitting on a gravemound or at a crossroads, going under the cloak could be done wherever one was, but both implied a distancing of oneself from the other human members of the community. The one who was sitting out was not to be disturbed, and in particular their name should not be mentioned (Aðalsteinsson 1978). Útiseta also became problematic, proscribed in Iceland in the laws of the thirteenth century, which remained in place until the nineteenth, in terms that name '...fordæðuskap ok spáfarar allar ok útiseta at vekja tröll upp ok fremja heiðni,' 'sorcery and spae-working (foretelling) and sitting out to wake up trolls and practising Heathenry', a wording which associated útiseta with gaining knowledge from other beings or spirits (we can treat the term 'trolls' as a derogatory re-working during Christian times). Referring to this law, Hastrup comments that 'By the act of sitting out, which was a metaphor for leaving the ordinary social space, it was possible to invoke supernatural beings'. While the penalty was death, no-one was convicted until Iceland's small witch-craze in the seventeenth century (Hastrup 1990: 391).

As with seiðr, members of today's Heathen community are attempting to rediscover techniques of útiseta, seeing it as a solitary practice, whereas oracular seiðr is a community ritual.

Men (and some women) appear also as practitioners of galdr, sung or spoken spells, which do not in themselves involve the shapeshifting, journeying or other shamanic/ecstatic components (and which together with knowledge of runes in the early modern period formed the basis of the few witchcraft accusations and convictions in Iceland – Hastrup 1990). However, that men could perform seiðr is evident. In chapter 7 I discuss how the ninth-century Norwegian king Haraldr Finehair, and his son Eiríkr called Bloodaxe, were responsible for the death of Eirík's brother Rögnvaldr *rettilbeini*, a *seiðmaðr*, and the troop of eighty *seiðmenn* with whom he was associated. Rather than representing a purely individual relation between people and the spirit world, the practice of seiðr and útiseta appears now associated with gender and with political power, and these dimensions will be explored in subsequent chapters.

Other, perhaps associated, political dimensions are evident also in today's community, as will become apparent. However, many people are enthusiastic about the techniques, and about their potential for use in healing and alternative medicine, as well as divination. They also see journeying and útiseta as a way to gain personal knowledge of the cosmology of the World Tree, Yggdrasill, and of deities and other wights, and so to explore the possibilities of religion together with conceptions of self and spirit.

Approaching the spirits

It is important, here, to return to the idea of 'the spirits', evaluating them from the practitioners' viewpoint – external, independent beings who may (at times) assist but require to be negotiated with, cajoled, even fought. Political dimensions of seiðr lie therefore in both 'everyday' and 'otherworld' realities. Bil's references to plant-ghosts, or helpers, as tricky, potentially dangerous, but assisting him as 'comrades in arms', have been already noted. A return to this discourse of the reality of spirits can indicate some of these 'spirits' that may be met with, and the ways in which seið-people are called on to interact with both human and spirit worlds, mediating between these.

'Spirit beings', therefore, may include ancestors, deities, plant or animal 'helpers', but refers also to various others associated with places, people or practices, who may help or hinder. While these are often 'explained away' (within psychology or anthropology of shamanism) as archetypes, fragments of the seer's personality, or remembered or reconstituted cultural expectations, within contexts of active shamanistic accomplishment of meaning these beings are met with as real, external entities who are not subject to the 'control' of the seeress. (This is discussed as a possible association for the term 'ergi' by Blain and Wallis (2000), and will be further pursued in chapter 7.) Suffice it to say here that seers in trance interact with 'spirits', treat them as 'real', and that this spirit-reality is presented as one reason for the careful construction of oracular seiðr, as will be discussed below.

At times, seers seek spirits in quest of knowledge; at times, spirits seek the seer. Often there are 'ancestors', and they may be helpful, interested, even approving or guiding. But spirits may be 'there' for their own purposes, at odds with those of the practitioner: disease spirits, for instance, or those associated with other problems, that may move between 'realities' even as the seiðworker does. After experiencing strange, toothed 'monsters' (described in chapter 5) I asked Bil's advice.

> I've encountered the beasts you describe several times. The mouths and the size of the creatures are always different (unless it's one I've come across before). They vary greatly in both looks and personality. Some were not friendly disposed towards me, some were filthy (carrying disease, I'm guessing), some were enemies, and one lived in my house for a long time never bothering me, but bothering people who slept over even knocking one out of bed. My guess is that they are troll. Never travel with companions (that I've noted), large variety of personality, never seen one in the daylight. Got into it with one and came out ahead (but sick afterwards), been chased by a few. The one who lived in my house was fine (very protective of the family, but a minor thief on occasion – didn't much like company over).

Heathen seer Ybjrteir discusses incidents when spirits have been difficult or dangerous. During an oracular seiðr, a participant asked a question of an ancestor, who turned out to be 'not a pleasant or good wight', came into Ybjrteir's body and refused to leave. The seer's sprit helpers told him how to expel the invading presence from his spirit-body (indeed saying, 'just shit it out!') and so he learned a way to deal with a hostile invasion. For this seer, seiðr is not only 'high seat' but includes 'trance and healing work'. He has met hostile spirits during these forms of seiðr also:

> I did a co-journey with someone that I thought was experienced ... and she wondered why she was involved with a well. During the journey I encountered one of the most frightening and I believe dangerous creatures...I have no idea if it is any mythical story...but it was a white snake with yellow eyes and yellow markings...I immediately became nauseated and cold...when I came out of the trance my hands and body were ice – PURPLE – my friends had to get me into a warm shower.

Such are not the kinds of spirit-beings that practitioners hope to meet, though this may be necessary to effect healing or protective seiðr, or 'deghosting'.

Examples of very different spirit-beings have already been met. Some are immense, powerful, the Maurnir (female etins or giants) who 'ate' Rauðhildr being a case in point. Rauðhildr considers there are things she can now do which directly result from that experience of dismemberment and re-constitution (at the behest of Loki, another 'spirit being'). She is, within her seiðr community, sought as one who has knowledge, skill, whose seiðr practice and 'performance' *works*. She engages with Wyrd on behalf of the community, and this is recognised.

Those Maurnir are not lightly to be sought, and she has met them only once since that time. But even spirits closer to the practitioner can be difficult, dangerous, not entirely predictable, as shown by Bil's multiple spirit-helpers. Indeed, only the seer's fylgja – animal ally or personal spirit-helper – can be regarded as reliable. There are others who appear: beings who have knowledge, especially if a querant asks something relating to a deity. Much of the work that Winifred described to me, for instance, involves deities, and she becomes a mediator, conveying information to others that is not intended for herself. Several seiðfolk have reported 'god-possessory' experiences, not necessarily having sought these out. Ybjrteir described a situation in which god-possession was unintentional, but appropriate:

> there was no expectation of it...someone just asked what Freyr wanted to teach him and Freyr stepped right in....it is as if another being has just comfortably sat down into your skin

with you...you are aware in the trance of them speaking through you and there is no fear, unlike the uncomfortableness of the angry dead man's spirit. The other time was Ullr. I do have to say after a Deity possession, my energy was high for a couple days after...both spiritually and physically. It was a nice side effect.

Hrafnar's god-possession experiences should be likewise described. These commenced, members told me, when, intending to celebrate an academic achievement by having the achiever welcomed into a party 'as if' he were Óðinn (by quoting appropriate lines of Eddic poetry) they found that the personality they were dealing with was not that of their friend: he was possessed by the god. They investigated rituals of possession (intending that this should occur again only deliberately), drawing on practices from Umbanda – including learning that the gods often like 'to party', but that the one who is possessed should strike a 'deal' with the god before letting her or him 'take over', part of the bargain being that if the god desires to drink or smoke, she or he should 'take it with them' when leaving: which possessing entities seem to do. During possession, the deity may give guidance to people within the room, as the mood takes her or him. A participant-observer's description of Hrafnar Odin-possession, reads thus:

> In effect, the possessed become the horse vehicle for the god. ... the possession ceremony, which lasts about one and a half hours, follows a strict procedure. It begins with an explanation of what is going to happen, so that all persons present are fully aware of the format, any dangers, and the responsibility involved. Everyone is then purified with smouldering herbs, candles are lit and each person is blessed with appropriate runes, in preparation for the journey. A horn of mead is passed around and each participant makes a toast to Odin, giving either informed consent in the wish to become a horse of Odin or passing the opportunity on this time. Singing then follows to invoke the god, again based on Nordic sources. As they become possessed the participants pick up garments that have been made available to them and that are characteristic of Odin, including a wide brimmed hat, a cloak, and an eye patch to represent his missing right eye. They may also hold a tall staff and carry a tobacco pipe and drinking horn. ... Odin moves

among the non-possessed to give oracular advice. Dialogues occur between Odin and devotee, with questions asked and answers given ...when people may be challenged by Odin to change their ways or take on advice that is unexpected, a profound and empowering experience. Being a trickster God though, Odin can also play devious tricks on people; the advice is not always 'good'. At the end of the rite Odin returns to *Asgard* (the realm of the *Æsir* gods in Norse mythology) and the possessed waken from trance.

(Wallis 1999b: 84, also forthcoming, a)

More often, in oracular seiðr or private journeys, the being is simply spoken with, negotiated with: the seiðworker remains herself, a mediator, thus able to meet and describe deities, wights, spirits.

In chapter 3, I indicated how a practitioner new to the 'high seat' or seiðhjallr experienced the Völva – or at any rate *a* völva, a seeress – emerging from a gravemound to give him understandings of what *was*. His account further illustrates how practitioners see or meet their spirits. He did not expect this experience.

I have never thought that sort of thing would happen. I was expecting to meet Woden or have one of my helpers appear. As it was they appeared well before then, and all of them were supporting me on the way

He described the seeress:

And then you know the mound appeared, just this green turfed mound, very sort of – reminds me of a painting by Rousseau – just sort of very *there* amongst this blackness and then there was a tree there, yew tree there, and then the seeress comes out, and I could see in the distance, and it was definitely in the distance, rather than very close, a hall, which was shimmering gold-like as well. And the seeress appeared, and she was dangerously thin (laughs) mainly because she's dead I presume! But at the same time sort of wiry with it. Sort of she came out hobbling but she sort of almost trotted back in, you know.

I had asked for more description, the seeress' face, and how she appeared.

I didn't see her face. I think I may have seen the very base of it, and it was bony, bony and aah, pale, pale. And she was wearing a grey rag – a grey cloak type thing... I think she started off being very hunched over and therefore small, and then as time went by she got increasingly animated.

This seeress appears to have dictated the pace of the seiðr, and required to be negotiated with, which had its effect on the practitioner:

Then towards the end, the end being as much the – it started off the seeress wanting to leave, and I, with a sort of Woden, Woden hat on, you know in the Völuspá, said 'no, we're here, there's more, you've got to help these people, these people are needing you'. So she reluctantly came back and then after that it was me that was waning, I felt myself visibly shaking and I kept having to sort of focus myself and to, concentrate to get the stuff.

... I found it difficult to get back to the gates, and it was very appealing to stay behind, and as if she was sort of, Hel was pulling my legs, to keep me there, and I was kind of willing, really, for a while longer, so you know, a struggle to get back.

From the seiðworker's perspective, this völva was not 'called' or invoked, she was simply *there*, presumably (if one 'takes the spirits seriously') for her own reasons. I discussed this experience through email with Rauðhildr. She commented on her own experiences with 'The Völva':

She does things for her own reasons and becomes involved for her own purposes. The Maurnir sheltered her in their cave from before Ginnungagap for their reasons. She saw the world created. She knows and doesn't tell anyone, except maybe Vor the necromancer of Frigga.

She is also not above playing some pretty nasty tricks.

I requested further explanation. Writing as if 'in a seiðr trance', she told me:

There is a resurgence in the power of the Volva and the Maurnir to interpret creation to us again. But they have not moved with us in the stream of our world and are still exacting the older price for services rendered. Does this make sense? It seems as though I am typing in a seidh trance.

They are the only ones who know the beginning of our story. Because we have no context for the end without the beginning we are starting over. We will have to embrace the mysteries of the coming into being of the worlds through the lens of our knowledge here and now before moving along the path of the religion of the ancients to the never ending conclusions of the confining of life in the parameters of understanding.

This is why the Volva comes now, I see, she is safer to approach than the four. She is 'dead' in the sense that she is a cast-off garment, a face that no longer could speak to / interpret for creation to the created.[8] A new face she wore, again, cast off for another. Until that other was not the one to bridge the gap to the beginning, and was cast off in turn. One Dis, One spirit, interrupted ...

Thus, mutually confounded by the world as it is in its present face, we and she look again to the most primal face and begin at the beginning. Learning our letters, the runes, as keys to the cosmos; learning our numbers, the Norns as weavers of fate, taking our measure the goddesses and gods with guidance and occasional counsel. Counting our fingers and toes and naming them, meeting the wights and the mighty dead once more for the first time. Learning to remember primal terrors so as to be taught survival and that fire is hot.

And the resistance to seidhr arises again, because seidhr proves that we do not have the answers and that humankind is not wise without 'other' and our fear of our own frailty makes us shun the practice just as it did our 'ancient' kin of faith, who were beginning to know enough to be too proud to be seen not to know.

The 'spirits' met with, then, encompass a wide range, in addition to the plant and animal 'helpers' previously encountered. Some appear closely connected with individual seiðworkers, but others seem to be involved with the re-awakening of seiðr: they may have long-term goals which do not necessarily coincide with those of practitioners or audience. Yet others are incidental, problematic, once again pursuing their own aims. All are, to the practitioners, very 'real'. This interaction with the spirit world is something that is taken account of in the construction of 'ritual' for today. As indicated previously, Hrafnar have been challenged on why they involve practitioners in a complicated 'journey' in their oracular seiðr ritual. In an email discussion of seiðr, Rauðhildr explained it thus:

> My reasoning for going to the spirits, rather than calling them to us is not grounded in anything but my darker self, my suspicious nature and my mistrust of the behavior of other human beings. This culture has no training or grounding in how to respectfully treat the spirits that come. Forgive this harshness, but I have seen a great, disrespectful stupidity in many pagan communities, including our own.
>
> If the wights are offended it can damage the luck of the offender for life. There are dozens of cases of this in folklore and myth. My feelings about this are simple – Not on my watch, never. Even if the individual does something to richly deserve it. Not on my watch.
>
> If the wights are sufficiently angered, they can turn on the seer/ess as well. I will not willingly endanger my own luck, or the luck of another seer or his/her well being. I will not endanger my own well being without profound need.
>
> I will not call spirits into a place where I do not know and trust every single person. It is too easy for someone who has no respect for anybody else to find a way into a public seidh. If you don't think it is possible for problems like the ones I have mentioned to pop up, then you have never been asked a trick question by a malicious soul, asked the exact same question by the same questioner at the same event six years running (to the rage of certain spirits who told me I was not allowed to answer it), nor have you had to watch your seer be asked to tell a questioner what kind of ice cream he had for dinner.

Did the 'ancient heathens' not have problems of having to mediate between wights and 'stupid people', she was asked? Not in the same sense, she replied, as there was an awareness of, and respect for the 'reality of spirits'.

> They had a culture of 'faith' that those raised in the modern world lack. A respect that spirits could affect their world. . . . I have been in a space with a wight, normally kindly, who was disruptive and angry because of a single person in the space.

Things fell down and broke when the individual entered. When the individual left, everything was wonderful and peaceful again. I immediately went and put down an offering as an apology for bringing the person into the wight's space.

Several people got sick right after that and had coughs that hung on weeks. Again a case of a kindly wight being dangerous.

Whatever academics or other observers may think of their work, these seiðworkers are themselves 'taking spirits seriously' and can discuss their encounters in ways that make sense to other seiðfolk elsewhere, who recognise the same beings in their own practice. In understanding the meanings of seiðr for its participants, it is necessary to admit this reality, for them, as they undertake these experiences that appear so meaningful both for themselves and for those of their communities who watch and listen, bring their questions, and evaluate those 'seeings' for their usefulness within their own lives.

Seiðr as contested practice

As this and the previous chapter make plain, a direct equation of seiðr as shamanistic practice today with seiðr of the past is not possible. Today's practices are being constructed from evidence which though not scanty, is rather patchy and incomplete, fragments scattered throughout the sagas and Eddic poems. The nature of people's relationship to seiðr – as something specifically 'constructed' consciously – implies that the processes may be better described as 'neo-shamanistic': not directly embedded in everyday-cultural understandings of the cosmology of the Nine Worlds or of what seeresses do, a product of a 'fact'-based knowledge that can be articulated, rather than 'habitus' (see e.g. Vitebsky 1995a on differences between 'neo-' and 'traditional' shamanisms), though for some practitioners cosmology and the everyday are becoming closely interrelated. Questions arise about meaning and contest-ation, in both past and present. Dimensions of, and debates around, seiðr give interesting examples of how discourses and competing definitions are played out, how people create their understandings of self and community, self and spirit, within a context of spiritual tradition and today's research. The construction and practice of seiðr show people actively involved with their lives and their identities; as they themselves would say, creative agents in the formation of their own Wyrd, constructing meaning in otherworlds and in their daily lives.

In subsequent chapters some of the sites of contestation will be further examined, before returning to a consideration of seiðr and academia, and similarities between the journey of the seiðworker and that of the ethnographer who sets out to chart a largely unknown terrain; and to questions about shamanism and academia. First, however, I return to personal perception: my own account of experiences with seiðr and my insertion into seiðworkers' discourse and practice. I ask you, therefore, to step into the world of the beginning-seiðworker, and to suspend academic doubts, as I recount how I came to make my own journey in the mound.

Chapter 5

The journey in the mound

Narrating

Every story is told for an audience. Pieces of the narrative that follow were addressed, initially, to various audiences: friends, colleagues, co-workers within seiðr. The account of my first encounter with oracular seiðr was written for two friends; later, part of it was incorporated into a paper given to the Society for the Anthropology of Consciousness (Blain, forthcoming) and used again, together with Jordsvin's narrative of visiting Hel's realm, at a folklore conference (Blain 2000). Other pieces come from fieldnotes, from poems, from email discussions, from a website I constructed to share with others who journey in quest of knowledge of self. The narrative is, of course, partial, selected for the particular readership of this book.

Storytelling, though, is constructed within audience participation, feedback through which the narrator becomes aware of how her words affect her listeners. A move from academic mode into storytelling is dangerous, in a mostly academic book. Yet in the interests of taking both spirit and human research participants seriously, my own experiences require to be presented. These form part of my understanding of community and consciousness, and inform the processes through which I approach other people's narratives. At times my experiences echo those of others: at times those others, heard later, become an echo or a counterpart to my own.

In what follows I describe something of my own journey, and something of those others – human or otherwise – whom I have met with, on the way. I move from an interested spectator, to a beginner, a seiðworker, a guide, and once again return to ethnography, within contexts that include seiðr in quest for my own knowledges, and for healing, as well as the oracular practices described elsewhere in this book. Largely absent from this account, though, are the discussions and debates with other practitioners, some very considerably more 'expert' than myself (for instance discussions with Bil about the strange, toothed beasts I met as described later in this chapter, entheogen use, and healing-seiðr, or with Rauðhildr about Woden and the seeress in the mound). These emerge, at times, in other chapters. In the meantime, this chapter serves to indicate that the narratives of 'what is seiðr' and 'doing seiðr' constructed elsewhere have their being within practitioner dialogues, and that the perceptions shared with me as part of my research were given in the understanding that I partook in at least some of the experiences related.

This chapter is also a reminder that seiðr is being reconstructed, or 'reinvented', newly for today, within contexts of post-modernity in Britain, the US and elsewhere. There are no 'master shamans' whose knowledge and practice we can draw upon, but simply those who have tried to put something together and who discover, one way or another, that 'it works', giving them insights and under-standings, ways to approach their own lives and at times touch, heal or guard those of others, ways to create and assist communities. The experiences I describe include many that are solitary, individualised: but such is not the overall focus of seiðr. Unlike some other Western neo-shamanisms, this is not merely a tool for self-discovery or self-help, but for engagement, mediation between human and spirit communities, where the spirits encountered have 'their own agendas' and are not necessarily benign.

Some of the experiences narrated here are discussed or drawn on elsewhere in this book. They are not unproblematic. As indicated in earlier chapters, within the linked communities of participants there are questions and disputes over what is experienced, how far it is 'external' to the seeress or 'shared' between participants, how far it reflects or is informed by practices described in the sagas. The final instance related here, of 'the Völva' emerging from her mound to give answers to a seer, has been quite extensively debated between participants. Based in the discourse of 'taking spirits seriously', was she indeed a 'seeress' and to what extent were her answers trustworthy? What was her stake in the proceedings? Why did she appear (for the seer did not 'summon' her)? What is the 'use-value' of seiðr perceptions? This chapter, though, gives my own impressions: those of others are elsewhere in this book.

Experiencing

The first time I was present at an oracular seiðr was in summer 1996, at a festival, Trothmoot, held at the Gaia retreat centre near Kansas City. For some years I had been reading about seiðr, on the internet, and corresponding with people about it via email, witnessing, some time previously, major disagreements on an email list ensuing from descriptions of seiðr as 'shamanism', reading accounts by Heathens of these contested terms. Oracular seiðr was, I thought, something I should see, and learn about, as an academic researching identity in Earth-religions, to grasp how people constructed the realities they worked within. I knew the story of the seeress Thorbjörg. I knew the basics of how the seiðr séance was constructed, following Hrafnar's deductions from the literature, and had some familiarity with anthropological material on shamanisms and consciousness. Two friends were interested in pursuing this further, incorporating a more shamanistic practice into the small 'kindred' we had developed previously, and I had asked for, and received, training materials from Jordsvin, whom I was interviewing as part of my research. I read up on neo-shamanic journeying, dipped briefly again into some of the anthropological literature on shamanism, and was ready to face the unknown. In participation in neo-pagan guided meditations, I had discovered a talent for assisting others, through voice and imagery, into light trance states. Having worked with altered consciousness within circle rituals and on my own, I could, to some extent, visualise the 'journey'. I was eager to see the session, report back to my friends, and use this experience as part of my ethnographer's construction of 'Heathenry', another aspect to reconstructed religion, part of post-modernity's diversity of spirituality. I did not envision myself as a seiðworker.

It was late at night, after the other events of the day, and the room was dim, candlelit, still warm from the exceeding heat of Kansas at midsummer. My brain switched into 'taking notes' mode as people were seated and the seið-folk began the preliminaries, chanting a rune-row, invoking deities, singing the journey song, drumming and singing the songs that called their power animals. In near-darkness, Diana narrated the journey down beneath the roots of the World Tree, to Hel's realm, and Winifred sat in the high seat, her face veiled, and in trance went through the gates.

I had been working hard, visualising the journey and taking

mental notes. What I did not expect was the very strong pull, experienced both as a yearning and as a direct physical tug to the pit of my stomach, to follow her. Remembering the instructions, I concentrated on visualising the gates before me, closed. Diana had said the seeress would remain connected to us, by a silver cord. I felt the cord, an umbilicus between myself and Winifred, felt its tension. Questioners stepped forward, and listening, I felt that attachment, that pull. Some asked of jobs, some of relationships, health, future meetings, relatives. One asked of a severe health problem and the need to face her mortality, and I listened in the half-world of trance, before the gates, profoundly moved. When Winifred left the high seat, I felt my body doing work, drawing her back, lending my own strength. With a second seeress in the chair, I was more able to distance myself. Now there was no call to enter the gates, though I could sense that later, at another time, there would be. The seeress was tiring, and still there were questions. Diana, taking the high seat, called to me to stand behind her and 'shadow' her, giving protection and physical stability, should she sway in the seat.

After the session, I walked to my tent, up the steep rocky path to the campsite. Though we had been 'talked back' from the gates, up to the World Tree and through a tunnel of trees to the 'consensus reality' of sitting in our circle of chairs around the high seat, I could sense that I was moving in another reality, walking back from Hel's gates, and used the sensation of physically climbing to help my return from the light trance of the audience-participants.

Seeing

Armed with more information I returned to my small working group, and some weeks later, in Thorgerd's living-room, we journeyed to the gates and spent time sitting before them, to familiarise ourselves with the journey there and back. On the second journey, in July 1996, a raven sat on a gatepost, its head on one side, eyeing me. Somehow its slightly ramshackle farm gate was superimposed on my visualisation of the great gates of Hel's realm: a farm gate similar to the ones in the countryside of the burial cairns in my own land. I was conducting the narration to Yggdrasill and down beneath its roots, acting as guide for my friend, Amber, singing her through Hel's gates while Thorgerd drummed. We were not attempting a question-and-answer session: rather we were familiarising ourselves with the landscape and the process, mapping out the territory. Amber went through the gates, moved around, saw – a hall, with two men talking: what more she saw and described is no longer with me – and returned.

Thorgerd drummed some more, for me, as I moved through the gates. *Seeress, what do you see?* I sat on our improvised high seat with a shawl over my head, waiting for something to happen and wondering whether the experience of guiding Amber had brought me too much out of trance. At first there was nothing, no sensation, resolving into greyness, then shapes, as if surrounded by rocks, boulders that I could not touch. I walked amidst them for some time, trying to move onward. Then my waiting friends remembered to sing for me... Did I see a path and a tree? In later visions I did. This first time, I was within a hall, filled with people, and a bright gleam of gold. But the people did not see me, for I was not of this place, but I moved through, and out...

...into a strange place, a plain of whiteness, bright and cold, not snow, simply whiteness all around, with no markers, no features. Then came the raven, flying back and forth, black against the white, glossy feathers reflecting the light, then returning to me, sitting on something – what, in the whiteness, I do not know – with its head on one side, again looking at me. It had a white streak on one side of its head. There were no words. It was flying again, and I moved on, in my person's shape, rather clumsily through the white veiling brightness, on a path that I knew to be there, and now there were some shapes, geometrical and changing, and the raven flew farther...

Three ears of grain were before me, clear and distinct in the foreground, and as I looked beyond, an image, a place, a glen or valley between hills, with in it a flowering meadow. In the centre was a log, and on the log one who sat wrapped in his great grey-blue cloak with his hat over one side of his face and with his travelling staff at his side, who looked at me in greeting. I paused, drawn, wishing to go further, but something in his face, or his movements, told me it was not yet time for me to be there, and I found myself back before the gates, with Thorgerd and Amber, filled with the purest delight, the most utter happiness I had known: delight in the knowledge that I could do this, and, most of all, that I had met the one whom I recognised, who had spoken to me before in words and sensations, the Wanderer of the worlds who seeks for knowledge where it is to be found.

On the next journey we experimented with questioning, and I found that I could wait, in darkness, for a question and, with some difficulty (due to the wish of my academic's brain to analyse rather than speak the vision) relay what then came to me. At the end the guide gave me space to go where I would, and once again the raven was there and I was back in the meadow; and this time I sat, sheltered by his cloak, and he called me 'daughter'.

Meeting

Several others who met with us for ritual had become interested in what we were doing, and we agreed to run a animal-ally ('power-animal') meditation. I had received a copy of Diana's seiðr workshop, and I planned to use the meditation from this, a little modified to suit what we had been doing. Both Amber and I already knew our animals – so we thought. We arranged a session where Thorgerd would drum for us all, and I would narrate, take over the drumming when we reached Yggdrasill so that she also could participate, and watch: then a few days later Thorgerd would drum for me alone.

As I began the narration to Thorgerd's drumming I could see with double vision: the room of participants, of whom I was attempting to retain awareness, and the tunnel of trees that led downward, downward, to the plains of Midgard. As I talked of the tree Yggdrasill, and the squirrel Ratatosk that ran up and down, I could both see and touch the rough bark before me. Thorgerd's drum ceased and I began a slow beat, as steady as I could make it, directing them to turn from the tree, and move where they would, across the plain, to forest, hill or stream, to where their ally in animal form, their friend, fylgja, spirit-helper, part of their own spirit, waited for them. Even as I continued to drum I felt myself moving also, the raven came to guide me further onward, and I could see and hear other creatures – a blue jay screeching, as I recall – even before I let the drum fall silent.

Several came by me. Most clear was a vixen, who trotted purposefully along, on the grass by the edge of the forest, and across a little mound. She was not for me, but for another of my company, this I knew. I became aware of some kind of large, white-ish shape half-seen in the woods; a great cat; another, smaller, of which the claws were its most prominent feature. There were many birds. For a little while I flew among these, all the while knowing that there was something more. I returned to the grass by the forest's edge and waited, sitting and gazing into the shadows beneath the trees.

A stag came out of the forest, his antlers tipped with gold by the sun's rays. *Oh, beautiful!* I thought. *Are you for me?* He looked at me and moved aside, and behind him another creature trotted out to look me squarely in the eyes. A wolf, with the changing grey/brown/hazel/green eyes that could have been those of a person overlaying the yellow eyes of a wolf. It came to me that I should have known this.

I returned, shocked, briefly, to awareness of the room and its participants. All seemed well, and in trance. Then I was once again by the forest's edge, standing by the great predator with my fingers on his fur, as he twisted his head to look round at me again. *So soft, despite the rough exterior.* I was surprised by the softness and thickness of his pelt. Then I was riding bareback, as if on a horse, with my arms around the great beast's shaggy neck, feeling the warm soft hair, and I remember laying my head down on the wolf's back as we sped over land and sky, rejoicing in strength and softness and speed.

Then back, to an awareness that some of the group were stirring from their trance state.

I returned, flying again with the cloud of birds and the raven that had first greeted me. Then I stood again at the forest's edge, and took leave of my guide with his thick soft fur, and agreed to meet again, soon, for he had much to show me, as he let me know without words. I returned to the great tree and, surfacing, took my drum, struck three loud beats, and commenced the narration of leave-taking and return. We looked at each other, dived into finger-foods we'd brought, shared, and ate to 'ground' our beings in the tangible reality of hunger and food, then I asked, 'whose was the fox?'

The purposeful vixen had been for Thorgerd, the white beast for a man who thought, though was not sure, he had met a white goat. Others had met with a lion and a lynx. The stag was connected only with my own vision, as I was to discover later.

*   *   *   *   *

A few days later, Thorgerd drummed for me alone and as I lay wrapped in a blanket, she recited the narration to take me to the plain of Midgard and the World Tree. This time the wolf was waiting, and again I rode on his back. Then the world changed, and I changed, and now I became a wolf, part of the pack, with cubs which may have been my cubs, and I watched them play and I played with them, then, leaving them in the den, ran with the pack through the forest, tracking our prey.

We found the great stag of the woods and tracked it, purposefully and wordlessly, which seemed to take a long, long time, running through the forest with a joy of life and movement, and common purpose. Thus began a long journey. Space prevents inclusion of the entire account, from my fieldnotes. Also my doubts re-emerge, about ability to present feeling, sensing, experiencing in ways that a non-shamanic audience will grasp. Suffice it to say that it took time. My first 'initiation' was to run as a wolf with the pack, blending 'self' and 'other', to track and kill the stag. We pulled it down, and ate, tearing at skin and flesh with strong teeth. Then we slept.

Next, waking or dreaming, I was in bird shape, and flying, high, onward, then walking as a person, and then once more with the wolf, again riding on his back, as he commenced a journey, running faster and faster, first on land towards the mountains, and then through the air, and now the wind howled like a wolf and all around were other shapes, wolves and horses, spirits on the wind . . . As I rode with the Wild Hunt, I saw many things, before standing on a mountain top to have some questions answered by the Wanderer's many words, and become, myself, challenged before I experienced my death by both spear and noose, absence of breath, blackness, which was understood and welcomed.

Much later, I was flying high over a chequered world of field and forest and town, with here and there the black smudges of smoke. There were again many words, though I cannot now remember them, but it was important that I see this world and know something of the problems that beset it. Then down, lower, to where many did battle, and the ravens waited to feast.

Then I stood alone and robed in a circle of great grey stones, waiting, and the wolf came for me, and I rode, and the world dissolved . . .

I sat up, returned, dazed, in Thorgerd's living room, as she finished the narration of return to the world of the living. She said, 'You were very far away . . .'

Speaking

I found that in oracular seiðr the journey was less clear, as I was conscious of the audience, wondering about their level of comfort, their level of trance, attempting to facilitate their experience, except when I sang the runes or sat in the high seat. The almost formulaic ritual 'performance' led to its own state of altered consciousness, different from that of the solitary or facilitated journey. I would go through the gates, wait to be sung onto a path, and see first many people, then a tree, and by the tree I could find answers, though they came slowly when people asked, and speaking, requiring to withdraw sufficiently from the deep trance state to be able to articulate with physical tongue, throat and lips, was hard, and has since become still more hard.

Then came a journey several months after I first went through Hel's gate, early in 1997. This journey was different from the start. As I did the narration to the gates, it seemed increasingly that this was for the others, I was facilitating their journey, but though I felt myself moving into a light trance I did not see the gates. Sitting on the high seat with the veil over my head, I was in a mound, at once seeing the one who dwelt there and being myself the dweller in the mound, buried there long before. To the questions, answers arose within the mound, from the glitter of flecks of gemstones in the soil, from images projected onto walls of stone or earth, from patterns formed by stacked stones before me. At times my awareness seemed to incorporate a large hall of feasting people, who yet formed part of the mound – howe, barrow or cairn, I did not inquire at this time. When Thorgerd, a craftswoman, asked of her work, I heard the ringing of hammer on anvil, and saw the dwarf-smith who laughed when I passed on the question to him. My friend had asked this question before, which was why he laughed. In the mythology, dwarves crafted the finest objects, and forged precious metals.

Two days later, sitting at my computer, the images returned to me.

Around me earth
above me roots, turf
darkness encircles
and the scent of moist soil,
mould
with a freshness of new life
as seeds stir in soil
waiting rebirth
a fresh spring, a new year

Here is silence

Yet now I turn, to hear the clamour,
of hall bright-beaconed,
laughing and boasting,
feasting with noisy cheer
those who wait with me,
laid in this mound, or come
from where they fell
to join their kin...

... Fires glow in the encircling darkness
bellows-blown;
deep in the earth
a dwarf-smith forges gold...

Here was a silence of many words.

Listening

Over the next two years, the walls of the mound became clearer, stone-built, so that at times the answers lay in the patterns of their arrangement and positioning. In an example from my fieldnotes, an account describes waiting on a 'high seat' constructed from cushions, while my guide drummed. The wolf came at this point, the guide talked me 'through the gate' and I was on my own. It was dark, with a little light which seemed to be from a flame or fire set within the place where I was. I could see stones of the walls, reflecting the flame. I was in the mound, and the walls were stones.

The first question concerned a job. I 'saw' first a woman who stood holding a straight staff, which she held planted on the ground. She seemed to be a guardian. She was standing on the bank of a stream or small river, and animals were coming to the river to drink. I wasn't sure what they were. Some may have been cats, and other small animals seemed a bit like mice. The river ran quite fast, but they were all able to drink, and the woman remained on guard, on the bank. Then the vision changed: another woman now sat at a table and sorted some small flakes or leaves, mint or another herb, putting some into small packets and lining them up on the table. I could not describe her, because the focus was not the woman but the little green leaf flakes. But when I spoke of this, the picture changed back to the river and the guardian on the back, but now I could see a bird on a rock in the stream, like a wagtail, long tail wagging up and down. I gave some more description of the scene, and there were more animals there. The waters were healing, and moving on.

The questioner asked what message Freyja had about what she should be doing. There was a sensation of a very large animal with very large horns, which I couldn't quite see. The concentration of the trance gained intensity, and I was falling into the darkness of the vision. I was aware of opening my eyes, under the veiling scarf, to blackness, no light at all, while retaining the sensation of falling into the dark, or into the mound. Closing them I was in the presence of the aurochs; 'Audumbla', my mind echoed. I could see the horns, but not the whole animal. The shape of the horns changed, and there was the face of a deer, somehow very female, my wolf very briefly, then the cats of the goddess' chariot, gold-brown and a little striped, and I knew that these were not domesticated animals. I recalled that there had been a question – what should she be doing? – and was aware of formulating it, and then there were words which did not come from the cats or the aurochs, although the power of the aurochs was in them and I was not describing but speaking for another. The exact words are hard to recall, the only hazy part of the experience. The sense of being that was behind them was what absorbed my attention. However, the gist was that the querant had healing hands, something about gathering herbs (and I was returned briefly to the little flakes of mint), but that she had to use her gifts and she had to speak about it. There was more, an elaboration. The questioner pointed out that speaking and gathering herbs didn't pay the rent and asked Freyja how she saw this being possible. For some time there was no image, simply a sense of power together with exasperation – why does she ask this, why doesn't she understand? – and I found myself re-emerging, asking what the querant should do, reformulating her query. Then I saw one of the cats, looking very puzzled and a little put out, and again I felt I was falling, though not so strongly as before, and saying with some exasperation that the querant had to *do*, the implication being get on with it, get the word out there about herself, keep working at it, take a chance.

I do not remember coming out of Freyja's presence. I do know that I returned to a 'resting' state, in the mound, with the wolf beside me. I tried opening my eyes again, and again there was darkness. The second querant asked about whether she would make a planned move to another country, or should seek work locally. The answer was fairly straightforward: grey skies, stormclouds and wind, what seemed to be the patterns of a hurricane, a line drawn across the sky; then someone who leaned over a table with a chart or map on it, in a laboratory, wearing a lab coat, planning some detailed work, then others were there also. Outside the storm was still raging. I could see trees bending in the wind, and they were in leaf. I said that it seemed that she should seek work where she was, that there would be some kind of technical or scientific work, and that there was not a real possibility of going away for some time.

My guide's question also concerned work, whether the small jobs she was getting would grow into something else, whether the seeds would finally sprout. The answers were very visual: first a pattern, a geometric shape like a 'V', golden-brown, faceted and multi-layered, which remained there in the darkness when I opened my eyes, then with them closed turned so that I was looking into it, and from the centre grew a small sprout, which gained strength and produced a flower, like a buttercup, which I viewed head-on. The flower changed to become crystalline, like a pattern of quartz crystals. I reported that seeds might sprout but that the result would not be direct, but transformed in some way.

There were no more questions for me, and I rested in the darkness, again seeing the wolf, then returned through the gates. I opened my eyes under the veil, to the brightness of a candle on the right. The guide drummed. I felt rather dazed but recovered fast and on leaving the high seat, drummed briefly to get my bearings before asking Thorgerd if she would take the high seat.

Even at the time of writing the fieldnotes from which these descriptions are taken, the day after the event, I did not have a good memory of what Thorgerd said, other than in her answer to me. My focus was on her and on the pattern of question and answer, not on the details of what she saw. To my question, she described a meadow with a picket fence across it, a very large meadow. Cats were moving through the fence, although the gaps in the fence seemed too small for them. They were like ghost-cats, shadow-cats, moving and merging one with another. She was tired, and I brought her back after this answer, without seeking clarification.

A month before this séance, I had attempted a personal exploration which produced a series of images, including Hebridean sea waves, caves, terns flying and a squabble between different birds for something, an eagle. Emerging quite clearly were the pillars of Staffa, which I had seen once, on a boat trip from Oban in my mother's company. Several days later I journeyed again, chanting a tune which had come to me some months previously and gelled in my mind after the Staffa journey. Now I found there were words, and images to go with them. Gulls and terns, whitecaps on the wind-whipped seas, fish, an eagle (seemingly a sea-eagle rather than a golden eagle or osprey) and the wolf, who ran swiftly over the rocky shore and up into the hills behind. My drum sang its own song, and my voice seemed to echo with harmonics, amplified by the nearness of the drumhead.

Two weeks later at Thorgerd's house, I drummed again and sang a rune-row, then used my new song as the method of trance-induction. Thorgerd drummed for me during trance. Jumbled visions merged one to another: several animals, the wolf, a distant friend, interspersed with the stone circle that had been a part of my visions since I began this project, and the stacked stone and earth walls of a tomb, the mound of the dweller of my earlier poem. Here I was revising past memories through present experience. I had entered this vision with questions, and near the end a small figure appeared, a woman cloaked and hooded, her face aged and almost skeletal yet at the same time filling out with the flesh of youth, small in distance as if viewed through a reversed telescope, yet near, present beside me in the mound. It seemed that she was Heiðr, the seeress (or at least *a* seeress), and answers formed to my questions, before it was time to leave.

I had begun to suspect that my mound had a physical location, and knew where it might be. On a trip several years previously, I had glanced briefly into the chambered tomb, and left, because of pressures to not spend time there, to continue on a family visit, return to the car and drive to where we were to spend the night in a Scottish bed-and-breakfast. I had at the time made a promise to myself, or to the place, to return: which I had through reading and through the internet, but never in person, though I was beginning to, now, in the seiðr trance and in dreams.

And an opportunity arose. In June 1999 I reached my destination, tired from a sleepless transatlantic night-time flight, yet successfully reliant on public transport to reach a small West of Scotland village. There were many things in the area that I wanted to see, but when I arrived my first destination was the burial cairn that I remembered. In the late afternoon of a bright summer's day I entered, gazed around, noting the stacking of the stones, the way the sun entered the chamber. I stayed there a little while, reflecting, and started to chant a rune-row, but it seemed to me that the air was dead, the sound did not reverberate, this sound was not right for the place. I took some photographs, with results that later astonished me: though I could not, at that time, sense it, there was an energy here that was living, bright, vibrant.

Two days later I returned. I walked around the outside, taking more pictures, then put away the camera, and spent some time feeling myself become part of the landscape, the scenery, the ambience of this place. Then, taking a deep breath, I climbed down into the tomb.

It was cool, cold on the stones striking into my bones, a relief from the heat of the late afternoon, becoming colder, and then I no longer was aware of the cold of the stone where I sat. I chanted a little, the song that had come to me some months before, which seemed to fit. Over and over, then silence. I studied the walls, the stacked stones, the large stone slabs of the base, the capstones. Some present-day constructions of meaning were evident in the scratched graffiti, some older than others, though. In the stillness I waited, and my song still echoed: stillness, silence, eyes closed now, heart rate increased, a waiting of anticipation.

Thoughts, impressions, voices: a face that changed to become another, and another, and that one a child, then changing again, though with likeness one to another, hazy, with a memory of dissolution, of burnt bone, of merging into the others, into the walls, into the floor. The community was here, and I was of them, looking out over the valley and awaiting something – what? Fragments of my poem from the mound surfaced, though these people were far older than their descendants of whom I'd spoken then. But I did not know, then, where I had waited for words to come, waited for rebirth, waited for those who would uncover walls and floor, let the light into this place that with my eyes shut or even open had become so dark, despite the sunlight that streamed behind me, to warm my back and counter the effect of that so-cold stone: a warmth that I no longer needed, absorbed into this community, part of these presences that permeated walls, roof and floor.

I understood that there were sounds in the silence, voices, whispers, and I was part of the sound.

Remembering

From my seiðr experiences, too many impressions remain with me
to detail here. I will sketch only a few images that appeared –
though whether seen, heard or otherwise sensed in a deep-trance
blending of senses, is not clear to me: 'seen' or 'heard' are everyday
understandings of separate, documentable perceptions. Some made
no sense to me, only to the querant. A white mask with curling lips,
Buddha-like; a person who walked with a staff, leading others
around a spiral, maze-like hillside track; a wild cat in a cave. I
learned that the details were important and that I should attempt to
relate them, during or after the seance. Undertaking a healing
journey for a friend, I received a strand of spun yarn and grain to
feed his deer-fylgja, and found a blue bead for him to hang on the
thread, with its counterpart, later, in the physical bead that another
friend produced for him.

I made a new staff of yew wood, carved with rune-verses. I learnt
to sit leaning forward with the staff supporting me, so that it
became a branch of Yggdrasill, a connection to all the Nine Worlds,
and I could sway, falling into the vision, focusing into its intensity,
sometimes resting my forehead on the staff. At time, now, it seemed
I could see those strands of Wyrd, connections, fine gold wires
shimmering, or rough home-spun. They led to strange places,
through the walls and entrance of the mound. There were some
instances when I could reach out to those threads, touch them,
smooth them, cause a ripple which moved along the strands, but I
knew this was not to be lightly done. At other times the engagement
with Wyrd was through interaction. In seeking guidance for
querants I found a creature, large-toothed, open-mouthed, seeming
to threaten them: from my non-involved position I could stretch out
a hand to close its mouth. In a private trance-session, months later,
a beast appeared, akin to the other, and now I could see it more
clearly – white, red-spotted, with thin neck, open mouth, bent on
pursuits relating to someone of my acquaintance (I knew not
whom); when I closed the mouth, it disappeared.

There are images, too, of a different kind, from when others
made seiðr. Again at Trothmoot, I watched the seiðfolk, Jordsvin,
Winifred, Rauðhildr, Diana, and it was to Rauðhildr that I
addressed my question. I was living in Canada, about to undertake
a journey to Britain to see family, friends and places. How would
my journey change me? Seated on the high seat, and in Hel's realm,

she asked my permission to journey elsewhere, to Hlidskjalf, where Óðinn sits to view the Nine Worlds: then described how she looked out to where I was or would be. But she could see no outcomes, gain no sense of what would be. She saw, instead, trees, waving in the wind, thick, green, concealing: they were calling me, she said.

Over a year later, now returned to Britain, I sat with staff in hand to guide a seer's first venture to Hel's realm. Others of the small gathering sang the journey song, chanted and visualised the rune-row, we invoked Freyja and Óðinn, I narrated the journey to Hel's realm, and the seer went through the gates. He described a yew-tree, a mound, a hall shimmering in the distance. ('I am not going there,' he said emphatically.) The mound opened, and from it came the seeress, wiry, bony – though I was 'outside the gates' I could sense her, almost see her, and she gave or prompted answers to the questions we asked, some 'making sense' only to the querants.

I was about to move, to take up my present job. What was most important that I should remember, in my move? There was a pause, and the seer's somewhat puzzled voice said, 'cats?' Then he continued: I had been right to return home, called by the land and the trees; I should live out of the city as soon as I could; I would have good students; most importantly, I should retain links to those I knew... and there were cats again, many of them.

Later, long after the session was ended, I found others of the company discussing how they had seen the gates of Hel's realm. For the seer, one had been made of human bones. He described it for my ethnographer's tape-recorder, and in a later communication the cats – uncountable shadow-cats, running from behind him, from the mound, from the seeress, out to the gates of Hel, merging and melding.

Thoughts, impressions, voices, ideas; now once again as an ethnographer, I sit at my computer and spin the narrative strands, concepts, discourses, into an account for presenting to an audience, attempting to find words that reflect the peculiar sensations and perceptions of these 'otherworld' experiences. I draw on the ideas that come from others, informants, participants of all kinds. In attempting to 'take seriously' both the spirits and all those who engage with the spirit world, I turn next to the context of seiðr, then and now: to look at areas where understandings are created and some of the processes, and contestations, that surround their construction.

Chapter 6

Re-evaluating the Witch-Queen

The women of the sagas

An understanding of seiðr and Northern magic, in the old literature or today, requires consideration of the times and places referred to, the political struggles taking place, and the location of people as seiðworkers or clients within frameworks of everyday life and work including dimensions of gender and social class: and further a recognition that neither gender nor class are static properties of individuals, but constructed and reconstructed by and within the community. Today's gendered processes are not those of the tenth century, or before. Nor are they those arising after Christianisation, at the time of writing of the old accounts.

This book is not a work of history or literary criticism. I do not examine the sagas to determine their 'truth', their literary construction, or even the devices used by the authors to tell their stories. I have no expertise in this area. The major analysis of seiðr in the texts is that of Strömbäck (1935). Here, rather, I examine instances and words, and attempt to reflect some sense of the variety of description of seiðworkers and the embedding of this description in context and processes of the times of writing – in order to understand how discourses of the time of writing, and their contradictions, decontextualised, become those of the present, interpreted and recontextualised, as today's readers draw on past to shape present and future. Multiple readings of the saga material are not only possible, but inevitable within today's multivocal society, as each reader, academic or practitioner, brings to the material their own awareness of gender and sexuality, society, community and individual, Heathenism, Christianity, and centralising political processes.

In what follows, I am not regarding the sagas of Icelanders as 'historical'. Much ink has been spilled over whether they reflect reasonably accurate accounts of the times of settlement or conversion to Christianity of Iceland, preserved in the oral tradition, or whether they are essentially 'fiction'. My assumption, here, is that however 'accurate' they may or may not be regarding characters and events, what they hold are understandings from the thirteenth and fourteenth centuries of how the writers' ancestors might have lived; and when many descriptions tally, we have a sense, therefore, that these were possibilities open to women or men, filtered through cultural change and shifting political circumstances. The accounts, in the versions read by most of today's Heathen practitioners in North America or Britain, have been further filtered through the interpretations of nineteenth- and twentieth-century translators, though a number of practitioners both in English-speaking and, more obviously, in Scandinavian countries and in Iceland, are reading (today's normalised versions of) Old Icelandic texts.

Seiðr appears in some of today's contexts as 'women's magic'. The tendency within reconstructionist communities is to view seiðr, or magic, as essentially unchanging: spell-casting, shape-changing, done by individuals and either approved of or disapproved of by society. Arguments arise, as previously indicated, over whether seiðr was 'evil magic' and 'women's magic': connections between the two may be seen in terms of Christian misogyny. Yet examining the extent to which seiðr was associated with women, and (with other magical or shamanistic practices) seen as 'evil', cannot be so simply done. Practices were constructed over centuries, reconstructed within changing political and economic circumstances, and people used them, deliberately, within communities and societies to specific intents and purposes. Here I look at some of the women who 'did seiðr', and in the next chapter, some of the men who were and are seiðworkers, and how perceptions of the gendering of seiðr affects its practice today.

As indicated earlier, most of the accounts of seiðr or magical practice, from the sagas, are of women. Some detailing of their exploits is required, here. They appear as part of the action, influencing events, sometimes as central figures. Some have been mentioned already: Heið, in *Hrólfs saga Kraka*, Þórdis the seeress and Þórveig the spell-caster, in *Kormáks saga*, and (with further details below) Oddbjörg of *Víga-Glúms saga*, Kjannok of *Heiðarvíga saga*, Heimlaug of *Gull-Þóris saga*, and others. In chapter 4 I indicated that the accounts could be regarded as pointing to realities for women, part of a cultural framework in which ecstasy, magic and prophesy could occur, in which women could ask spirits to assist them. It is time, now, to enquire further about these women, and how what they did appears to relate to their communities.

I earlier mentioned Þórdis. In the *Saga of the Water-dalers* (*Vatnsdæla*) the same spákona Þórdís uses her power to resolve a dispute in court. 'She had foresight and could see into the future, and therefore was chosen to arbitrate in important cases' (Jones 1973: 118): when one party will not accept her judgement, she uses magic to cause them to adopt her peaceful solution.

In *Víga-Glúms saga* the seeress Oddbjörg is described as 'gleðimaður, fróð og framsýn'; 'a cheerful person, wise and capable of seeing into the future' (Hollander 1972: 57). However, it is said of her that she will give good or bad 'spá', foretellings, depending on how she is treated, and when she predicts misfortune for two young boys she is shown the door of their grandmother's house: her prophecy is, of course, borne out by the saga. In *Heiðarvíga saga*, Ólöf, called Kjannok, is said to be 'vitur mjög ok kunni mart gerla að sjá . . . fróð og forn í skapi', 'very wise and could see many things clearly . . . learned and leaning to the old ways'. She charms her foster-son so that he takes no harm from weapons.[1] From *Gull-Þóris saga*, there is Heimlaug the völva who dwelt at 'Völva's-steading' in Comb-heath. She gives the leading characters information which may be gained from far-seeing, receiving a gold finger-ring for her knowledge. (Icelandic from Netútgáfan, n.d.).

The later legendary sagas and short stories, which are fiction, told for entertainment value, reintroduce the seeing-women, but now their magic is akin to the 'witchcraft' or spell-craft, supernatural events or powers of later Western fairy-stories, which appears, often seemingly without cause, to create a circumstance which drives the plot, rather than the embedded magic or seeing from within the community. The instances of the 'norns' in the *Þáttr of Norna-Gest*, or the seiðkona Heiðr in *Arrow-Odd's saga*, given in chapter 4, are examples.

Seeing was not all that the women could do. We have accounts of people shapeshifting, using their abilities to hide themselves or others, causing illusion to be cast. *Völsunga saga*, the longest of the legendary sagas, holds many instances of magical practice: for instance the mother in law of Signý turns herself to a wolf, by 'tröllskapar sakir og fjölkynngi', spell-craft and *fjölkynngi*. Signý later consults with a 'seiðkona', and Signý and the seiðkona exchange shapes.

I will examine several instances of women's magical practice, from the Icelandic sagas, in more detail, before turning to an consideration of Gunnhildr, the Witch Queen of the title of this chapter, and how she, and the others discussed, become part of the construction of today's perceptions of women as magic-workers within seiðr communities.

The evidence of the sagas

Eyrbyggja saga holds an extraordinary amount of folklore about magic, much of it associated with women. First, there is the story of the rival *fjölkunnig* (much-knowing) women, Geirrid and Katla, who each have an interest in the young man Gunnlaug. When he comes to grief, riding home one night, Katla accuses Geirrid of being *kveldriða*, a night-rider who has magically attacked Gunnlaug; but Geirrid is cleared in the ensuing legal action. Katla gives her son Odd a charmed tunic whereby no weapon can wound him. In a fight, a woman attempting to separate combatants has her hand struck off, and Geirrid states that Katla's son has done this. A group attempting to bring justice goes to seek Odd: three times Katla disguises him, so that first he seems to be a distaff where she is sitting and spinning, second a goat she is grooming, third a pig sleeping by the house. Each time the searchers realise, after leaving, that they have been tricked. Finally they take Geirrid with them wearing a blue cloak, and Katla realises that now no *sjónhverfing*, delusion or optical illusion produced by her magic, will work. Geirrid places a bag over Katla's head, Odd is found, and he and his mother face death for what are perceived as the problems they have caused.

Other magical workers named are *Þorgríma galdrakinn* (translated as Thorgríma witch-face, Thorgríma the witch, though 'magic-face' might be more precise) and *Þorgunna*. Thorgríma is mentioned by name on several occasions: in one, she is asked to bring a storm to cause trouble to another character. Thorgunna is a wealthy woman whose possessions arouse envy, and when she dies another woman takes some of the prized goods, against Thorgunna's expressed wishes. Thorgunna's magical abilities are revealed when she walks after death, gets food ready for her corpse-bearers when hosts are inhospitable, and over a period of time causes hauntings and deaths until her property is retrieved.

Finally, an unnamed elderly woman, considered to have had foreseeing (framsýn) abilities earlier in her life, predicts a problem with a bull-calf that is borne out when it causes the death of her foster-son.

One of the magic-workers best-known to today's reconstructionist community is found in *Gréttis saga*. This saga is also rich in magical or supernatural occurrences, involving giants or trolls, *draugar* (the walking dead) and so on. Grettir, the hero, famed for his strength, is a social problem, a disruptive element within the society from which he is eventually banished. His death is accomplished with the aid of an elderly woman, Thurid (Þuriðr) the foster-mother of Grettir's foe Thorbiorn Angle (Þorbjörn öngull). She first foretells his death: it is unclear whether she has 'seen' his death or whether the words are themselves a spell that helps bring it about, and equally unclear (at least to today's reader) whether her position, lying in the stern of a boat covered with wraps, indicates that she is engaging in a form of útiseta or merely that she does not want Grettir to know, until the last moment, that she is present in the boat. Sitting up, she says that the remainder of his life will be without health or good luck, increasingly until his death.

Grettir casts a stone at her, breaking her leg, and says that he knows some evil will now result to him from her *fjölkynngi*: which is the case. Thurid later charms a log, using runes and galdr (spoken charms), walking backwards, widdershins around the log, before causing it to be pushed into the sea where it drifts against the wind to the island where Grettir is living out his exile. A servant there collects it for firewood, and Grettir, attempting to split it, finds that his axe turns to wound his thigh; the wound becomes gangrenous, incapacitating Grettir so that Thorbjörn and others finally succeed in killing him. His brother claims that his death has been caused by the old woman's spell (*galdrar ykkrir og forneskja*, 'your charms and old-time lore') and *fordæðuskap*, usually translated 'witchcraft'. Thorbjörn is accused of sorcery, exiled from Iceland, and 'Var þá í lög tekið að alla forneskjumenn gerðu þeir útlæga', at that time the law was passed that all old-lore practitioners (sorcerers) should be outlawed, says the saga.

This is another case of an elderly woman who had earlier 'known much' but whose practice had, apparently, ceased with the coming of Christianity. Yet, as the story says, she could remember her earlier skill, which she puts to use on behalf of her own kin-group. The eventual accusation is against her foster-son, not herself.

Gunnhildr: political dimensions of magic

So now we return to Gunnhildr, queen variously of Norway and York, later known as King-Mother, described as working seiðr, learning seiðr from two 'Finnish' seiðmenn, and being the 'most-knowing' woman of her age. She is a historical figure, a woman who exercised power in a man's world, and the accounts are written from the points of view of those who were her opponents. Her reputation is bad. In the sagas of Icelanders she is portrayed as initiating the chain of events occasioning feuds in which first Gunnar, then Njáll and his family become enmeshed, by a spell she casts on a lover who wishes to return to Iceland.

Gunnhildr can be understood both as a historical personage and a literary fiction. She appears to have been the daughter of a Danish king, Gorm the Old, and his English wife Thyra, and sister of the Danish king Haraldr Bluetooth (Jones 1984). Yet she is identified in *Egils saga*, *Njáls saga*, and *Heimskringla*, probably following the account in *Ágrip af Nóregskonungasögum*, as daughter of Ozur Toti, an indication that by the time of their writing she had passed from history into folklore: a translator of Ágrip speculates that her recasting as a 'commoner' is in part due to 'Icelandic hostility toward Gunnhildr, whom they may have wanted to have had more humble origins' (Driscoll 1995: 87, note 15). Her first appearance in *Heimskringla* and *Egils saga* tells of her being trained in 'magic' by 'Finns', implying that she was learning Sámi shamanism. *Haralds saga hárfagra* tells of how she was found with two 'Finnish sorcerers', whom by sending to sleep she betrayed to their deaths at the hands of followers of Eiríkr called Bloodaxe, the King's son: she then married Eiríkr.

She bore at least one daughter and seven sons, in a period of stormy politics involving the sons of Haraldr Finehair who competed for power during their father's lifetime and after his death. She was variously queen in Norway and at York. Much of *Egils saga* deals with the feud that developed between its hero and Eiríkr and Gunnhildr, during which Gunnhild's son Rögnvaldr was slain. She is known as Egil's implacable enemy. Chapter 59 of *Egils saga* recounts Egil's visit to York, when Gunnhildr spoke for his death, and took the shape of a swallow, twittering outside his window to hinder composition of his 'Head Ransom poem', her plan being thwarted by the arrival of his friend Arinbjörn. The saga implies that Gunnhildr has 'called' Egill to York, by setting a seið-spell on him.

After her husband's assassination in Northumbria, Gunnhildr with her children travelled to Orkney, and later Denmark, remaining a major player in political intrigue. Eventually her son Haraldr became king of Norway. Several of her sons, including Haraldr, died in battle, and her sons were ousted from rule by Earl Hákon of Hlaðir (around 970 CE). Gunnhildr ended her days in exile in Scotland: however, an account in the *Saga of the Jomsvikings* relates that after journeying to Denmark in pursuit of a marriage with King Harald Bluetooth (unlikely, as he was her brother!) she was drowned in a bog. This was to result in a fresh interest in her in 1835 when a body was discovered in the bog (Fischer 1999; Glob 1969).

> The historians of the 19th century were never in doubt. The peat-diggers had found Queen Gunhild and despite her bad reputation – she was, after all, of Royal blood – King Frederik VI arranged for a beautifully carved coffin at St. Nicolai Church in Vejle.
>
> (Fischer 1999: 9)

Though the woman's body found was later dated as Early Iron Age, the legend of the witch-queen had been given new life.

The episodes of *Njáls saga* and *Laxdæla saga* occur during the kingship of her son Haraldr called Greycloak, when she institutes a sexual relationship with a visiting Icelander, Hrútr, who is in Norway to claim an inheritance. As the story goes, Hrútr is not given much choice, his uncle Osur saying, 'I know Gunnhild's nature. The moment we refuse her invitation, she will hound us out of the country and seize all we own.' (Magnusson and Pálsson 1960: 42) *Njáls saga* tells that Gunnhildr wins the inheritance for Hrútr (who rewards her by returning to her half) and later lays a spell on Hrútr, when he seeks to return to Iceland, so that his marriage there will remain unconsummated. The resulting divorce sets in motion the chain of events of the saga. Her portrayal in *Njáls saga*, as in *Egils saga*, is overwhelmingly negative. *Laxdæla* (chapter 19) is kinder in dealing with the episode, which it portrays as a love affair without mentioning the spell. *Laxdæla* states that when Hrútr's nephew Óláfr 'the Peacock' travels to Norway, Gunnhildr and Haraldr show him favour for his uncle's sake, though adding as a piece of gossip that 'some say' it was for his own sake also, implying that his good looks led to a 'special relationship' with Gunnhildr. Discussions of *Njáls saga* have tended to view Gunnhildr as a 'destructive prima donna' (Lönnroth 1976: 76) introduced into the story as a literary device, giving clues to thirteenth-century Icelandic identity by indicating dangers to the hero, providing a contrast between the known world of home and family and the king's court.

> At the King's Court there is more romance but even less security than at the Allthing. The king sits in his hall surrounded by beer-drinking warriors as the Icelandic visitor arrives to have his heroic valor tested. Evil royal advisers and beautiful but dangerous women lurk behind the throne
> (Lönnroth 1976: 59).

This accords with Hastrup's (1985) structural analysis of mediaeval Icelandic culture and identity, which draws on concepts of *innangarð* and *útangarð*, the worlds within and without, community and wildness, known and unknown. In these saga accounts, Gunnhildr is of the útangarð.

Historically, Gunnhildr and her children received Christian baptism in England, though how seriously she took this is not related. She was a patron of poets, commissioning the Eiríksmál on her husband's death, and may herself have been a poet, though the one verse accredited to her is an unlikely praise of King Hákon, Eirík's half-brother, who had caused her family's exile in York (Jesch 1991).

Of all women, says Snorri in *Haralds saga hárfagra*, she was the most fair and most skilled in magic. From this mention onwards, she is spoken of as *fjölkunnig* (much knowing), as *hamram* (shape-strong) and as a worker of seiðr. The accusations levelled against her by her enemies are those which Loki charged against Freyja – witchcraft and nymphomania. *Ágrip* calls her 'of all women the most beautiful; a woman small of stature yet great of counsel,' (Driscoll 1995: 9) but makes plain that in the eyes of the (probably clerical) author of this history, her counsel was 'wicked' (*illrǫðug*) and she was to blame for her husband's reported cruelty.

A task faced by researchers and today's seiðr practitioners, alike, is evaluating the accounts. For our understanding of the concepts and their applications, it may be that the 'historical fiction' is in some ways more important than the actual woman – of whom very little is known, although one assumes that she must have been quite highly regarded by at least some of her contemporaries: she was always able to find refuge and support. In the later accounts, Gunnhildr has become the archetypal sorceress, 'the prototype of evil and revenging women in the old Norse corpus' (Jochens 1996: 180). The accounts in *Heimskringla* and possibly *Egils saga* were written by Snorri Sturluson, a descendent of Egill, around 1230. The *Njáls saga* portrait of Gunnhildr, from around 1280 (Magnusson 1975), continues the trend. Her daughter Ragnhildr who married Arnfinn, son of Þorfinn earl of Orkney, appears in *Orkneyinga saga* as another political, scheming, woman. Gwyn Jones points out that 'In fact, there is no evidence that Eirik, Gunnhild, and their royal brood were greedier, crueller, more devious or ambitious than their fellow contenders for rank and riches in Norway' (1984: 122, fn.).

Today, Gunnhildr has the name of a woman who used her skills in politics or magic to further her own interests, sometimes cruelly. Today's readers know her through the elaborations of thirteenth-century saga-writers whose chief business was to tell the stories of their own ancestors, her enemies. Jesch (1991) has pointed to misogyny inherent in these accounts, and Jochens (1995: 180) comments that 'the earliest Old Norse narratives offer a more nuanced portrait that include references to her beauty, pagan beliefs, magical knowledge, and cunning'.

This is the background against which today's seiðworkers see themselves and their magical/shamanistic practice. Academia has emphasised negative evaluations of seiðr, and many accounts within the Heathen community have likewise positioned seiðr as something to be regarded with suspicion, even fear.

Past and present: evaluating the seiðwomen

Today's practitioners are working, therefore, with conflicting definitions of seiðr: 'evil magic', or constructive; something done by women, or a special skill that anybody might learn; valuable or destructive according to discursive constructions within the community. Some say that 'seiðr' should mean *only* evil magic, with activities of journeying and divination more properly termed 'spae'. There are the arguments that seiðr involved 'messing with people's minds', changing memories or personality characteristics, turning (or threatening to turn) 'the world upside down' (from Ljót in *Vatnsdœla saga*, which may refer to an earthquake or personal turmoil), with Gunnhild's curses given as evidence. Yet these accounts can be read as attempts to defend, or to avenge. I asked the seeress Rauðhildr about such 'negative' views, and how she saw her practice in their light. Her response:

> I agree that defense/vengeance can be read into some of these accounts.
> One might also note, the mind and the sword can be equally deadly if wielded 'properly'. I find it interesting the judgments made about death by magic as opposed to death by the sword and how that difference bears on opinions of the practice of seið.

I made reference, in chapter 3, to the account of the seiðkona Þurídr *sundafyllir*, who called fish into the sound, thereby bringing life, not death: and speculations that this seiðwoman and the Greenland Seeress were effectively dealing with the threads of Wyrd so that they acted to restore balance within the community and its environment; engaging in shamanistic practice, performed for the community, going beyond telling the future to engaging with its construction. Rauðhildr gave me a present-day example of 'fishing' seiðr designed to benefit individual or community (also in Blain, forthcoming). On a Californian fishing expedition, one person had caught no fish.

> I touched his line and 'sang along it' to the fish. I asked them to please give one more of their kind to this good man. I said he would make offering to the gods and wights of the sea for the prosperity of all their folk in return. I sang of the man's worthiness to receive such a gift. How a great fish giving himself to this man would bring honor to all parties. I sang of his power and his bravery as a warrior (the gent was a Vietnam Veteran). Lastly I thanked them for listening to my song. I took my hand off the line and a fish hit his line so hard I heard the line slap against the side of the boat. Two minutes later he had the fish on the deck. I don't like the practice, but on the big trip boats, they will sometimes club the fish. But this one didn't need it. The gentleman knelt down and touched it, said 'thank you' and the fish stopped moving. It was very powerful. No more

than two minutes after that, the boat limited out and the lines were pulled out of the water and we headed home.

This active construction is something emerging frequently in Rauðhildr's discussions of seiðr, an important aspect of what she is doing. Stephan Grundy instances Þurídr *sundafyllir* as an example of 'socially constitutive seiðr', others being the accounts of Þórdis spákona from Vatnsdæla (as previously mentioned), using magic to bring about a peaceful solution to a crisis, and 'another Þórdís, in Gunnars saga keldugnúpsfífls [who] uses seiðr to force Gunnarr to pay the weregild for her brother whom he has slain, since there is clearly no man in the family to bring him to law' (Grundy, pers. com.).

Grundy relates this socially approved use of seiðr to the relation of women to the law of the times, and its mechanisms for enforcement.

> In these examples seiðr may, I think, be seen as the way in which a woman could complement a not always adequate power of law, just as men at times had to complement it with fighting. In this regards, I might suggest that some of the horror felt towards seiðr had something to do with the fact that it was usually performed in secret and normal methods of defense against it could not be used. Hence it bore a whiff of the moral taint associated with secret murder – and in these 'socially constructive' examples, we note that the primary operators are female and therefore permitted means of enforcement or redress other than physical challenge to the offender.
>
> (pers. com.)

The suggestion here is that seiðr used for community construction or protection was acceptable when done by a woman, but that men were expected to seek other forms of redressing the social balance (see also Dubois 1999). Seiðr in this account parallels the use of strength or weapons, and indeed seiðr can be seen as a means of strength or a weapon, one which is hidden. As Rauðhildr said, 'the mind and the sword can be equally deadly'. This concept of seiðr as hidden, therefore less acceptable for men, is further pursued in the next chapter.

So for at least some within today's Heathen community, seiðr, defined as use of hidden skills which enable the practitioner to contact spirits and with their aid to 'see along' the threads of örløg or Wyrd or actively manipulate those threads, is legitimate and acceptable practice when performed for the benefit of the community. For others, though, it remains doubtful, seen as devious, unfair advantage, or as a way of gaining power when more legitimate (or socially acceptable) means have failed. They cite a verse from the poem *Völuspá* which almost all practitioners have read (in various translations): its interpretations display contestations of 'women's magic'.

Heiði hana hétu	hvar er til húsa kom,
völu velspáa,	vitti hún ganda;
seið hún kunni,	seið hún leikin,
æ var hún angan	illrar brúðar.

(Kuhn and Neckel 1962: Völuspá 22)

Verse 22 introduces the name 'Heiðr', giving what information we have about this entity. The manuscript sources are not in total agreement, with 'seið hún hvar er hún kunni', and 'seið hún hugleikin'. A nineteenth-century interpretation has 'vél' (deceit, artifice) in place of 'vel' (well or pleasing), and as diacritical markings are not present in the earlier versions, either reading is possible. All the more scope, therefore, for today's interpreters.

Translations available to practitioners vary.

Heith she was hight	whereto houses she came
the wise seeress,	and witchcraft plied
cast spells where she could,	cast spells on the mind:
to wicked women	she was welcome ever.

(Hollander 1962: 4)

Larrington's translation is probably the most read among today's Heathens. She gives:

Bright One they called her, wherever she came to houses,
the seer with pleasing prophecies, she charmed them with spells;
she made magic wherever she could, with magic she played with minds,
she was always the favourite of wicked women.

(Larrington 1996: 7)

A translation in an article in the Heathen magazine *Idunna* gave:

> She was called Heidhr when she came to houses, a volva
> prophesying well/deceitfully, she knew gand-craft, she practiced
> seidhr where she could, practiced seidhr, playing with hugr, she
> was ever dear to evil women.
>
> (Gundarsson 1995: 9)

The translation by W.H. Auden, frequently met with on the
internet, especially on Heathens' webpages, reads:

> Heidi men call me when their homes I visit,
> A far seeing Volva, wise in talismans.
> Caster of spells, cunning in magic.
> To wicked women welcome always.
>
> (Auden and Taylor 1981)

People making seiðr today in North America and Britain are
likely to have read one or more of these, and whichever one they
have read carries its own implications. There are some obvious
differences: The fourth half-line produces multiple sets of possible
meanings, in the above translations. Was Heiðr 'enchanting staves'
or 'charming (people) with spells' or 'knowing gand- (staff or wand-)
craft' or 'wise in talismans', and all from the phrase, 'vitti (or
perhaps 'viti') hún ganda'. So the debate goes on – exasperatingly to
some of today's Heathens who seek 'truth'. 'Anyone else wish
someone would just translate it all just as it is?' was a recent
comment on an email list. Yet, between the meanings of the original
author and the meanings today's reader takes lies a wealth of
interpretation and reinterpretation, which forms part of the context
of today's seiðr practice. All share the common element of the last
line: Heiðr, the archetypal seiðworker, was specifically welcomed by
wicked women.

Heiðr, discourse and interpretation

When members of the community raise the question of why Heiðr
was associated with wickedness, or evil – as they do – they ask
questions such as 'What does the text say?' or 'Could it be a
Christian interpolation?' But no text here is definitive, and the
dating of the poem is debated. For the community as a whole, there

are no easy answers, and so the debate about whether seiðr (or Heiðr) is intrinsically 'evil' continues. Meanings shift and change within changing contexts of practice. Every interpretation or translation relies on previous decisions as to which version was 'better', and there is no simple answer.

In approaching understandings through discourse and narrative, meanings of a text are constituted by many people, including writer and reader, and any or all that come between, within the specifics of (changing) context. The text becomes a site of contestation. Sometimes within Heathen interpretations the part of the editor, scribe or redactor is recognised: many agree that the Eddas are not sacred scripture, (not absolute Truth for all times) but the inspired poems of various individuals who lived in their own times, their own places. The meanings that today's readers bring to Eddic analysis are not necessarily those that their creators would recognise.

As a practitioner, I explore the context. The preceding verse introduces Gullveig, Love of Gold or Intoxication-of-Gold, who came among the Æsir. Three times she was burned in the hall of Hár, yet remained living. The common interpretation is that Gullveig became Heiðr, with interpreters mostly in agreement that Gullveig/Heiðr is also Freyja,[2] who came among the Æsir after the war of Æsir and Vanir, and who, according to Snorri, taught seiðr to the Æsir. Gullveig/Heiðr was burned, but lives. As Heiðr, she comes to houses, she foretells, she knows the magic called seiðr.

Why was she burned? The commonest interpretations within the Heathen community (and academia: see Schach 1983) are that she brought to the Æsir the love of gold, which caused problems so that the Æsir attempted to remove the problems by removing Gullveig; or that her magic caused problems for the Æsir, with the same result. Less negative viewpoints are that as she shines more brightly after the burning, there may be an association with 'thrice-refined gold'; or even a parallel with Óðin's ordeal on Yggdrasill, if it is the 'initiatory' experience of burning that enables her to have the knowledge of seiðr.

Some academic interpreters see the verse as an example of late-Heathen distrust of magic or seiðr, misogyny, or indeed both.

> It may well be... that this description of Heiðr (especially the last lines) sounds strange in the mouth of the sibyl who is declaiming the poem. But in fact it demonstrates that the poet

let his zeal override the thought of what would be the most natural thing for the sibyl to say. It was not only that Heiðr had an evil purpose among the Æsir, but also that sibyls and enchanters were already unpopular with many people in pagan times.

(Nordal 1978: 44–45)

Jochens reads the phrase as indicative of late-Heathen misogyny:

In the divine world, we now see evil associated with Gullveig and Heiðr...the two new names stand for female being who are associated with evil. Heiðr may simply mean 'witch.' Gullveig, the personification of gold in female shape, brings into the world the first war... As Heiðr she offers magic to the gods, and her art is appreciated by 'wicked women.'

(1989: 353)

The most problematic phrase is in the last line *illrar bruðar*. *Bruðr*, literally 'bride', is glossed as a generalisation for 'women', actual, past or potential brides. Dictionary definitions (Zoëga 1910) of *illr* give (1) ill, evil bad; (2) hard, difficult (3) close, mean, stingy. Yet the same dictionary glosses *illþræli* as 'wretched thrall', thus introducing another potential understanding of 'illr'. Some of today's Icelandic Heathens have suggested it be read as 'wretched' or 'unhappy' (Jörmundur Ingi Hansen, pers. com.), giving the sense of 'unhappy young women', or perhaps simply 'unhappy people'. From this, Heiðr becomes one bringing relief to people in need!

The phrase may have had more than one interpretation, even at the time of writing. I am attempting to understand meaning within contexts of the political and material circumstances in which women and men lived and had their being: semi-isolated farmsteads of Iceland or Norway or Scotland, the long dark of winter nights. Numerous commentators have pointed to a relative equality between women and men, at least in terms of the household, at the time of writing, but this equality was only partial, especially in areas in which power was being centralised with all the implications of hierarchical organisation of power implied thereby. In many cultures those with low levels of political power choose to use methods of magic, identified as 'witchcraft' or 'sorcery', which may be an attempt to influence events or bring about their wishes: the claiming of power by those who have little. This is how Lewis (1989) describes instances of North African possession. The women who are possessed acquire some social power thereby.

Interpretation of interpretation

Permit me, though, to position these understandings within a discussion of interpretation. Anthropological narratives are full of such accounts – some, though, highly problematic in both description and interpretation where 'European notions of rationality and the discourse of an often positivist science have been used as a universal benchmark against which other cultures are judged' (Greenwood 2000: 39). Classical ethnography, interpreting 'witchcraft' in functionalist or structuralist terms of power-seeking and ill-feeling in the community, has tremendous difficulty in dealing with the effects of, for instance, shamanic healing ceremonies.

> In Anthropological writing, a Western ontology is still often taken for granted. When posing questions about experience, the patterns of Euro-American 'common sense' resonate so subtly with our working assumption that we fail to notice their cultural specificity.
>
> (Salmond 2000: 55)

Western dominant assumptions reappear as categories: the distinctions made not only between 'witchcraft' and 'shamanism', 'witchcraft' and 'sorcery', but between 'possession' and 'shamanism', being cases in point. (Lewis (1989) and others have pointed out that possession and shamanism may not be easily distinguishable, or indeed distinguishable at all, in practices of specific societies or their 'shamans': but the distinction remains in both popular and academic descriptions.) Alan Harwood (1970: xv) quotes definitions derived from Evans-Pritchard's work: 'Witchcraft...is "a mystical and innate power, which can be used by its possessor to harm other people". Sorcery, on the other hand, is "evil magic against others".' (Most often sorcery is believed to involve the use of 'medicines' to harm, in these studies.)

These words, 'witch' and 'sorcerer' had their roots in dominant Western discourses, both of 'good' and 'evil', and of 'rationality': 'witch' then was used as referring to a practitioner of potentially evil magic, and so supplied it as a translation for whatever local term ethnographers were presented with. Often word-meanings were gained first from other non-native personnel who had had reason to gain a fairly close acquaintanceship with Native languages – such as Western missionaries, who would have their own reasons for decrying local spiritual practices and practitioners. In addition to this circularity of definition, classical anthropology tended to ignore rapid changes taking effect in many societies studied, and tensions between colonial administrators' views of how a society should be run and local traditional practice. Indeed, especially in a situation of rapid change, those with less power may well choose magical means of bringing about results pleasing to them. These results however need not be negative for the community as a whole, and not only those of low status engage in such practices. The ethnographic work of (for instance) Taussig (1987) or Kapferer (1997) indicates complexities of meaning constructed within political dimensions, with 'magic' used and experienced in multiple ways. Favret-Saada's (1980) experiences in the Bocage indicate how much the interpreter/ethnographer becomes part of the multiplicity of meanings, and how those meanings are dependent on embeddedness within events and discourse. Lines cannot easily be drawn between negative and positive magic. I have already indicated that in saga accounts of seiðr, we distinguish 'positive' from 'negative' only in terms of who is telling the story, or who is its leading character.

Multiple contested meanings need not relate only to the present. Who would be these 'illrar' brides'? Wretched young women, evil sorceresses, people powerless (taking 'brides' literally) in a strange household, scheming to strengthen their own position? Should we believe, with Jochens, that by the time the verse was written, probably, as Grundy points out, by a poet with knowledge of both Heathenism and Christianity, patriarchy had gone so far that women who sought to further their own position were automatically 'evil'? This argument is not convincing to me. (Even if two or three hundred years later it might have more basis, it still seems too sweeping. Even in the mis-titled 'burning times' of 'witchcraft' trials and accusations in parts of Europe, realities in any village were more nuanced.)

Another, speculative, interpretation might run as follows. The primary cause of death for young women, until the present century, was childbirth. Dread of childbirth included not only concerns about dying (especially if close relatives had died in childbirth), but concerns about labour, its duration and intensity, including fear for the child as well as fear for oneself. The Icelandic sagas, chiefly concerned with matters of feud and politics and the doings of males, do not give details of difficult labours: but material dealing with Icelandic Christianity recounts numerous instances of women seeking reassurance regarding childbirth (Jochens 1995). When the outcome of an event or process is uncertain and factors other than skill are concerned in this outcome, people often have recourse to magic to seek knowledge or to attempt to control events. It would be indeed surprising if childbirth and reproduction were *not* areas associated with magical practices. Ability to conceive and produce a healthy child was prized. In some other societies a women's position was not secure within a household until she had done so, though again the sagas do not, to my knowledge at least, explore this area.

Heiðr being welcome to *illrar bruðar* might be read then as an association with bringing relief – whether of the pains of labour or the uncertainty of a secure outcome, uncertainties of the ability to conceive and bear children, or all of these, is something that can be conjectured.

Is Heiðr a midwife?

Most scholars consider that Gullveig, Heiðr and Freyja refer to the same Goddess.[3] Now, many Heathens speak of Freyja as a goddess whom women asked for help in childbirth. Grundy points out (1996: 60) that 'Only once, in Oddrúnargrátr, does she appear as a patroness of childbirth; a prayer to hold in giving birth calls on "kind wights/Frigg and Freyja/and many gods".' Further, if this poem is late, the reference to 'Frigg and Freyja' may be an attempt to make the poem seem archaic and Heathen. A Christian poet may not have known what goddesses would be called upon in childbirth, but put in the names of the two most important, or the first two that came to mind. This cannot be regarded as evidence that Freyja was indeed called upon to assist childbirth. However, there is another, rather tenuous, link, indicated by Näsström, from the poem *Húsdrapa*. Heimdallr recovers Freyja's magical necklace, Brisingamen (which Näsström (1996a), connects with the shining sea, and with Freyja's name 'Mardöll'). The jewel is referred to as *hafnýra* or sea-kidney (which Näsström (1996b) identifies as a dehydrated palm fruit, conveyed from the West Indies by the Gulf Stream, with a brownish red colour, and associated in folklore with fire), which Näsström finds was used in folk-medicine to facilitate deliveries, and in Iceland called *lausnerstein* (delivery stone, 'loosening' the baby from the mother).

Evidence associating Freyja/Heiðr with childbirth is therefore unclear, though tantalising. The suggestion that Heiðr is a midwife, whether magical or practical, remains purely speculative.

In the meantime, some other intriguing possibilities remain. If Heiðr is concerned with reproduction – or with making such reproduction possible – the concept of 'empowering staff' may be reconsidered also. Some researchers have associated 'staff' and 'penis' (see Jochens 1996). (Could *illrar bruðar* be read as 'unsatisfied women' whom Heiðr could help?) Yet what I have read of these comments suggests Heiðr as disempowering rather than empowering, fitting the stereotype of the witch who renders men impotent. One could say, however, that if Heiðr, or her followers, had the one power – of arousing and maintaining desire – they may also have had the opposite power. One might think also of the spell which Gunnhildr was said to cast on her erstwhile lover, Hrútr, preventing genital sex with his wife Unnr through over-engorgement (*Njáls saga,* chapters 6–8).

Five centuries after the likely date of composition of the poem, some European 'witches' were charged with causing impotence, miscarriages or the birth of children who were 'imperfect', preventing conception, and so forth.[4] Women who healed could be said to have the power of harming;[5] women who assisted childbirth, mitigating its pains, were in the eyes of some churchmen the greatest sinners of all. Yet even then the Scandinavian countries were on the periphery of the 'witchcraze', not its centre, with only a few instances (such as that of the 'Blakulla' trials in Sweden) showing the misogyny that seems to have been one factor among others, elsewhere. In other Northern countries, such as Scotland, witchcraft accusations came late, and were politically motivated. According to Hastrup (1990), Iceland did not have a true 'witch hunt' at all, and there, as in Finland, accusations were chiefly against males. Morris (1991) suggests that the 'Icelandic sorceress' did continue to practice 'witchcraft' – seiðr, midwifery, and folk-magic – but that this was not treated with the negativity which at times suggestions of 'magic' received in parts of continental Europe.

But when the collection of traditional poems to which the name Edda became attached – including *Völuspá* – was rediscovered in the seventeenth century, and even more when the stories and deeds of gods and heroes were lauded and romanticised in the nineteenth, circumstances were ripe for a reading of Gullveig/Heiðr as the 'evil witch', causing harm and sowing discord by her very being; and such readings have persisted up to the present day. Today, when our society appears to be more aware of contradictions and misogyny in some of its still-dominant narratives of women as evil, Heathens and scholars alike ponder the extent to which the *Völuspá* poet was influenced by 'Christian' ideas, or to which 'misogyny' was part of late-Heathen thought. Yet it seems to me that this debate is not necessarily pertinent to the verse at issue here. The words were written in one era, and read and interpreted in others, through filters of the intervening periods. Nor do we know the extent to which the verse might hold different meanings to different people, even at the time of its composition. For my own purposes, I prefer to interpret the verse:

> Heiðr she was called   when to houses she came,
> Völva well-foretelling,   empowering staffs;
> Seiðr she practised   Seiðr with thought playing,
> Joy was she ever   to despairing women.

The slant on Heiðr thus given is in accordance with how she appears to at least some Heathen practitioners today, and is one that 'makes sense' to many women. It is not presented here as conclusive or as a scholarly glossing of the verse: that is not my field or my purpose. In the spirit of experiential anthropology, I have examined my own situation and the understandings that result from it, reflexively, as a community practitioner, and attempted to show their construction. The community is divided on Heiðr and her meaning for today's practitioners, and this is linked to the ways that seiðr as shamanic-magic is received and explained today.

Women and magic, a continuing strand of practice?

There have been suggestions that the practice of the völva, going to houses, did not die out in Iceland, becoming instead modified within changing conditions of daily life.

Icelandic lawcodes never included proscriptions specifically against the practice of the völva. Today, interpretations both of the lack of such proscription, and the increasing targeting of male practice as unlawful, are disputed. To Jochens (1996), these indicate that men, including churchmen, took over practices of *spá* and rune-work, with this divination becoming increasingly problematic. However, Morris (1991) implies that 'seeking for knowledge' in Iceland remained part of the complex of activities that were appropriate for and performed by women: it became problematic only when men practised it, possibly (as I conjecture) for political reasons.

Icelandic Ásatrú's current *Allsherjargoði*, Jörmundur Ingi, indicated to me that women in Iceland maintained some of the practices associated with seiðr, often unthinkingly, as everyday activities, gendered practice, simply things that women do in their households and kitchens.

> I remember when I was a little kid living out in the country. . . the women would close themselves into the kitchen, to ah, to do some things that they were whispering about, and the men would simply keep away... and we were just little kids, we sometimes stayed in there, they didn't bother with us. They were doing some sort of little magic tricks which we didn't know was magic and probably they didn't know either ... from some signs or whatever, usually you know, whom they should marry or how things should go and so on, and so they have been doing it all the time.

The extent to which these activities would be considered *seiðr* is of course debatable. The word covers a range of meanings, not necessarily those of the Heathen period. Jörmundur, however, considers that women's magical practice was continued, as part of everyday life. On occasion possible links with seiðr or *spá*, could become more evident, as with the coming of the 'spiritualism' movement to Iceland in the ninetenth century, when, he says:

> . . . while this movement was sort of a fringe movement every-where else, it was here part of ah, high society. It was introduced into Iceland mostly by priests and lawyers...so right from the start, it got a socially accepted stamp on it, it was the in thing, to be an adherent of this, and very strangely what happened was that women would flock to this and all of a sudden, you would have mediums, women, everywhere, and the most astounding thing about that was that the way they were conducting these seances, what they were doing of course, was that you can read the story of the Völva, in the saga of Eirík

the Red, and they held the ceremony exactly. So I have the theory that women were doing this all through the Christian era, they were simply having little ceremonies like that without even realizing that this was religion. This was just something that women did, and men didn't interfere in.

Again, interpretations of spiritualism, in Iceland as elsewhere, vary (see e.g. Swatos and Gissurarson 1996). Yet, the words for a woman who does this kind of magic, völva, vølve, have remained; or, as in Scotland, the spaewife. They are re-emerging to describe today's practice, whether drawn from core-shamanism as described by Jakobsen (1999) and Lindquist (1997), or the reconstructions of Hrafnar and other Heathen groups, as discussed here. Dialogue between these constructed practices reveals considerable approachings, as each draws on the story of the Greenland Seeress, and beyond that on the concept of the being who worked magic for Óðinn, at his request, to foretell the fate of the Æsir and the Nine Worlds: and on the Well of Wyrd at the roots of Yggdrasill, the World Tree. Today's practice is shared by men and women. The Scandinavian groups use the same word, vølve, to describe both, some reconstructionists preferring seiðkona and seiðmaðr. I turn, therefore, to contestations of gender and sexuality surrounding those men, and women, who do seiðr today: and to further debates over the relationship of seið-practitioners to 'the spirits' and who or what those might be.

Chapter 7

Ergi seiðmen, queer transformations?

Many of the accounts of seiðr, as earlier indicated, are of women practitioners, to the extent that scholars and practitioners alike speak of seiðr as 'women's magic'. I have, however, referred to accounts of men who did seiðr, and how they might be regarded. The term *ergi* can be interpreted in many ways (and was not only applied to seiðworkers). It appears in the literature as an insult directed differently to men and to women. In this chapter I examine some of the ways that the term was applied, and is regarded today. I also look at related controversies, which include the status of seiðr as either 'indigenous' practice or 'borrowed' from the Sámi during the Viking ages, before returning to implications for today's practitioners.

Shamanism and resistance

First, some men who made seiðr: a twelfth-century account, *Ágrip af Nóregskonugasögum,* details the many sons of Haraldr Finehair, king of Norway.

> [T]he twentieth [was] Rögnvaldr *reykill*, whom some call Ragnarr. He was the son of a certain Lappish woman called Snjófríðr, the daughter of Svási, king of the Lapps, and took after his mother. He was called a sorcerer – that is to say a soothsayer – and he lived in Haðaland and practised sorcery there and was called a warlock.

> xx. Rögnvaldr reykill, er sumir kalla Ragnar, er var sunr Finnkonu einnar er kölluð var Snjófríð, dóttir Svása Finnkonungs, ok brá hónum til móður sinnar. Var hann kallaðr

seiðmaðr – þat er spámaðr – ok var staðfastr á Haðalandi ok
síddi þar ok var kallaðr skratti.

(Driscoll 1995: 4, 5)

Rögnvald's mother had secured the interest of King Haraldr,
according to *Ágrip* and to Snorri's *Heimskringla*, by magic, when
offering him a drink of mead. On her death, the king kept her body
beside him, richly dressed, for three years. Her son the 'sorcerer'
was, from this text, a *seiðmaðr*, 'that is to say spae-worker
(*spámaðr*)'. His death is related by Snorri:

> Eiríkr *blóðöx* planned to be the king over all his brothers, and
> so wished he and king Harald; father and son were always
> together. Rögnvaldr *réttilbeini* had Haðaland; he (had) learning
> in *fjölkyngi* and became a seiðman. Seiðworkers were disliked
> by king Harald. In Hörðaland there was a seiðman who was
> called Vitgeirr; the king sent him a message and told him to
> stop making seiðr. He replied and said:

> > There's no harm
> > if we do seiðr,
> > children of ordinary men
> > and ordinary women,
> > when Rögnvaldr
> > straight-leg does seiðr,
> > Harald's famous son,
> > in Haðaland.

> And when Harald the king heard this, then by his advice Eirík
> went to the Uplands and came to Haðaland and burned his
> brother, Rögnvald, in his house with eighty seiðworkers, and
> this work was much approved.
>
> (*Haralds saga hárfagra*, chapter 36, my trans.)

This event may be seen as part of political processes of
centralisation of kingship, together with Eirík's removing a close
relative who while unlikely to seek the over-kingship, might support
another claimant among many half-brothers hoping to succeed
their father. The later king Óláfr Tryggvason is also said to have
caused the death of eighty s*eiðmenn*, and while Snorri uses the
masculine pronoun 'þeir' for them, older sources seem to have
described them as including males and females (Jochens 1996:125);

the word *menn* (singular *maðr*) meaning 'people'. Here again it is likely that politics played as great a part as religion. ('Eighty' probably indicates 'a large number', not a precise count.)

There is little information about Rögnvald: he had a personal connection with 'Finns' or Sámi; he performed seiðr as part of a large group of others involved in this practice; and his seiðworking was not liked by his half-brother and father. One may speculate further on reasons for this dislike: Rögnvald's 'making seiðr' may have been viewed as permissive sanction for others' seið-practices (as implied by the poem). Why Haraldr Finehair did not like seiðr can only be guessed: I have speculated that any form of shamanic practice introduces unpredictable elements into political decision-making (unpredictable, that is, for those who do not themselves speak to 'the spirits') and suppression of shamanic activity can be found in Western colonising (and missionising) in North and South America, and more recently Soviet suppression, with occasional co-opting, of Siberian practices. The shaman's 'reasons' for advising various courses of action are neither obvious nor explainable to those who, once again, do not themselves speak to the spirits. Shamanic activity is localised and predicated on local loyalties. There are, therefore, many reasons why those bent on extending their spheres of influence might seek to obliterate local shamanisms and their practitioners, and why the local practitioners, adjusting their practice to changed political conditions, might at times reinforce their 'difference' from the governing classes or powers (see e.g. Taussig's (1987) discussions of nuanced adaptations of South American practitioners) and at other times become part of the 'system' for dealing with those unpredictabilities which were not so politically threatening – small-scale charms, the uncertainties of childbirth, weather and crops, etc.

There seem to have been few attempts to examine the history of 'conversion' to Christianity of North and West Europe as complex interweavings of religion in the service of politics, possibly because the dominant assumption has been, until very recently, that Christianity was on the whole 'a good thing', bringing progress, enlightenment, truth, justice and better treatment for women. The converse view that Christianity was responsible for bringing a flood of ills in its wake, including repression of sexuality, denial of goddesses, subordination of women, and leading eventually to the excesses of capitalism and environmental degradation, is held by many Pagans, including some Heathens and neo-shamanists today.

It can be traced to nineteenth-century romantic movements, and reappears in much neo-pagan writing (see e.g. Markale 1986).

Application of post-colonialist and discourse theory would tend to suggest more nuanced interpretation of specific, local practices and events, within changing contexts of climate, power and technology, and in situations where 'boundaries' between 'cultures' and 'religions' are permeable, not fixed. Anthropology is producing new understandings of missionising and conversion elsewhere (e.g. Salmond's (2000) account of missionaries and Maori), and it will be interesting to see what relations of politics, religion, power and resistance emerge within the history of European conversion in the next few years. As I am not a historian, I do not attempt to engage with these historical processes, other than speculatively: my focus is on the construction of practice today, and I engage with the past to understand the present. Like other seiðr practitioners, I am handicapped in my search for meaning by a lack of nuanced interpretations of the past. I therefore am here attempting to provide a context for Rögnvald – and Vitgeirr – to understand the complex meanings, including what appears as progressive 'demonisation', surrounding men making seiðr.

The evidence of the sagas

In *Gísla saga Súrssonar*, 'Þorgrímr hastened to his seiðr and built a scaffolding and worked *fjölkyngi* with all *ergi* and *skelmiskáp* (devilry)' (chapter 10). Kotkell of *Laxdæla saga* uses both seiðr and galdr (sung spells, often associated with rune-magic, and more often associated with men): Kotkell builds a seiðr-platform, ascends it, and with his sons chants galdr to raise a storm. Other male practitioners are positioned as *fjölkunnigr*: an example being the magic-worker of *Kormáks saga* who sleeps by the door and knows the business of everyone in the hall, a way to keep safe those present.

These accounts indicate that at the time of writing it was understood that men could, and had, engaged in seiðr practices. But there is no male equivalent to Þorbjörg, or Þordís spákona, or Þuriðr *sýndafyllir*. Men appear in the sagas engaged in shamanistic practices, but this is rarely elaborated upon, and if called seiðr (rather than *útiseta*) never positioned as 'socially constitutive'. The one detailed account of seiðr by a male is of Óðinn, from *Ynglingasaga*.

Odin could transform his shape: his body would lie as if dead, or asleep; but then he would be in shape of a fish, or worm, or bird, or beast, and be off in a twinkling to distant lands upon his own or other people's business ... Sometimes even he called the dead out of the earth, or set himself beside the burial-mounds; whence he was called the ghost-sovereign, and lord of the mounds...

Odin understood also the art in which the greatest power is lodged, and which he himself practised; namely, what is called magic [*seiðr*]. By means of this he could know beforehand the predestined fate of men, or their not yet completed lot; and also bring on the death, ill-luck, or bad health of people, and take the strength or wit from one person and give it to another. But after such witchcraft followed such weakness and anxiety [*ergi*], that it was not thought respectable for men to practice it; and therefore the priestesses were brought up in this art.

(*Heimskringla*, trans. Laing 1844/Online Mediaeval and Classical Library (OMACL))

Several points emerge from this account. It is not clear exactly what is indicated by seiðr. Some techniques of 'faring forth' are addressed, which seem to fit well with the accounts of *útiseta*, discussed in chapter 4. Necromancy, calling the dead from the earth, is separately dealt with. Óðinn could know, by means of seiðr, the course of people's lives, and cause various things to occur – all, apparently, things benefiting him, not the recipient (except when this recipient receives another's strength) – but how this 'seiðr' was done is not said. Finally, we are to understand that seiðr was not appropriate for men because of the *ergi* that followed, and therefore was taught to women. Snorri was writing 200 years after Christianisation, and the development of the concepts he incorporates is unclear: however, the tone of the passage adds to the general implication that seiðr and those engaging with it are dangerous, ambiguous – and that it was generally performed by women. Additionally, the tone of the nineteenth-century translation used above – the translation most accessible to practitioners because it is available on the internet from OMACL – indicates an unwillingness to deal with the concepts of either *seiðr* or *ergi*, which did not fit in with the romantic, nineteenth-century notions of a Viking 'warrior god'.

Jochens (1996) examines both older material (e.g. *Völuspá*) and later material (e.g. *Ynglingasaga*) to suggest that seiðr was initially women's magic, with its practice by men seen as problematic, effeminising or *ergi* (even for Óðinn), possibly because it included female 'receptive' sexual activities. She speculates on actual or symbolic ritual sex practices, involving the seeress' staff. She suggests, however, that men were able to take over the (not sexually implicated) practice of spae-working while retaining community standing, male spae-workers (including Christian priests) being described approvingly in the later Icelandic literature. Without necessarily agreeing fully with Jochens that magic within Germanic communities was originally a female domain, appropriated by males during an increasingly patriarchal period prior to Christianisation, it is still possible to see gender and gender-constructing processes as part of a dynamic marginalising of seiðr. Jochens points to a gradient from the respect with which the seeress Veleda appears to be regarded, as described by Tacitus (*Historia*, book IV) to descriptions of female spell-workers in the Icelanders' sagas (such as Katla in *Eyrbyggja saga* or Ljót in *Vatnsdæla saga*). In Jochens' view, this movement towards seeing female workers of magic – and male workers of female magic – as 'evil' had occurred by the time the *Völuspá* verse about Heiðr, previously discussed, was composed.

Men and seiðr today

We are back, then, with concepts relating seiðr with women and ambiguity. This has not escaped the attention of those reconstructing seiðr today. Diana Paxson initially saw high-seat seiðr as 'something for the women to do' while men were engaging in 'playing Viking'. Men had competitive athletics, women had magic. But in today's climate of equal opportunity, some women engaged in 'Viking games', some men tried out the experience of seiðr – and experiencing something new and different, found a calling for themselves as seiðworkers.

Elsewhere, writers and shamanists were already exploring seiðr. Bates' (1983) *The Way of Wyrd* describes a young cleric sent to (still Heathen) southern England in order to find out about the 'Old Religion'. Essentially coming as a spy, then, he meets a shaman and becomes the shaman's apprentice. The shaman's activities are based on the 'charms' in Old English texts, the Lacnunga and Leechbook (see Storms' (1948/1975) *Anglo-Saxon Magic* for texts and commentary). Bates' novel influenced a number of men and women, notably in the UK. More recently, a number of non-academic authors have turned their attention to 'Northern Shamanism', Fries' (1996) *Seidways* serving as example. 'Northern Shamans' have emerged in Britain, North America, and Europe – in England 'Runic John' interviewed by Wallis (1999b and forthcoming, a), or in France Yves Kodratoff, who has written extensively about his blending of runes and seiðr into healing rituals (Kodratoff 1998). They have derived their practices from the literature, from merging basic Heathen or Pagan rites with more obviously 'consciousness-altering' practices, or from using 'shamanic' techniques derived from academic descriptions of shamanic practice or basic neo-shamanism texts together with what is known of rune-magic and meanings, within the cosmology of Wyrd, Yggdrasill and the Norns. Books such as *The Well and the Tree* (Bauschatz 1982) *Runes* (Elliott 1989), or *Anglo-Saxon Magic* (Storms 1948) are therefore among 'source texts' for would-be 'Northern Shamans' who often look to Óðinn, or Woden, as a shamanic deity.

So, people were practising 'seiðr' before the development of oracular seiðr by Hrafnar, or the adoption of 'core-shamanism' techniques within Scandinavian, Saxon or more generally 'Northern' cultural contexts. (Several of those who since received training from Hrafnar were constructing their own shamanistic techniques, or 'talking to spirits' before adopting the form of the oracular seiðr.) Many of the individual workers of the past 25 years have been men. Malcolm, in Scotland, is an example: initially taught 'Northern Shamanism' by a Swedish 'Tattare' (tinker or 'gypsy') practitioner in 1981, he says, 'I call what I do seiðr, because that's what Sven called it'. His work today is a blend of Sven's teaching, what he learnt from Hrafnar workshops and manuals, and his researches in literature and folk-practices.

Bil, in the south-western US, has formulated his practice from Sámi teachings and personal research, owing little to Hrafnar or core-shamanism. Material from his extensive on-line interviews and discussions indicates development of his practice, and communities in which he works.

> I've been Ásatrú over 25 years, but I wasn't the kind of person you would have wanted your kids to emulate. In a nutshell, to get where I am today, I had to lose everything: wife, family, home, job, children, and, finally, my own life.
> I was one of those people you see sometimes who are like

living corpses – shells of people with nothing inside. It was during that period that things began to happen. In essence, I was given or offered a deal and I took it. I went through two years of debilitating illness (pneumonia and pleurisy being the worst) always governed over by the ghosts. At first one, then another, then another, and so on. Looking back I think they came in stages or phases. They told me they were 'remaking me.' (I can think of a lot easier ways of getting remade, though.) Sometimes they came in my sleep. A lot of the time they came when I was awake like images cast up on Saran Wrap in front of me (I still work that way, with my eyes open and body moving).

Some of them were ghosts of animals, trees, and herbs (most, I found out later, could change their appearance at will). They told me my luck was gone, was spent. My life was in their hands. I asked them 'What will you do if I fight it? Do things my own way?' They didn't care; they were running the show anyway – they said 'Go ahead. It won't change a thing.' My pneumonia came to me on Dec. 18th at 3 PM and left on Sept. 3rd (the following year) at around 3 PM. They informed me that medications were meaningless (I tried anyway); they were rebuilding me. They choreographed the whole thing and never missed a beat.

About a month after the pneumonia left (I had 9 ghosts who followed me by then), I ran into Ailo Gaup. He showed me what it was all about. Between him and the ghost of the plant that I call the Little Red Man of the Forest (you call Fly Agaric), I became whole. However, I still don't have a life of my own. I still have 9 ghosts who follow me plus the Little Red Man, plus others who come and go, and WE make up my life.

There are constraints that I follow closely: taboos, you might say, but not quite since I'm not punished if I break them. I follow these because it is part of the team effort. A lot of the neo-shaman crowd like to talk about their purposes in life; I can't, though, because I don't have one. I am a luckless person. (Happy as a pig in mud, though.) I live with a wife, a new child is on the way (Jack is his name), a dog, a cat (and a ghost-cat who still comes back to visit), a rabbit, 9 following-ghosts, and a constant entourage of others.

Seiðr, for me, gave me life, but I don't consider soul-wandering to be the only part of what it is that I do (it's a small part but significant). I am stuck between. I'm either a ghost living in a body or a physical being whose soul has its roots in the Otherworld. I'm amoral (life and death aren't separate states for me so according to some I lack a driving force behind 'morality' as it's commonly practised). I work with the dying a lot especially Christians, but I work with anybody. My only job is to help (that's what I'm given) even if it means being instrumental in someone's dying.

Weird life, this. I wouldn't trade it for anything (I couldn't anyway – not mine to trade). I've not really been accused of the 'ergi thing' nor is that one of my constraints. I've been accused of plenty of things, however, even of coming back from the dead (which isn't true – I'm still a dead man). Christians can come up with some doozies once in a while, too, but none of it makes any difference anyway.

Personally, though, I'm enjoying participating in the whole thing.

Thanks for the curiosity. It's fun just rambling on about stuff I wouldn't normally talk about.

Be Whole,
Bil

His teacher is a Sámi *noide* practising in the American South West. Bil's work (see Linzie n.d.) involves 'wholemaking', working in trance to reconcile people's bodies and spirits: definitely affecting their lives. He is interested in seiðr as healing practice: not documented in the sagas, but seeming likely as it fits in with practices of protection and general 'knowing', and possibly-related Siberian shamanic skills.

As indicated in his account and in those given previously, seiðr does not emerge as a notably 'safe' practice (see also Wallis 1999b). People who engage with seiðr see this, and may have little wish to become community seiðworkers. Even those who feel called to it, may not seek the high seat for some time. Those who do, however, express satisfaction similar to that of Bil, above, or Winifred (in chapter 2). Jordsvin has been already introduced as a practitioner of oracular seiðr.

I'm a satisfied customer . . . it has enriched my life... And, ah, I am satisfied it's real. I'm happy with it. It seems to be a service to the community. Do I enjoy doing it? Yeah. I like my animal spirits, I visit with them. I like the journey work, I've gotten

directions through the underworld journey on how to get to see
Ran and Eigir and how to see the Svartalfar and their forges. . .
you start building up your own cosmology, within a cosmology,
you start learning how to do things, and I'm very happy . . .

But both men and women who engage with seiðr at some point have
to deal with the concept of the 'ergi seiðman' (Blain and Wallis
2000). They have read the material, they know the reputation, and
ask what are the implications of *ergi* for practice today.

The ergi seiðman?

Some non-practitioners take the view that regardless of practices or
ideologies 1,000 years ago, today gender and sexuality should not
matter in the organisation of human activities, and hence that
questioning links becomes dubious. An example is a recent letter to
the journal *Pomegranate* from a long-standing 'Northern Tradition'
leader in the Western US:

> There is no evidence that the practice of seidh makes you
> 'unmanly' (neither does being gay for that matter – where have
> you people been for the last 20 years?). But because these
> practices involve being 'possessed', and since genuine posses-
> sion is virtually impossible to control (ask any Voodoo drummer
> or Pentecostal), there is plenty of evidence that you can be
> 'unmanned' by these practices.
>
> For the difference between 'unmanly' and 'unmanned' please
> consult a dictionary.
>
> Any genuine psychic experience can 'unman' anyone (male or
> female), and being a man who embraces his anima is not going
> to give you special dispensation to avoid this.
>
> (Priest 1999: 3)

These comments touch on some central issues within seiðr and
shamanism, addressed within this book.[1] My point, however, is not
whether seiðr makes male practitioners 'unmanly', but how seiðr is
experienced by practitioners and by others in the community, for
whom it may be performed; how past interpretations – and
reinterpretations of those interpretations – affect the discourse and
development of seiðr as shamanistic 'performance' today; and just
possibly, whether men have to become *able* to be 'unmanly' in order

to practice seiðr (a reversal of Ms Priest's formulation). There are indeed indications that both men and women engaging with seiðr, but particularly men, were viewed with suspicion in the past – and that this 'suspicion' was expressed in terms decrying deviation from the hegemonic masculinity portrayed in the (later-written, post-Christianisation) sagas. Use of the term 'ergi' is notably explored in Meulengracht Sørensen's (1983) work on *nið* and *ergi* (of which the English title is *The Unmanly Man*).[2] The challenges have their echoes in experiences related by men today who seek to justify their practices as they are creating them. But to appreciate this is to examine the insertion of seiðworkers into the discourses and practices of their times – now or in the past.

Much of today's Western society remains homophobic. Heathen and Pagan culture is not immune from this homophobia, although some sections of the alternative spirituality communities do attempt to consciously combat it. As Wallis (1999b) points out:

> Many Heathen neo-shamans in Britain and North America, in contrast to being 'safe' and 'Westernised', confront and challenge conservatism both in Heathenism and wider society. Heathenism writ large is a conservative paganism with moral, ethical and spiritual values adhering to 'middle' England and America. 'Traditional' family values are sacred and the issue of same-sex relations remains controversial.
>
> (Wallis 1999b: 207)

Indeed, one British Ásatrú organisation holds as official policy that 'homosexuality' is 'anti-family'.

Today's seiðworkers include gay and straight practitioners: for them, in their practice, sexual orientation is not an issue. How seiðr connects with their community identity, however, is. Malcolm puts it thus:

> I'm playing around with the idea that male seidr-working may be connected with loss of aggression, or potential for violence, and that this may be related to the meaning of 'ergi' ... I'm no Icelandic/Old Norse scholar, just someone who is trying to see if his own experience corresponds to some apparently very cryptic statements about male seidr practice in the old material.
> ... And it is an issue I feel I need to look at. Having been practising seidr for a good while now, the 'ergi' accusation gets

thrown at me on a regular basis, usually with some very uneducated and childish interpretations along with it.

An exchange on an Ásatrú email list (which both Malcolm and I had joined) included an expressed comment that 'seiðr is for women and gay men'. The speaker was not attempting to prevent the practice of seiðr: rather he was completely dissociating himself from it. It was 'other'. His unwillingness to read anything that might relate to gay practices or identities extended to regarding any use of the words 'homosexual' or 'gay' as 'flaunting' of such practices: any discussion of non-hegemonic sexuality, *or of seiðr*, thereby became suspect. Two years later, in 2000, during an email discussion involving seiðr and *ergi*, the list moderator had to issue a strong reminder that homophobic statements would not be tolerated.

Jordsvin, as a well-known gay seiðworker, is on the receiving end of such comments: that Heathenism is not immune to the homophobia of the wider society is evident from his experiences.

> I occasionally get bigoted rants via email, usually from young males high on testosterone and bravado, usually with blatant homophobic content. Large sections of the Heathen community really need some education on this matter.

From these experiences, the situation of seiðworkers within today's society is not unproblematic. Seiðr practices exist in tension with dominant discourses of suspicion against men who do 'female' things, which permeate Heathen, as other, communities. For those who come to Heathenism as 'a conservative paganism with moral, ethical and spiritual values adhering to 'middle' England and America', seiðr is dangerous, problematic, with the seiðworker as an ambiguous figure: a 'seeress' can be romanticised, but men who do 'women's work' are difficult to reconcile with the model of the independent 'Viking'. Hence the 'rants' received by Jordsvin. So, here, I look further at relations of present and past, how today's Heathens weave a strand connecting the two, tendencies to view both seiðmen and seiðwomen with some ambivalence, and, not least, how *ergi* becomes a way of relating to the worlds, 'a process of identity and a means of dissonantly 'queering' the perceived socio-spiritual norms of the present and the past' (Blain and Wallis, forthcoming).

Ergi *or* argr *as insult*

First, a look at the verses in which *ergi* is most evident – and most well-known among today's Heathens. In *Lokasenna*, Loki has arrived, uninvited, at a feast. He proceeds to insult other gods and goddesses, who return the favour (until Thor arrives, late, and uses force rather than words to expel him). During the exchange between Óðinn and Loki, each uses the epithet *argr* of each other. Opinions on interpretation differ.

(Óðinn says)
. . . eight winters you were, beneath the earth,
a woman milking cows,
and there you bore children,
and that I thought was *argr*.

(Loki says)
But you once practised *seiðr* on Samsey
and you beat on the drum as witches do (*völor*, volvas,
  seeresses)
in the likeness of a wizard (*vitki)* you journeyed among
  mankind
and I thought that showed an *arg* nature
            (*Lokasenna*, 23 and 24, based on Larrington 1996: 88–9)[3]

Another god, Njörðr, refers to Loki as an *ás ragur* (translated by Larrington 1996: 90 as 'pervert god') who has given birth to children.

One interpretation is that the accusation against Loki, relating specifically to sexual activity, gives a meaning for *argr* of becoming sexually 'female'. (In one story from Snorri's *Edda*, Loki became a mare, and bore a foal; the story of being a woman for eight winters is not known.) This interpretation implies sexual contact, 'passive' or 'receptive' homosexuality, suggesting that Óðinn also had engaged in 'receptive' sexual practices. The counter-argument is that *argr* refers not to one specific set of behaviours, but more generally to practices not within the normative 'masculine' repertoire. Loki did something 'not masculine' (giving birth, milking cows) and Óðinn did something also 'not masculine' (performing seiðr, beating a drum, journeying as a *vitki* or sorcerer, activities associated in this culture with women). This distinction, therefore, is between sex and gender practices.

The words 'passive' and 'receptive', in this discourse, require consideration. They are today's words, and imply a direct equation of homosexual practice with a model of heterosexuality that is heavily reliant on 'active male, passive female' constructions: a twentieth-century psychological/psychoanalytic elaboration of nineteenth-century ideas about womanhood, severely critiqued from feminist and queer theory approaches today (see, for example, Butler 1993). But they remain part of the discourse of both academics and Heathens who read these passages: part of a general, partly institutionalised, assumption of heterosexuality as 'natural', homosexuality 'deviant', and of male and female 'normal' heterosexualities as distinct, based in character traits that are biologically related directly to XX or XY chromosome combinations. However, queer theory approaches can point to the 'constructed' nature of *all* sexualities, diversely socially sanctioned within specific cultures – thus giving other readings of *ergi*, in contexts of changing times and diverse styles of masculinities or femininities, whether in present or past. I shall return to this point later in this chapter.

Initially, it may be more useful to regard *ergi* as primarily an insult, that can be used to convey the meaning (pejoratively) of 'homosexual' or of 'acted upon sexually', or simply 'coward', without specifying any of these. *Ergi* applied to women is most often read as 'sexually promiscuous' (Meulengracht Sørensen 1984), but can be construed as 'taking the initiative sexually'. In this sense Freyja is *ergi* (Høst, pers. com.).

Classic examples of such insults, between men, occur in the first poem of Helgi Hundingsbani (in the *Poetic Edda*), in which two warriors – Sinfjotli and Gudmund – engage in a 'flyting' or insult-battle: giving detailed and contextualised descriptions of the other warrior: castrated by Thurs-women, daughter of a Troll-woman, milking goats, a mare for a horse, performing the work of slaves, being sexually 'used' by the speaker – and, paralleling Loki's insult to Óðinn, being a völva.[4] The whole draws on discourses of gender, sexuality and status current at the time of composition, in ways that are stylised and specific to the 'flyting' genre within which the poet was working, and hence indicating the most deadly of insults that one man could give another – or at least a twelfth-century conception of the 'deadly insults' of an earlier period, used for purposes of entertainment and education. For let us not forget that these are poems, told for the poet's own purposes which one presumes included getting some response (such as shock or laughter) from the audience.

The words *argr* and *ergi* do not occur in these insults: rather, the context of the 'insult' verses can be summarised using them. Use of *argr*, *ergi* or *ragr* to an actual opponent carried penalties in Icelandic law. If the use could not be justified (i.e. the opponent could not be shown to be indeed *ragr*) the speaker could be banished, according to a legal code of *c.*1100–1200 CE:

> Þav ero orð þriú ef sva mioc versna máls endar manna er scog gang vaðla avll. Ef maðr kallar man ragan eða stroðinn eða sorðinn. Oc scal søkia sem avnnor full rettis orð enda a maðr vigt igegn þeim orðum þrimr.
>
> (*Grágás*, 2, 392, given in Meulengracht Sørensen 1984: 100)

Most of the uses of the words, including those in *Lokasenna*, seem of this nature: the extreme insult, linked dubiously to 'actual' behaviour of the one insulted. And this is how *ergi* is interpreted by some of the men who perform seiðr today. Bil says (also quoted in Blain and Wallis 2000):

> There is no reason to doubt that homosexuality existed at the time of the Vikings and that, at least, 'effeminism' and cowardice were two character traits which were frowned upon and that both were lumped into the category of 'ergi.' Also, it is fairly easy to tell that the seventh to twelfth-century Norseman used the term as an insult. True connections between the terms 'ergi' and 'seið' are speculative at best.
>
> I think that an in-depth study of 'the practice of insults' might be in order. It would seem . . . insults were not only to force the emotional hand of the insulted but were also (for third parties) 1) fairly common, 2) often involved sexual innuendoes, 3) contained a small grain of truth wrapped up in embellishment, and 4) rhetorically misdirecting leading the listener to make a character judgement based either on the embellishment rather than the 'grain of truth' or to make an altogether incorrect assumption about the insulted.

Malcolm, practising in Scotland, relates that the word *argi* is still used there today.

> I can remember the context of two uses. First was one where I was challenged (aged 15 or so) to fight someone, and refused,

and was accused of being 'argi'... Oddly, when backed into a corner, dealing with it by throwing the attacker into a puddle, and refusing to 'give him a good kicking', was still considered 'argi'. I got the impression that what was meant, was 'cowardice', in terms of holding back violence considered to be 'appropriate'. My relatively non-violent solution was considered 'argi', just as failure to fight at all was.

The second situation was when I was in a village talking to someone much later in life (in my 20's or so), and hearing a young man spoken of as 'argi' because he asked the police to deal with a threat against his sister, instead of dealing with it personally.

'Argi' here apparently implied 'coward, unmanly, not using the resources men are expected to use'. Within a context of present-day Heathenry, such terms carry mixed messages, positioning speaker or referent within discursive contestations of gendered identity, sexuality and power. *Ergi* may still be used as an insult; alternatively it may be used by a practitioner to try to uncover, or explain, the meaning of his (or indeed her) own seið-work or the ways in which the practitioner's identity is changing or developing: hence, it becomes part of the vocabulary of some members of the seiðr community, to indicate a perception of potential for community/seiðr involvement. In this sense, the *ergi* person is one who moves between the worlds, deliberately transforming 'self' in specific relationships with people and other beings: not necessarily gay, but certainly 'queer' in the sense in which Wallis (2000: 253) uses this term to describe neo-shamanism, following Halperin (1995: 62) in saying 'queer' is 'by definition *whatever* is at odds with the normal, the legitimate, the dominant'. To examine this, I will further investigate some of the comments of today's seiðmen, before considering theories of shamanisms and gender, and returning to political dimensions of practice.

Ergi *as seiðr practice*

This conception of 'queerness' returns us to the practice of seiðr today, and the experiences of the seiðworker. Reclamation of *ergi* often relates directly to the shamanistic/shamanic nature of seiðr. The seiðworker becomes an intermediary and interpreter between the community of human people and those of spirits, including ancestors and deities, associated with the human community or the land. Many seiðworkers, and other shamanistic practitioners, point out that this involves a loss of 'ego' or an abnegation of self or of privilege. Bil, and others, relate this to the concept of *ergi*.

> My sexuality is heterosexual. I was never approached by the ghosts who follow me to change that in any way. I was, however, severely 'lambasted' for carrying too much of a 'macho attitude' and was forced to make many changes in that area – so much so, that folks often wonder, now, if I am homosexual or not. . . My eccentricity doesn't stem from sexuality or sexual preference but mainly from the fact that I have no emotional reactions any longer (I have emotions; I just don't demonstrate reaction with them, that's all).
>
> (Bil)
>
> Personally, I resonate with what Bil is saying, to an extent. I do react less than most people, very much so...Perhaps this is because emotion is so important to the seiðr work I do. It's like the fuel for the tools I use, so maybe I'm conserving it?
>
> (Malcolm, discussing Bil's statement,
> taken from Blain and Wallis 2000)

Jordsvin, though, suggested that 'gay men may have an advantage in practising seiðr, that they may be more 'called' to it, be a little better or learn it a little easier'. It has been noted that people who are marginalised within their society are in a position where they must attend to levels of meaning that escape from, or that are not obvious to, those privileged by dominant discourses: indeed much feminist scholarship points to those in disprivileged positions developing multiple ways of understanding the world. Dorothy Smith's (1987) 'bifurcated consciousness' comes to mind.

Thus, in indicating how he came to be a seiðman, Ybjrteir told me that (after communicating with spirit-beings as a child):

> Then puberty came! I wanted to fit in, so I learned to wear two selves – the part of me that I kept hidden that could talk with and see other things and the part of me that I showed to my parents and friends at school. ... at high school I was a great student, played sports, had girlfriends; while, at the same time I had other abilities and that I was Gay. This is the beginning of learning how to switch forms back and forth.

Those who are marginalised may draw on their specific understandings in ways that elude those in more privileged positions. If in today's society, women and gay men are more used to dealing with multiple understandings of social relations, and interpreting one understanding in terms of another, this may constitute an advantage in shamanistic practice. But it is also an overt political positioning, relating to processes of secular, as well as spiritual, power, and to attempts to claim locations – identity politics existing within a Western perceived need to categorise and name practice and theory, as recognition is given only to that which is categorised.

The Western term 'homosexual' is recent. Foucault (e.g. 1980a and b) points to the nineteenth-century invention of 'homosexuality' as a social construct, a way of labelling personal awareness of sexuality, and of categorising and pathologising people while institutionalising specific kinds of heterosexualities: creating therefore a category of pathological 'deviance' and a normative system of binary opposition. The term then became centrally part of the conscious awareness of people generally, a measure of social acceptance and a major identity focus. It becomes, now, difficult for either practitioners or researchers to understand seiðworkers or *ergi* without reference to today's categories: a difficulty that has plagued other accounts of multiple or alternate genders, notably understandings of 'berdache' or 'two-spirit' practitioners in North America. Likewise, Herdt (1996: 24) points also to 'misinterpretation and labelling in the third-gender roles of Polynesia from the time of Captain Cook to the present'. Simply put, it becomes hard for Westerners to see sexuality as part of nuanced social relationships, informing all relationships (not only those which are overtly 'sexual') in siting and shaping 'selves'. In the case of seiðr, too, the relationships formed are not only with other humans but with those 'spirit' figures that are equally difficult for researchers to deal with. Seiðworkers, therefore, are anomalous figures, working within a broad cultural framework in which dominant discourse rejects concepts of 'the spirits' or 'deities', and yet within specific contexts or learning paths where spirits or deities are the teachers. Within indigenous shamanic practice, the shaman's spirit 'helpers' may indicate possibilities or work to be done, set the pace and give directions. Western society rewards male autonomy, and there are issues here of suspension of control. In accordance with indigenous shamans, and in contrast to Western society's expectations of them, these seiðmen give accounts of working with spirits and relinquishing 'control'. These experiences compare with anthropological descriptions of shamanic practice – texts with which seiðworkers are familiar.

So, some seiðworkers, male and female, have suggested that in the past, *ergi* may not always have been an insult; and further, that it can be used to describe the state of 'making seiðr' or an orientation to the Nine Worlds that enables seiðr. This is connected with the multiple gendering of shamanisms elsewhere, and it is to this that I turn next.

Many genders or 'changing ones'?

Many researchers have attempted a theoretical understanding of shamanism as incorporating an ability to move between 'realities' generally considered 'male' or 'female'. The 'third gender' concept as introduced by Czaplicka is that 'Socially, the shaman does not belong either to the class of males or to that of females, but to a third class, that of shamans'. She indicates that by clothing or ritual observance ('taboos'), Siberian shamans might by incorporating characteristics of both males and females hold an in-between location. However, she continues: 'Sexually, he may be sexless, or ascetic, or have inclination of homosexualistic character, but he may also be quite normal' (Czaplicka 1914: 253) which, while indicating a distinction between 'gender' and 'sex' that more recent researchers have found useful, also re-essentialises a two-sexed Euro-centric 'normality' of binary opposition, repositioning all other 'inclinations' as deviant. Czaplicka's 'third class' thereby appears as one in which the shaman is privileged to engage in 'deviance': which could be a suitable description of how 'shamans' (and at times poets, artists, and others who engaged with a reality outside that of normative everyday experience) were regarded by early twentieth century European society, but not very convincing when applied to descriptions of practitioners.

Applying a 'third gender' concept to research among the Inuit, Saladin d'Anglure sees shamans existing 'on the border between sexes/genders' (1992: 148). His ternary or triple model is based in Inuit descriptions of the changeability of gender: not something fixed at birth, but something 'unstable and changeable' (147) and rather than adopting Czaplicka's 'in-between' third gender, his culturally specific model indicates a third sex/gender dimension shown at right angles to a male/female axis and involving spiritual components different from those associated with either 'females' or 'males' within Inuit constructions of gender.

The most familiar term for the 'third gender' practitioner is 'berdache', indicated in a number of studies of Native North American and other 'shamans' or 'medicine people': often critiqued (Epple 1998) but used despite or because of the plethora of specific cultural names, e.g. the Zuni *llamana* (Roscoe 1991), Navaho *nádleehi* (Epple 1998), Mohave *hwame-* and *ayaha-* (Roscoe 1996), for those who occupy third- or fourth-gendered locations within their respective cultures. Some 'berdaches' themselves use the word, others seeing it as a remnant of colonialism prefer 'two-spirit'. However, while the terms are used often of shamans, it is clear from descriptions given by anthropologists and two-spirit practitioners that the two-spirit very often, perhaps usually, are not themselves engaging with altered states of consciousness as shamans, although holding specific responsibilities to both human and spirit worlds. However, the institutionalisation of two-spirit locations within a number of cultures (male berdaches documented in 150 North American Native nations, female in half that number (Roscoe 1996)), together with expressed negativity towards seiðfolk and other shamanistic practitioners from cultures in which a binary, heterosexual gender duality is institutionalised, indicates that some questioning of the commonly accepted models and linkages of sex, gender and altered consciousness is in order, and that the social relations surrounding the two-spirit may shed some light on the *argr seiðmaðr*.

Roscoe attempts a multi-gendered model. He finds the concept of 'gender-crossing' to be wanting, pointing to berdache status as multi-dimensional, and saying that 'the most reliable indicators of berdache status were its economic and religious attributes and not gender or sexual difference alone' (1996: 335). He locates female and male berdache 'roles' as third and fourth genders, and abstracts from North American instances a model of 'minimal conditions' enabling berdache social relations to develop, relating to gendered division of labour; a belief system in which anatomical sex is conceptualised as 'unstable, fluid and nondichotomous' and in which gender is not determined by anatomical sex; and 'the occurrence of historical events and individuals motivated to take advantage of them in creating and shaping gender identities' (1996: 371). He further hypothesises that:

for a given society in which multiple genders were present, it would take not only the elimination of the economic dimension of such statuses but a lapse in the belief systems rationalizing them and the introduction of a dual-sex ideology to effect a full collapse of such roles

(Roscoe 1996: 372)

Questions arise whether the society that produced seiðr can be conceptualised as one in which a multi-gendered worldview was breaking down within the kind of situations Roscoe hypothesises, and whether the reinvention of seiðr and other western 'shamanisms' today are enabled by reassessments of gender and sexuality. Further, there is another dimension in applying this already multi-dimensional model to shamanistic practitioners, which is that of the spirit-connections of seið-practitioners now and in the past and ways in which these also are 'gendered'.

One researcher attempting a queer theory approach to the concept of *ergi* is Solli, who refers to the *Ynglingasaga* passage about Óðin's seiðr, seeing tension between Óðinn as 'warrior's god' and as *argr seiðmaðr*, the 'unmanly performer of seid' (Solli 1999a: 342). Her resolution is through a third-gender concept, examining various discussions of gender location. Among these is Czaplicka; yet Czaplicka, as I have indicated, appears to employ a frame of (more or less fixed) male ways of being, (more or less fixed) female ways of being, with the shaman being 'allowed' from the first into the second. It may be that a more fluid using of these concepts is possible, without imputing a doubtful monolithic unity to 'Old Norse' culture, over generations, even centuries. This Solli implies in seeing 'shamanism [as] . . . also the technique of transformation' (1999a: 345).

Transformation, though, applies to society as well as shaman. There is a need to understand Óðin's 'gender status' constructed within changing political/spiritual environments, and a need to look at how we 'know' about Óðinn. Solli views him bridging between Æsir and Vanir (seeing Vanir as fertility/earth gods, Æsir as war/sky gods, a view shared by some Heathens though not all) with, as aforesaid, tensions in the literature between Óðinn as 'warrior's god' and seið-practitioner. Yet as Grundy (1995) indicates, Óðin's association with war or battle may be connected not with his own 'masculinity' or abilities in war, but his status as death-god. As giver of death, he is giver of victory to the side with fewer dead. The association of death, ancestors and seiðr/shamanism runs throughout the material, including the passage where he hangs on the tree Yggdrasill, thereby gaining knowledge of the runes.[5]

Each part of the material was written within a context, from that of court poets praising patrons who traced descent from Óðinn, to that of the thirteenth-century politician Snorri Sturluson and his systematisation of the material. A dynamic treatment of the literature locates it within specific relations constitutive of 'male' and 'female' practices, themselves fluid over time (and without universal meanings even at any given time). Within this fluid approach, multiple genders in the ninth or tenth century may have been 'othered' by the thirteenth, in a religio-political scene that was not leaving much room for shamanistic understandings (or indeed female and non-hegemonic-male understandings).

Solli (1999a) suggests evidence for 'third gender' of seiðworkers from a verse in the *Shorter Völuspá*, in the poem *Hyndluljóð*. Translated, this gives:

> All the völvas are from Víðólfr (Wood-wolf)
> all the vitkis from Vilmeiðr (Wish-tree)
> the *skilberendr* (or *seiðberendr*) from Svarthöfði (Dark-head)
> the giants all come from Ymir.[6]

The poem purports to give the family descent of a person, Óttarr, with the insertion of genealogical information about the gods, and this peculiar verse which Solli interprets as about seið-makers: female *völvur*, male *vitkar*, and *seiðberendur* who are third gender, 'two-spirit'. *Seiðberendur* is usually translated 'seiðmen', but the meaning of 'berendr' is, says Solli, 'a very coarse word for female genitalia in old Norse' (1999a: 344). Seiðwoman and historian Gunnora Hallakarva had earlier alerted me to this word, indicating a legal proscription (from the *Gulaþing* lawcode) against the use of the word *berendi* of men.

> '... Item three: if a man compare another man to a mare, or call him a bitch or a harlot, or compare him to any *berendi*'. *Berendi* is used to indicate a female animal, one which bears young, though the narrow sense of the word is used to refer 'to the sexual parts of a female animal, particularly a cow', and there are examples of it in this sense in Swedish and Danish dialects. It is derived from the verb *bera*, 'to give birth'.
> (Hallakarva, pers. com., citing Ström 1974: 9 fn. 3)

Like *ergi*, the word, then, would be an extreme insult. Yet, the derivation from 'bera' may also imply a seiðworker actively giving birth to the seiðr; which concurs with Gunnora's further statement that 'to me the term seiðberendr evokes a sense of "bringing seiðr forth from within oneself"'.

Additionally, rather than implying female, male and two-spirit seiðworkers, the verse may refer to three types of magic (and their practitioners). Particularly, a *vitki* engages in spoken spells or rune-work, and in notes to Sigurðsson's edition is interpreted as *galdramaður* (Sigurðsson 1998: 402, also reading *seiðberendur* literally as 'þeir sem fremja seiðr', those who make seiðr). A reading of three types of magic may give a völva's seeing-magic, not necessarily with spirit-intervention; *galdra*-magic using spoken charms or runes; and seiðr-magic. Yet this in turn may be read as more nuanced, with gradation from respected seeresses, suspected runic magicians, shunned and insulted seiðworkers, and to conclude the verse, giants who all come from Ymir. A gendered distinction here need not be that of three types of seið-practitioners. *Völva* implies a woman; *vitki* a male rune-worker; yet *seiðberendur* need not in itself be specific, perhaps implying further possibilities – potentially linking gender and magic with action, agency, performance, bringing forth, as Gunnora suggested, from within oneself. (I am not disputing Solli's reading of 'seiðberendur' as an offensive term, but suggesting further room for investigating ambivalence, in present or past.)

Agency leads to the question of both gender and shamanism as performativity, active accomplishment of meaning: gender does not reside in biological sex, neither is it confined by binary opposition of 'roles' which can be breached only because the shaman has a sort of cultural permission to do so. 'Gender performativity' (see e.g. Butler 1990) implies gender as doing, creation, meanings actively accomplished by shaman and community rather than transgression of fixed boundaries.[7] Gender and sexuality are actively constituted within, and constitutive of, specific sets of social relations, which for those practising seiðr today include spirit as well as human communities: and many differing relations can be so constructed. Experiences and constructions within altered-consciousness states shape practitioners' understanding of 'self', gender included: where gender is fluid, malleable and changeable, and practitioners of seiðr find their lives transformed in many ways by the experiences they undergo. These experiences include, as shown in chapter 4, meetings and negotiations with diverse spirits, possibly involving levels of spirit or deity-possession. Thus for 'James':

> seiðr focuses on both 'male' and 'female' deities, Woden and Freyja, in rituals of possession. The rituals also involve spirit creatures, including two lynxes, and a berdache. With these helpers my experience transcends conventional understandings of gender. At times it can be described as experiencing female, or male, or both. It is sometimes difficult to express how the experience is gendered. This is something I am still learning to come to terms with, explain and interpret.
>
> I think many people (especially men) would find seiðr disturbing because of how it makes them feel (apart from the radical change into shamanic consciousness), going beyond stereotypes of male, female, gay, etc. For me, seiðr with Freyja allows an integrating understanding of what it is to be male, female and other, multiple possibilities. That is empowering and affects how I live with my reality, world, local and spiritual communities. It changes who I am.
>
> (Taken from Blain and Wallis 2000)

Some have questioned whether possession is found in the old literature. Paxson thinks that it can be found, offering as an example the story of Gunnar Helming in the *Story of Ögmund Dytt*, who 'impersonates' the god Freyr. Gunnar, having fallen out with Norwegian king Óláfr Tryggvason, goes to Sweden where he meets a priestess (*gyðja*) travelling the countryside with a wagon containing the god Frey's statue, who is spoken of as Frey's wife. Gunnar goes into the wagon to fight Freyr, takes his place in the wagon, travels with the gyðja, and the people are delighted that not only can 'Freyr' now walk around, eat and make merry, but the crops grow better than ever before, and Frey's wife is pregnant. The king, hearing about this, sends Gunnar a message that he can return home, which he does bringing his priestess-wife. Paxson considers this story may be read as indicating the possibility of a person becoming possessed by the god, letting the god speak through him when needed.

The story holds several possibilities: a reading of 'possession' implies the priestess may travel with a 'shaman' (Gunnar's fight with Freyr being a fight with the previous shaman) who acts as the vehicle for god-possession. Alternatively, I suggest 'Frey's wife' can be read in light of Siberian spirit marriage (see e.g. Eliade 1964): Perhaps the shaman-gyðja has a spirit-spouse, Freyr, and a human-spouse, Gunnar. Writing for a Christianised audience, though, the writer implies that if Freyr is said to speak, this is either (demonic) magic applied to the statue, or Gunnar's impersonation, rather than the gyðja relaying Frey's messages. As Wallis (forthcoming, a) points out, these explanations need not be in conflict.[8]

I have introduced this story to indicate some of the complexities involved in spirit-relationships, and different ways in which these can be interpreted depending on the narrator's location and perspective. Further, in 'spirit-spouse' situations, the gendering of the 'spouse' need not be obvious: introducing further complexity, but reaffirming that relationships constructed in both spirit and human worlds take their own forms.

In reading the mediaeval material, today's participants recognise that it was largely written by those for whom, for whatever reason, the seiðworker was 'other'. Just how much 'other' is what I next consider, exploring a suggestion that the 'exotic' or shunned nature of seiðr is due not to 'third gender' locations of practitioners, but to its 'foreign' origin.

Seiðr as a Sámi borrowing?

Dubois (1999) uses seiðr as an example of practices which, in his view, entered the cultural complex from elsewhere to become assimilated, modified and adapted (in my paraphrasing) as part of the conceptual/magical apparatus available within Heathenry/ Heiðni. He contrasts this adaptation of seiðr with the coming of Christianity, in which the initiators, converts or priests, did not seek to merge Christian and non-Christian practices, but went to some lengths to avoid incorporating pre-Christian understandings and activities.

> Seiðr thus demonstrates a dynamic process of religious exchange operating in the Viking Age in which individual ritual elements – and sometimes even practitioners – crossed cultural and economic lines, becoming reinscribed within the worldview of the recipient community. Seiðr replicated strongly shamanic rituals among Sámi and Balto-Finns, but it also became assimilated into the preexisting repertoire of religious practices and mythology operating among Scandinavian pagans. This

assimilation effected its own substantive changes on the tradition, rendering it a new entity, the product of religious syncresis.

(Dubois 1999: 137)

Earlier, Dubois states that 'Seiðr practitioners are frequently depicted as foreigners, people with Sámi or Finnish connections or (more rarely) links to the British Isles' (1999: 128). The specifics of seiðr and *hamfarir* – journeying in other shape – are associated with 'foreign' practitioners, particularly Sámi or 'Finns', and occasionally Hebrideans. It may be that specific practices and practitioners are imports. However, the framework within which they are described is one in which most people accept the practices, and in which an animist world-view seems to have been quite prevalent. Indeed Dubois says as much: a range of spirits could be found in rocks, trees, waterfalls, houses, natural features or artefacts, within Nordic, Anglo-Saxon, Finnish, and Sámi beliefs and practices. Offerings to *Dísir* and other clan spirits point to a focus on ancestors, and the concept of the *fylgja*, the following spirit attached to one's self at birth, provides another of the components associated with an animist world-view. Therefore while it seems likely that components and practitioners of Sámi shamanism migrated into 'Nordic' practice, it seems to me that the development of 'seiðr' cannot be viewed only as a Sámi loan, however assimilated. Shamanic practice elsewhere, as previously noted, is creative and adaptive; seiðr practitioners would develop and change their practice, within specific socio-historic circumstances, in association with Sámi practice and within regional constructions of gender accomplishment. Sámi practitioners, described in (e.g.) the twelfth-century *Historica Norwegiae* and recent ethnographic accounts (Pentikaïnen 1984), were as Dubois says mostly male, though often with female assistants; the seiðworkers of the sagas were generally female. (There may even be a connection with Norse women training as 'assistants' to Sámi, but practising in their own right and their own way (Blain and Wallis 2000).) Evidence for indigenous practitioners comes from 'Viking age' burials where staffs, similar to those described for seeresses, have been found. Price (2000 and in press) details numerous sites in Scandinavia in which either staffs have been identified, or objects previously otherwise classified may be re-interpreted as 'shamanic' staffs,[9] sometimes associated with other 'shamanic' items such as a talisman pouch at Fyrkat containing bones of small mammals and birds, and henbane seeds. Most are from burials identified as those of women, but one in Norway is of a man, and in several others no attribution has been made, or the staffs are not in a burial context. Importantly, many of these burials appear to indicate high status: however their doing of 'seiðr' may have been viewed, these were not merely marginalised practitioners of a 'foreign' art.

Rather, the claimed 'foreign-ness' of many practitioners, in the sagas, may be read as the author's distancing him or herself from such 'queer' practices: practitioners are 'othered' by description as Sámi or Hebridean, just as they are 'othered' by having the saga 'hero' positioned in disbelief, or as Quinn (1998) indicates, showing distaste by ignoring the seer's advice or warning (which is, however, later borne out by events). Earlier shamanic/shamanistic practice is also suggested by the burial described by Hjørungdal (1989) from Hordaland in West Norway, which included a wooden staff hypothesised to be that of a seeress, dated to around 550 CE (Ingegerd Holland, pers. com.) several hundred years before Rögnvaldr and his colleagues were burnt out by the king who did not like seiðr.[10]

In indicating a context of shamanistic awareness within Northern and Western Europe generally, we can go back further yet. Coles (1990, 1998) interprets wooden figures found from the Neolithic to the Iron Age in terms of shamanism and understandings of gender and ambiguity: in this she suggests possibilities of 'links with Scandinavian rock art, with the north-western European bog-bodies, and with the god Odin of northern mythology' (1998: 164). She suggests links between the wood from which the figures are made, and gender: there are clearly-male figures of oak, a clearly-female figure of alder, and several of yew or pine which are ambiguous, thus giving yet another slant to later gendered practices. She draws on material from Siberian shamanisms (Anisimov 1963) in which such wooden figures are described. In the ambiguous yew-wood figures she sees a possible association with (or precursor to) Yggdrasill and Óðinn. While this is, once again, speculative, the combination of the wood and gendered ambiguity is at least suggestive – particularly when it is added that several yew-wood figures (with date ranges 2351–2139 BCE 1096–906 BCE, 606–509 BCE; Coles 1998: 164) appear to be one-eyed.

What these and other assorted pieces of evidence may indicate is some sort of indigenous shamanic practice across Northern Europe with, one presumes specific local patterns, associated with gender ambiguity, developing gradually within later 'Norse' contexts and with considerable Sámi input into the various strands of seeing, *hamfarir* and protective or attacking magics, all requiring some sort of alteration of consciousness and communication with spirits, that came eventually to be associated with *seiðr* – not as monolithic 'Northern Shamanism' or a single 'ritual form', but as sets of linked, complex practices possibly undertaken by different practitioners within communities. It remains entirely possible that elements such as the use of the seið-platform were relatively recent adaptive 'borrowings', indeed part of a 'dynamic process of religious exchange' and 'decentralised, circulating flow and exchange of religious ideas' (Dubois 1999: 137), the flow being multi-directional. However, to me it seems likely that 'cultural' boundaries and 'worldview' were less sure, more permeable than earlier accounts assumed, meanings and 'performance' of practices more fluid. Ambivalent interpretation of seiðworkers at the time of saga writing need not indicate doubt about a 'foreign' practice. The roots of seiðr – and of distrust surrounding it – may lie deep in the northern landscape.

However, whether seiðr is a 'borrowing' from Sámi practice, or 'indigenous' fluid practices developed and changing over time in multi-directional, multi-vocal exchange with Sámi and other practitioners, may not be the most telling of its features for today's practitioners. More important are the nuances that surround seiðr practice, whether past or present. In this we can see seiðr as part of a complex of activities including seeing, runic or spoken magic, and out-sitting. But the associations of seiðr with spirit contact, spirit marriage, spirit-possession, and the ability to manipulate thought, or Wyrd, always problematic, seem to have been increasingly so for men.

> The underhanded, covert workings of seiðr must have represented a further reason for male aversion to it, at least in public. In a society that valued a forthright male manner and a ready embrace of outward conflict, a ritual allowing the secret manipulation of another's will would violate ideals of proper masculinity... Such trickery is typical of Óðinn... but it appears more problematic for his male disciples.
>
> (Dubois 1999:137)

While the 'ready embrace of outward conflict' may be more

apparent than real – the sagas may draw on conflicts as the exception that makes a good story, and Byock (1982) discusses numerous ways of conflict-avoidance evident in sagas before violence occurs – as I have indicated, others too have suggested that these 'underhanded' ways of operating go against hegemonic masculinity, though they may be valued when undertaken by women denied the legal remedies afforded by the Icelandic system to men. Some seiðworkers today would dispute that these techniques would always have been seen as 'underhanded' but in working with seiðr today they know the saga passages, and the reputation that seiðr acquired.

And whatever was the case in the tenth century, distaste for seiðr arises in some sections of society today: as evidenced by the messages Jordsvin received and the internet exchanges I described earlier, and Rauðhild's mention of 'resistance to seiðr'. The activities of 'contact with spirits' and the descriptions given here are counter to hegemonic assumptions about what people can and should do. In a world that values rationality, acquisition of belongings or artefacts, and advancement through institutionalised gendered social hierarchies, shamanistic practice is threatening because it allows for possibilities of creating meaning outside the circumscribed 'choice' of 'legitimate' socio-economic activity. Many neo-shamanisms appear in the West as individual practice, forms of psychological 'self-help' that marginalise the practitioner while exoticising the 'other', the 'primordial traditional shaman'. Seiðr inverts this procedure by being community practice, and by drawing directly on the cultural and historical roots of the societies within which it is practised today. It reminds us that the ancestors of Western society were not 'rational' in today's terms, and that they dealt, or were forced to deal, directly with death, transformation and knowledge, in ways that are non-normative in today's society. So today's practitioners, male or female, create relationships with ancestors and 'spirits', and in living these become changed by the experience. Within this 'queer' fluidity of meaning and shaping of self and community, conventional labels of 'gay' or 'straight' need not apply.

Queer theory and the *ergi* seiðman

I have here examined many possible meanings or implications of *ergi*: I would add one more, from experience and observation. I have watched a number of seiðworkers, men and women, sit in the 'high seat' and go through the gates of Hel's realm, and wait, in a deep trance state, for questions. Some have been described in this account: I watched a seer leaning on his staff, swaying from side to side, seeking focus and answers. Reflecting on this while reading Meulengracht Sørensen's (1983) *The Unmanly Man*, I was struck by the vulnerability of the one in deep trance, who willingly rejects all means of protection and defence within a physical place. She or he has become entirely reliant on others.

It seems to me that the charge of *ergi*, applied to men, may relate to this extreme vulnerability. Within a world in which direct, physical, expression is paramount, and physicality is the measure of a man, the seer has abrogated manhood. That the seer is holding the attention of all present and communicating with spirits – negotiating with them, at times striving to wrest a solution from them – is, for the literalist, not obvious (though it may be central to the identity of the seer). Meulengracht Sørensen interprets the word, and the associated charge of *nið*, as political, within the contexts of the writing of the sagas and the rather extreme examples of violent maintaining – or taking – of hegemonic 'masculinity' given in, for instance, *Sturlunga saga*.

His account of *nið* (infamy) and *ergi* is an interpretation of the saga texts as incorporating concepts of (literal or figurative) 'phallic aggression'. In his understanding of the texts, often concepts of *nið* and the protagonist's attempts to free himself of this taint drive the plot of the sagas. He points out that seiðr (in the passage about Óðinn) was said to render its male practitioners *ergi*, and later says that 'witchcraft ... was closely associated with the practice of *ergi*' (1983: 55). (As he has previously said that one 'branch of meaning' in the '*ergi*-complex' is 'versed in witchcraft' (p. 19) this may be somewhat circular.) However, following this reasoning, at least in the sagas letting oneself become vulnerable would be *ergi*, and hence seiðworkers are *ergi*. In a context of increasing distrust of shamanic outcomes, and reliance on individual or family abilities for protection or defence, one who makes himself vulnerable, *ergi*, is avoiding proper duties and responsibilities associated with hegemonic masculinity in saga times. For women, the equations would have been a little different – the status of cultural protection afforded to women meaning that jettisoning awareness of physical threats would be acceptable in some circumstances.[11]

So there may be many reasons for seiðr or shamanistic practice to be seen as problematic, *ergi*, particularly for men. The seiðworker I interviewed after his first high-seat trance said, 'You'd be interested to know that I felt extremely *ergi*.' He was referring to the flow of information through him, and his openness to the spirits and to the people gathered. I, from a different position within the seance, could relate it to perceived vulnerability. These multiple interpretations need not conflict. Today's seiðfolk are reclaiming words, inscribing their own meanings as they find practices that 'work'. The context of today's practice, the 'safe spaces' in which oracular seiðr occurs, is not the context of the thirteenth century when accounts were being written.

The response of a seið-attendee, Einar, to a heated email discussion on seiðr, *ergi*, and *nið*, made this plain.

> Today, we have a totally different culture. Some of what may not have been acceptable in the tenth century is acceptable today. I've met a number of men who say that their lives are enriched by the practice of Seidhr or Galdr. Why not take what works (e.g., seiðr) and discard what doesn't (e.g., slaying an enemy if there is a dispute)? I say hail to those who take what they can use from the lore to enrich their lives. If it works, great! If it doesn't work or clashes with the law, etc., it's of little or no use!

Einar continued:

> Far too often the misunderstood 'ergi' accusation gets thrown about. . . . [I am] just noting that there are those who send private (and sometimes public) hate mail to men who practice Seiðr, etc. It is hoped that ... we can move beyond the hate and phobia of a few vocal people who spoil it for the rest of us by using a reconstructionist view without a modern critique.

Men and women who engage with seiðr today are shaping their own understandings of *ergi* as they deal actively with discourses of gender and sexuality, positioning themselves as active agents of change as they seek to understand their own worlds. Some are actively attempting to reclaim the term to describe themselves, their practice, their philosophy. Seiðr therefore is political practice, and 'queer' practice, existing within gendered political dimensions today.

Chapter 8

The dance of the ancestors

Summarising seiðr

This final chapter is an attempt to draw together and summarise some of the strands that have been elaborated previously. Here I return to issues of presenting understandings of seiðr and shamanisms, tensions between practitioners and academics, and engagement with post-modern discourses of reality and the critique of ethnography. How far do these interpretations hold, when the ethnographer deals with culturally contextualised spirits, and attempts to present her own understandings gained within the seiðr trance? Can this be done, or is academia too 'shamanophobic'? I draw, here, on my experiences of presenting material to an academic audience, and I examine some of the challenges that have been raised regarding engaging with seiðr and neo-shamanic practices, and the multi-sited nature of this kind of research.

Debates within academia parallel those within the communities themselves, and I again examine some of these similarities, revisiting the context of Western approaches to shamanism and to the 'Old Religions' of the North. Constructions of meaning move from seiðr as 'authentic', to seiðr as 'transformational', seiðr as 'recovering roots', and attempts to avoid appropriation. Finally, returning to ethnography, I again make use of the metaphor of the ethnographer as shaman, moving between worlds and being changed by the experience.

As part of today's post-modern explosion of spiritual expression, religions and practices of Northern Europe are being reconstituted or reinvented, in North America and Europe; and seiðr with them, as we have seen, though owing much to descriptions of shamanic practice, especially Sámi and Siberian shamanism. Descriptions of seiðr and its accomplishment today can be found on websites and in journals of Heathen and shamanistic groups: examples being the magazines *Idunna* and *Spirit Talk*. I have been asked to compose short accounts of seiðr for various audiences, for instance as part of the Pagan Federation's 'info-pack' on shamanisms.

Galina Lindquist (1997) describes how practices derived from the 'core-shamanism' of Michael Harner, and from others (following Harley Swift Deer) who have looked to North American indigenous spiritualities, are becoming 're-embedded' in the context, landscapes and cosmology and cultural knowledges of Northern Europe (in Lindquist's examples, specifically Scandinavia: this is happening also in Britain). Most of the people whose words and visions I have drawn on in this book have begun with an explicit exploration of Heathen cosmology, the Nine Worlds, the Well of Wyrd, the tree Yggdrasill, and the Æsir and Vanir. They are working, first, to construct religious practice and spiritual community, and they have stumbled across seiðr, reinventing it as magical or shamanistic practice, arising from the traces and descriptions in sagas and Eddas, and from remaining folk-practices in Iceland, Scotland and elsewhere. Others were already experimenting with seiðr for healing, but oracular seiðr in its present form was first practised within today's Heathenry in the US when Diana Paxson went looking for 'something for the women to do' while men were involved in performing 'viking games' and drinking beer, playing out the gendered, non-*ergi* stereotype of the macho warrior. The result was the creation of ritual and tranceworking that has moved from being a 'fringe' part of a 'fringe' religion, to being an expected part of Heathen gatherings, something that is displayed within the wider Pagan community as specifically 'Northern' practice, and conducted at large festivals by Heathen practitioners. Practitioners are sharing perceptions and experiences with those who derive their practice from Sámi and Siberian roots, and those drawing on the energies of land and nature spirits (Høst, forthcoming) and some interesting conversations are taking place.

Discourses of contested practice

In previous chapters I have discussed seiðr as contested practice within the religious movements that generated it, with its ambiguous and uncertain derivation from the old literature. The term's meaning is disputed. Within academia, also, challenges have been levelled at seiðr, seiðworkers, and those who would treat this as 'shamanistic practice'. These challenges appear to me as part of a (post?)modern quest for authenticity, sureness, roots, boundaries, and for definition of the indefinable. In addition to questions of sexuality and gender, dealt with in the previous chapter, they include: contested definitions of seiðr as 'shamanism', or past practitioners as 'shamans'; questions of whether today's practitioners are 'shamans'; challenges of 'inauthenticity' of today's practices; and challenges to the 'impartiality' of those who engage with experiential ethnography, exploring alternative consciousness and the Nine Worlds.

These deal with issues discussed in earlier chapters. I use these comments, now, as focuses for summarising earlier material, and exploring academic implications; and for examination of problematic relationships between seiðworkers, other neo-shamans, and the academics who profess to find their practices of interest in studying religions of post-modernity.

'Is seiðr "shamanism"?'

This question seems predicated on the assumption that a discrete something called 'shamanism' exists and can be clearly defined. Indeed, as discussed in chapter 4, there have been a number of attempts to define 'shamanism'. Most seem to agree that the term comes from the Tungus/Evenki word for a practitioner of particular kinds of work involving altered states of consciousness and relationships between 'spirits' and human community. Coming into European discourse through both Russian and German explorers' tales (Shirokogorov 1935; Flaherty 1992) the term 'caught on' among Westerners eager for stories of exotic practices of 'others', and came to be used of other Siberian peoples and extended more generally as an 'ism' to cover whatever the user wished to define as 'shamanism': based on an understanding of 'primitive religion' as *different*, *exotic*, and as such, definable. Eliade's (1964) definition of 'archaic techniques of ecstasy' is cited by academics and practitioners of core-shamanism or other Western 'urban shamanisms' that claim a grounding in research. Other definitions appear to grapple with some sort of 'essence' of shamanism, for instance the familiar one of Shirokogorov, of 'mastery of spirits' and the shaman therefore as one who controls spirits: or with attempting to explain it all away – a further definition, of shamanism as psychopathology that is culturally sanctioned, has arisen from older views of shamanism as psychopathology plain and simple. It, too, arises from a sense of the shaman as one who initially is dealing with some kind of problem (whether described as awakening by spirits, or as mental illness) which the shaman then 'masters'. A number of researchers have commented on the racism inherent in such stereotyping of shamans or peoples (e.g. Merkur 1992: 26).

Part of the debate over definition lies in the extent to which 'shamanism' and 'spirit possession' are differentiated. As Lewis (1989) and Merkur (1992) point out, shamanism and possession often occur together, not only within the same community but within the same individual, even during the same seance where a possessing spirit takes over the body of the shaman while her consciousness is elsewhere, for instance seeking answers to questions.

It is important to note that these definitions come from outsiders, people who do or did not usually engage with shamanic practice. However, those who are involved with core-shamanism (or many other neo-shamanisms) tend to deal more in practicalities, reproducing definitions close to that of Eliade's, which has indeed become required reading for sectors of the neo-shamanist community. Of Eliade's listed techniques or methods which he suggests define shamanism, entering an altered state of consciousness and ascending to the sky, or descending to the lower world, is paramount;[1] though as Heinze (1991) points out, Eliade's Christian focus tended to privilege the ascent to the sky.

I have tended to see attempted definitions of shamanism as saying more about Western approaches and discourses than they do about 'other people's' practices: and shamanism not as a 'thing' but as a concept constructed to meet needs of Western academics for definition. Ecstatic trance seems to be found almost everywhere, but in diversity, not sameness. Rather than seeing a universalised 'shamanism' I prefer to speak of specific 'shamanisms' that are not primordial or static. 'Shamans' are active agents, changing relationships and societies as they change consciousness.

'Surely the seiðwomen were not shamans!'

Merkur (1992) has pointed to the problem that each definition omits some people who are, by others' definition (including the definition of other shamans), 'shamans'. The approach that I have adopted in this book, and elsewhere, is one that avoids definition. In an article with Robert Wallis, we said:

> We feel the endurance of the term 'shamanism' espouses its potential for careful application, in an *approach* to shamanism rather than according to globalising *definitions*. Dowson's 'elements of shamanism' (1999) embrace diversity to avoid the metanarratives definition embodies. Techniques of trance are embedded in specific social relations: shamans enter a trance in order to engage with a spirit world, and this engagement is socio-politically supported by the community. By focusing on the socio-politics of shamanism, as well as 'techniques' or activities in the spirit world, we can discern cross-cultural difference as well as similarity. The ways that shamans and shamanic practices are sanctioned by their communities show how different shamanisms are across the world. The study of shamanism in this way is not monolithic (searching for the same thing everywhere, across space and time) because it emphasises difference. Neither is it vague: the shaman still assumes very specific social/spiritual activities.
>
> These specific shamanisms are neither static nor bounded, but change with time and circumstances, so that shamans are active agents of cultural change.
>
> (Blain and Wallis 2000: 398)

We received a comment that it was an 'almost non-definition'. I would disagree only with the word 'almost': the statement was not intended as a definition, nor were we trying to claim that seiðr either in past or present is 'shamanism' (that Western abstraction or ideal type). What we were saying, and I am asserting now, is that an understanding of seiðr (and some other neo-shamanic manifestations) is facilitated by drawing critically on the immense and growing literature on shamanisms; and can in turn contribute to understandings of 'shamanic' practices elsewhere. I attempt to engage with what today's seeresses do, and how they understand seiðr, community and self, by juxtaposing past and present, examining the ways today's seiðworkers use the literature, asking questions about relationships of seiðr to other possibly-ecstatic practices today and in the past. (A link with Sámi practice, for instance, appears quite strongly in both times.)

The seiðwomen were practising specifically according to what they had learned, within relationships constituted with other individuals and processes, and with the particular spirits they met in their practice. In the literature they appear at times embedded within community, whether acting on individual causes or engaged in 'socially constitutive seiðr': maintaining the course of justice, creating prosperity for the community, actively engaging with Wyrd rather than merely reporting it. We do not know about their training, or initiation. The sources – the Icelandic sagas – are late, and post-Christian.

If we do attempt a precise definition, such as Shirokogorov's (1935) concept of mastery of spirits, it seems to me that there is no way to decide whether the seiðworkers of the sagas were 'shamans'. Their relationships with their spirits are not described, other than in the situation of the Greenland Seeress who comments that because the song that calls her helper spirits has been so well sung, she was able to see further and know more than ever before (and as it is not she who sings the song, the question of 'mastery' here does not seem possible to ascertain). But she is very clearly entering into some kind of spirit-relationship, and doing so on behalf of the people who have requested her to 'see' for them. This relationship with the spirits is problematic for today's practitioners, who understandably want to gather more information than the saga gives. A number, however, are finding their own sources of information, namely 'spirits' whether of land or ancestors, who appear to them, in trance, as teachers and helpers, at times problematically. (As has been indicated earlier, spirits are not always 'nice' or of good will.)

'Don't today's people claim to be shamans?'

I know only one seiðworker who commonly and explicitly refers to herself as a 'shaman'. Others prefer the terms 'seiðwoman' or 'seiðman' or their Icelandic equivalents, seiðkona and seiðmaðr. For some, this is borrowed from the 'etiquette' of core-shamanism: the term 'shaman' is an honorific given by a community in respect of what you do, you do not call yourself a shaman, others will give you the status. Thus today's shamanists may pay respect to indigenous shamans and to the community-embeddedness of their practices (Wallis 1999a). One cannot be a 'shaman' without a community: serious 'urban shamanism' today is not work aimed at self-improvement or self-gratification (see e.g. Heinze 1991), although individuals' attendances at beginner neo-shamanic workshops or drumming groups may well be (see e.g. Jakobsen 1999).[2] Others do not use the term 'shaman' because it does not seem relevant, as they prefer to describe what they do in culturally specific terms. Yet others, such as Bil, avoid the term from a wish to dissociate themselves from the attendees at new-age workshops. Bil does on occasion use the word, comparatively, to explain what he does in terms of specific traditional shamanisms, including Sámi practices.

Scottish seiðman Malcolm says that originally he called what he did 'Northern shamanism', though he did not think of himself as a 'shaman'. The spirits with whom he works told him that he would know when he was a shaman, because the community would call him that. After eighteen years of practice within Northern cosmology he still does not call himself a shaman. Human members of the Pagan community sometimes do. His spirits, he says, do not (and he has learned that they themselves are the 'community' to whom they originally referred): but 'they have stopped laughing' when the humans use the term.

In/authentic seiðr today

A charge of 'doing it wrong' arises both from practitioners (about other practitioners); from non-practitioners within the Heathen community (as part of a quest for authenticity) and within academia (from those who seem to think that the point is to reconstruct a seiðr 'performance', to mimic those of 1,000 years ago rather than to engage in seiðr as explorations of community-consciousness and cosmology within a present-day framework). Critics rightly point out 'we don't know' what the seeress did. The literary sources are late and post-Christian. Nevertheless, the sources indicate that the concept of 'the seiðkona' was very much present in the awareness of thirteenth- and fourteenth-century Icelanders, with every indication that the phenomenon of seiðr was known and accomplished in Norway, Scotland, Sweden, Ireland and that it was a development of practices that were at least hundreds of years old.

The single detailed description of practice, the account of the Greenland Seeress, is indeed not likely to be 'correct' as a description of a specific incident: but the numerous accounts that refer to seiðr, or that give pieces of the puzzle, indicate that practices were known and widespread: building a seið-platform; holding a staff; the use of chanting; the giving of counsel that could not be known (e.g. about events taking place at a distance); and the related practices of travelling in altered shape, casting illusions, giving protection.

Today's seiðfolk are taking the pieces as and where they find them: scouring the sagas for details, drawing on the Eddic poems. They are also 'borrowing' and adapting from any source that seems relevant. Some have had Sámi teachers: but they frame what they do within the Heathen cosmology of the Well, the Tree, and the Nine Worlds. Some seiðr practices are becoming widespread within the community – many both women and men engage in journeying for personal knowledge or development. However, those who are seen as community seiðworkers are those who sit in the high seat, or engage with healing or 'wholemaking' for others, and who have been practising for some time. A small but increasing number are engaged in 'becoming a seiðworker', learning the techniques within the cosmological framework.

The learning is not only from human seiðworkers. The teachers are 'the spirits', especially ancestors and Landwights, and including the deities who themselves perform seiðr, Freyja and Óðinn. There may be a defined initiation, sometimes over a protracted period, followed by a period of learning – potentially life-long – in how to use the skills so gained. None of the people I have spoken with, not even Bil or Rauðhildr, describe themselves as 'masters of spirits'. The spirits are there, participants, helping or hindering, having to be persuaded and placated, or doing their own persuading: creating new sets of social relations which surround the 'shaman' or seiðworker. 'This is something I am still having to come to terms with, explain and interpret', said 'James' (in chapter 7). Similar statements have been made elsewhere, by experienced shamans:

> The shaman's path is unending. I am an old, old man and still a *nunutsi* (baby) standing before the mystery of the world.
> (Huichol shaman Don José Matsúwa, quoted by
> Schultes and Hofmann 1992: 138, cited by Gyrus n.d.)

To me it seems that the 'mastery of spirits' definition remains that of an outsider. What shamans, or seiðworkers, or other ecstatic practitioners experience is assessable, or accessible, only by an insider – human or spirit; for these spirits, to the ethnographer who seeks to map the terrain of seiðr, are party to the negotiation of its shaping. The seiðworker may experience these varied 'spirits' either as parties to the construction of a dialogue (in which information is given) or as possessory entities. In either case they can be spoken with: one might say even interviewed! However, this approach, which is dependent on treating seiðr or shamanic events and experiences as occurring within a 'reality' that can be mapped or described, taking 'spirits' seriously, leads to a further challenge.

'Have you jettisoned impartiality?'

As I am both a researcher and a practitioner, this may indicate that I do prefer seiðworkers' multivocal accounts of their practice, and interpretations, to those of Eliade or the 'master of spirits' concept previously mentioned. The later requires, I feel, some further deconstruction. A major strand in the Western concept of the individual, unique 'self' is that of control: which appears in many contexts. Before I saw, and participated in, seiðr, I had engaged with narratives of 'control' appearing within the discourses of many (not all) men as fathers, in a study of parenting in Halifax, Nova Scotia, which I linked (Blain 1992) to the construction of the liberal, rational, capitalist, usually male, individual discussed and deconstructed by Venn (1984). It seems strange to see this debate replayed regarding neo-shamanisms. Here several strands are interwoven, including not only the aforesaid western concept of 'control' but diverse readings of shamans' (or apprentices') stories of battles, or of 'performances' witnessed by Western explorers and missionaries. For the tales of the 'mastery' or 'control' of spirits are to me like nothing so much as the folk tales or Arthurian legends with which I grew up (Lancelot may work hard and be the best knight, but there is always another challenge and eventual defeat): or even the 'flytings' discussed in chapter 7. The enemy, defeated in (actual or spiritual) battle is defeated also with words, whether taunts or boasts. Or as a British shamanistic practitioner with whom I discussed this said:

> Now you've got me analytical, and thinking about the number of times I've spent a few hours in a state of general dread and

scrabbling near-competence, only to come out at the end and
SMS my wife with 'We won.' . . . A bit of healing is a bit of
healing, but if something kicks seven shades of crap out of you
and leaves you with bruises on your ribs, by the gods it was a
foe worth boasting about!

Further, if we view 'shaman' – or seiðworker – not as a one-
dimensional, glamorous but rather stereotyped figure, but as an
active agent of community construction, there is surely no reason to
suppose that all relations with all spirits will be the same. Taussig's
(1987) accounts of Colombian shamans' politically negotiated constructions have been referred to earlier: these and other 'traditional'
practitioners exist in a changing environment, using whatever
resources they can, constructing or reinventing themselves and their
social relations of practice within contexts of historic colonialism,
neo-colonialism, religious competition, spirit involvement and
contestation, environmental degradation, disease and death. In
such accounts, the shaman is 'negotiator and negotiated in a
deeply political process that destroys any belief in shamanism
solely as a safe or benevolent phenomenon' (Wallis 1999b: 45).
The enmity of other shamans, combated in trance, is part of this.
Whose spirits are more powerful? (See e.g. Vitebsky 1995b.) The
battle of Sámi noaides mentioned in the *Historia Norwegica* is a case
in point.
    The human-cultural context of seiðr – and most 'European' neo-
shamanisms – may be considerably less problematic, yet still
seiðworkers are involved with negotiating meaning and practice, in
the spirit as in the everyday world, where that meaning and practice
are immensely variable, and where the outcome is certain only in
hindsight. Previously-negotiated meanings ensure that there are
allies or associates who can probably be counted on, if appealed
to correctly or (e.g. in Inuit shamanic practice) challenged appro-
priately, and practice, as with other areas of social relationships,
increases skill.
    Here, though, I should add that the definitions given in beginner
'core-shamanic' practice also emphasise 'control', in this case
control through association with essentially benign spirits or guides:
consumer-shamanistic practice for middle-class urbanites.

[C]ore-shamanism emphasises that the shamanic state is
controllable. This is important in Harner's teaching of core-

shamanism to Westerners, because the path to becoming a shaman can be conveyed as safe and suitable for teaching in a workshop scenario. It may also represent an attempt to destigmatise shamanism following decades of oppression in indigenous communities by colonising cultures and religions. . . The emphasis on control in Harnerism promises the technique is safe to practitioners. It also reveals the Western need for 'control' (over consciousness, emotions, or money) where no such precedent may be found in indigenous shamanism.

(Wallis 1999b: 46)

From the accounts of Bil, chapters 4 and 7, or Rauðhildr, chapter 2, seiðr does not emerge as a notably 'safe' practice.

Reinventing Wyrd

Today, seiðworkers may be few in number, but they experience transformation of self and others, within negotiated relationships with spirits and with human members of their communities. They draw on understandings of cosmology and past practice, together with these negotiated relationships, to create their practices today. Their clients seek instruction on daily life in a complex urban society, once again based on understandings from practices of 1,000 years ago which may combine the attraction of the exotic shaman 'other' with nostalgia for a supposed past. Yet however audiences or clients view their work, seiðworkers are not reconstructing the past, but shifting across 1,000 years to weave Wyrd from past threads, in creating shamanic forms for the present and for the new millennium. They talk about fear and change, within meetings, the experience of trance, mingling everyday and 'extraordinary', known and unknown. Bil's web page gives an attempted answer to 'where does the seiðman go?'

> I have friends who only live in the Otherworld (who have no existence in the world of man), and I have enemies as well. We go places like anybody else: we go to the store, we go to work, we go visit the family inside the mountain, we go to Taco Bell, we go to the Land of the Dead. We see the same things that everyone else see; we just see a lot more of it than the average folk – that's all. Every single person interacts with ancestors, alfar, jötnar, and trolls of one kind or another every single day.

It's just that the interpretation by the average person is usually in terms of good luck or bad luck. We, on the other hand, can see the puppet strings. That's just the way it is.

(Linzie n.d.,
http://www.angelfire.com/nm/seidhman/seidgo.html)

They also talk about the ethics of seiðwork, remembering those other challenges – from the literature and today's readers – of seiðr as mind-control. Thus, the respected seeress Rauðhildr states her views on the practice of seiðr techniques within today's community:

It must benefit the practitioner in the long run.

It should benefit Midgard and the Gods when they touch directly with the practice.

It must be done safely with utmost respect for the Goddesses and Gods, the community, and the practitioner.

If something unsafe to the practitioner must be done for the benefit of the community and the Gods & Goddesses, it is the decision of the practitioner and hi/r allies so to do. They should be responsible in that decision and the community should support it if conscience will allow.

(Email discussion, 1999)

Shamans and anthropologists

Some researchers have described a curious 'double standard' – 'native informants', but not 'Europeans' or academics, can speak and theorise from within 'irrational' discourses of magic or spirit helpers (Blain 1998a; Wilson 1994). Others mention 'shamanophobia' (Dowson 1996), to which Wallis (1999a) adds 'neoshamanophobia', within academia: a reluctance to consider 'shamanic' constructions for human events. 'Magic is a virtual taboo in post-Enlightenment scholarship' say Arnould et al. (1999: 63). So, to speak of the human-political situating of seiðr is acceptable; to describe the politics internal to the seið-journey, as a form of 'truth' that can aid analysis (rather than a phenomenon to be analysed) is often not. 'Spirit-helpers' thus become culturally defined aspects of one's own personality, not external agents: part of the individualisation and psychologising of perception that pervades Western academic discourses of the rational, unitary self). In the Western neo-shamanic movement, it is common for practitioners to speak of Jungian theory, archetypes, and to individuate 'spirit guardians' and 'higher selves', entities that are attached to an individual person and may be explained as forming part of that individual's psyche, consciousness or subconscious. Similar discourses are used to explain academic understandings of the imaginal. (Is it 'real', or is it all in my head?) Researchers attempting to explain the 'otherworldness' of shamanic ecstasy and the images that appear have investigated neurological activity promoted by entheogens or by the stimulation of repeated sound (drumming, chanting) and movement, exhaustion, fasting and so forth: processes which are internal to the individual concerned.

But those who study shamanisms within context point out that the images are not the same in all cultures: not only the meaning, but what is seen or heard, changes. Even the experience of anthropologists, undertaking experiential research embedded within different socio-cultural contexts, changes – Michael Harner's terrifying entheogen-induced initiatory experiences of Jivaro cosmology (Harner 1980) are dramatically different from the experiences reported in this book. Perception and meaning are embedded within specific cultural and historic community inter-pretations. These shamanisms rely on similar possibilities (abilities of humans to remember dreams, to interpret images, to shift awareness in response to stimuli, and so forth) but the 'shamanic complex' differs in what is done and how this is interpreted (Hoppál 1987). But there is more. In shamanic cultures, shamanism is not one part or aspect of culture that can be examined or not, as the ethnographer chooses. Describes her experiences as an ethnographer among the Déné, Guédon says that 'Shamanism permeates all of Nabesna culture: the worldview, the subsistence patterns, and the life cycles' (Guédon 1994).

In the old material, as earlier discussed, seiðr is not usually described as central to the community. Yet in the sagas the possibility of magical action, of altered consciousness, of involve-ment with the community through seiðr, is there, present, and when it does occur it is non-remarkable. Though usually occurring on an individual basis (as do almost all activities in the sagas (Hastrup 1996)), at times it does have a community focus, as in the instances of Thúrid the sound-filler, the Greenland Seeress, and Thordís spákona. Altered consciousness, and the acquisition of knowledge or manipulation of minds or elements while in that state, is woven into the stories as part of the action. Relations constructed between people of the community include those that involve other beings, spirits, powers, deities.

However, the communities of today who have informed this book are deliberately constructed, rather self-consciously: groups of people who come together here and there, to link themselves with the deities of the Eddas, the Æsir and Vanir of Northern Europe and 'worship' in what they consider to be 'old ways'. Some have based their practice initially on ritual worship believed to parallel that of the 'Viking age'. Others associate themselves chiefly with spirits of land and sea, and only secondarily with the deities of Ásgard. Oracular seiðr was a deliberate construction. But however it arose, seiðr, for some groups, is now central to community practice and understanding of *how to relate to* deities and wights. Relations constituted through seiðr locate the seiðworker with respect to others – her clients, and the spirits she contacts. The seiðworker becomes a mediator between people and spirits, active in creation of community and knowledge. Winifred is an example:

> One of the most interesting seeings that I had was for a young man, and (the deity) Heimdall came for him, and it was wonderful ... they set up this whole thing where they went into a sauna together and had this man-to-man talk about how to be a man and follow the man's path, and the interesting thing was that I wasn't allowed to hear what they were saying to one another, but just to understand that Heimdall had this knowledge for him and that I had to pass it on to him... you know, sweat lodge and the whole, the whole deal and it was like, these are male mysteries and they're not for me, only the message was, it's my right to carry. But it was very warming to see a young man being taken in hand by Heimdall and set upon his man's path.

Approaches to seiðr and shamanism can look beyond the concept of technique or individual relationships, to shamanic practice embedded within social relations that include personal relations of friendship and community constructions of gender, ethnicity, sexuality and status: situatings of seiðworker and clients that are part-constituted by other beings, 'spirits', animals, deities.

Narratives of 'the spirits' and of the shaman as entering into socially constitutive relations with them, however, are what become most problematic for a Western rationalist audience, for whom non-belief in 'spirits' is axiomatic. I have seen a conference returning, time after time, to the question of 'do the spirits exist?' In presenting any material that relates to personal experience, I have to deal with the challenge of whether I have 'belief' in 'the spirits': a belief that would seem to discredit my credentials to do 'impartial' or 'unbiased' ethnography. (That non-belief also constitutes 'bias' would be seen as likewise irrational by adherents of the non-belief discourse.)

I could say that to my respondents, the 'belief in spirits' is real, and therefore it becomes part of the way in which they shape their world, create their realities, manipulate their consciousnesses: the ethnographer, however, standing outside, can see how the belief functions within the community. This has been the approach taken by many researchers – and shades into the view that such belief is appropriate for those studied, but not the researcher, which carries its own implicit ethnocentric assumptions of superiority (Wilson 1994). Two, linked, sets of problems become evident. Chapter 2 included an extract from an article prepared by Diana Paxson, author, and initial researcher, within the community, of oracular seiðr. In it, she moves back and forth between the discourse of 'spirits' and the discourse of 'rationality': furthermore, she says she did this when experiencing trance. She had to learn to set her academic brain 'on hold' at times. She, like Winifred and Jordsvin, Bil, Thorgerd, 'James', Malcolm, Susan, Rauðhildr, like the many others named and un-named in this book, like myself, is part of present-day post-industrial society, immersed in its dialogues, products of its education system, bombarded with information that supports the rational individual self and denies 'spirits'. Yet these seiðworkers author their 'selves' through a discourse which is contested even within their community of choice, making sense of their experiences and relating these also to their 'other' worlds: reflexivity, as Cohen (1994) points out, is not only the prerogative of the ethnographer.

Taking the view that 'they believe it, so I'll accept it as emic description' positions the researcher as having access to a 'truth' outside, and at odds with that of her participants. It is, to say the least, patronising. It may also, in the final resort, actively deny access to the 'realities' of participants (Turner 1994) – including the researcher's own experiences. And in distancing the ethnographer from this 'belief', it starts to reify 'emic knowledge' as fixed, static and unchanging, as generally shared, rather than as the specific construction of interpretations that each person, ethnographer included, engages in, and with.

For some time, my choice was to refuse to adjudicate belief, as I indicated in the introduction. However, 'belief' is, in my view, not a good description for the relation of shamanists and other beings that share the worlds of their lives. These beings are part of the relationships, partial creators of community endeavours. They are simply *there*: and in an ethnography of encounters with a spirit-world, the spirit-beings communicate their part. While shamanism may involve mimesis, 'performance', dialogue too is part of the process, and in interpreting 'extraordinary experience' I am required to take seriously not merely the human participants' perceptions, but the 'spirits' themselves. This has come to mean acknowledging publicly that I can understand only through experiencing, and that in my brokerings of knowledge from one group to the other, it becomes needful to say that 'I know' this experience not only as observer and repository of stories and confidences, but through direct connection, trance and seiðr seance, speaking for the spirits, speaking from the mound, dancing with the ancestors. Hence chapter 5 of this book.

I see Winifred and the others moving between the worlds, constructing meaning from discourse, relationships, surroundings: two images come to mind. Guédon talks of Déné concepts of place, location, without boundaries: the hunter moves from a 'home' point, out and back, out and back, creating knowledge of place that may be used and known also by others, from their own points of reference. Likewise, the 'shaman' moves from the safe place, out into the unknown *útangarð* and returns, to trace a different journey next time, and journeys intersect, mapping the territory in a way that is without boundaries. To me, the shaman becomes a metaphor for the ethnographer of post-modernity, moving through the worlds, moving between levels of analysis, in an attempt to reconstruct something in her own understandings, her own life, that approaches wholeness, an understanding of living that is complete, not fragmented, returning in her journeys to a pole of being, a World Tree.

I cannot create ethnography by appropriating local knowledges. (This was the old image of ethnography, that the anthropologist would go 'elsewhere' and come back with pure description, informants' stories and 'objective' observation. It never, of course, worked like that: the ethnographer's gathering of local knowledge being always partial, observations always situated.) My choice is to enter the world of the seiðworker, as a native-speaker: but simply 'going native', total cultural immersion, in itself is not enough. My understandings of seiðr include understandings of its links to the 'outside' world, and my own locations within these; and how 'the spirits' see these links. I seek to understand the construction of seiðr and its community, the contradictions and contestations therein, by understanding my 'self' as part/not part of that community, as situated within its relations, with my own knowledges that are not totally shared with others, though specific others have parts therein. Critical awareness and reflexivity are constructed in the inter-sections of the worlds, in the journeys; in experiencing ecstasy, and my attempts to communicate it in prose or poetry, here and elsewhere – and in the tension between these discourses and those of the academic world that I likewise inhabit.

This book has been a journey of many paths. 'Shamanisms' are being re-created on many levels, in many ways, as increasing numbers of people jettison 'established' religion and seek as individuals and as interlinked communities, for spirituality. Many turn to 'indigenous shamanism' still seen, mistakenly, as primordial, unchanged, a 'first religion'; but in this post-colonial world charges of appropriation, theft of culture and spirituality, have weight, and often people who are not part of 'indigenous' communities will seek to avoid appropriation. The quest for meaning, then, turns to the ancestors – and to those spirits of place, animals and plants, that people the landscapes, both physical and cosmological, in which the seeker feels most 'at home'.

We do not know, in North-Western Europe, how the earliest 'ancestors' conceptualised their spirituality. Cave art and rock-art may now be seen as 'shamanic', but it is only with the – relatively recent – writing of the sagas and Eddas that memories of a largely animist landscape start to reveal themselves in words. And there in the landscape, in mounds, hills, howes, barrows, are the ancestors. Yet the seiðfolk do not reconstruct the past, though their practices are based in it. It is from today's understandings of past, present, life and death, spun from a multitude of narrative strands that include those of the past, the Norns, Wyrd, that they go in trance to seek answers, to seek themselves. What they find changes them, and leads to questioning of everyday understandings that are otherwise taken for granted. Likewise my ethnographic journey leads me onward, from one site of practice to the next, and my personal understandings of self and other, community and friendship, are altered. Post-modernity may be, as Bauman (1997) says, about 'choice': but the choices are structured, layered by past meanings like words within the Well of Wyrd: by the networks of meaning, relations, social processes that people reconstitute in their daily lives, or by the *ørlög*, webs of obligation, that the Norns allot.

Notes

2 The saying of the Norns

1 This is an annual festival organised by The Troth, an organisation of Heathens based in the US.

2 I use these words deliberately, and in the sense in which Young and Goulet (1994) sub-titled their book 'The anthropology of extraordinary experience'.

3 Some Heathens do talk about archetypes, though those engaged in constructing theology generally do not. It has been pointed out that individuals use the word 'archetype' in diverse ways and that Jung's own meaning may not be too far from an Ásatrú conception of deities. In a recent debate via an email discussion list, it was pointed out that newcomers to Ásatrú speak of the God/esses as archetypes, while 'old hands' speak of them as 'real'. From the point of view of discourse analysis, part of this may be that exposure to Ásatrú discourse 'permits' a person to come to speak and think of deities existing independently of people without feeling they will be regarded as 'flaky'. In my interviews, some do use the concept of archetypes, and it seems that they do so to express something that has its being on a cultural or social level, rather than uniquely within the individual psyche (which is how the word is often used by neo-pagans).

4 Alternatively, the spirits may be called to the person who seeks their aid. This point is currently debated by the community, sometimes heatedly. In either case, the construction of the activity is one that involves active seeking or calling, followed by dialogue and often negotiation.

5 Snorri Sturluson, whose *Edda*, written in the early thirteenth century as a guide to help young poets who required to know their mythology, is the most coherent account of the mythology and cosmology of the North of Europe: though it is set within a euhemerised-Christianised framework, and may be over-systematised due to the author's familiarity with Greco-Roman mythology.

6 Varðlokur, of which the meaning remains obscure. Which 'powers' are to be charmed by it is not clear – god/esses, spirits, the dead, Landwights?

7 Gaining access to sources is a perennial problem, particularly for the

majority of Heathens who are without access to university libraries. A translation of *Heimskringla* is available on the internet from OMACL. It should be added in this context that many of the 'non-academic' buyers of paperback editions of sagas and Eddas are Heathens or Pagans.

8 Links with both homophobia and racism persist, and though the vast majority of practitioners dissociate themselves from 'racism', discourses of homophobia remain evident – as will be seen in chapter 7.

9 Some of this negativity has been disputed, for instance by Harwood (1970) who states that among the Safwa people he studied 'itonga' – the mystical power of magic-workers – was viewed as 'morally neutral', and that this people did not routinely see 'witches' as 'anti-social'. (p. 69), and suggests that an automatic reading of 'witch' as negative is a product of Western ethnocentrism. It is interesting that Harwood still adopts a definition of 'witchcraft' derived from Evans-Pritchard's word, which he gives as 'a mystical and innate power, which can be used by its possessor to harm other people' (p. xv).

10 Founder of the Foundation for Shamanic Studies.

11 These extracts are from an essay on this experience, which Ms Paxson sent me in response to a request for information. The account, with its commentary, was prepared in 1989 but not published.

3 The Greenland Seeress: seiðr as shamanistic practice

1 Larrington's translation, given here, is currently the most accessible translation to practitioners. Old Icelandic is:

Vegtamr ec heiti	sonr em ec Valtams;
segdu mér ór helio	– ec man ór heimi – :
hveim ero beccir	baugom sánir,
flet fagrliga	flód gulli?

(Kuhn & Neckel 1962: 278)

2 *Hyndluljóð*, 34 and subsequently.

Mart segiom þér	oc munom fleira,
vöromz, at viti svá	viltu enn lengra?

(Kuhn & Neckel: 293)

3 *Völuspá*, 28 and many subsequent verses. Old Icelandic given by Kuhn is:

vitoð ér enn, eða hvat?

4 Lindquist's preferred spelling is seid, sometimes sejd, present-day Scandinavian usage. The Heathens I have spoken with in Britain and North America, for the most part, use the Icelandic form seiðr, often transliterated to seidr or seidhr, although the word also appears as seith and seide.

4 Approaching the spirits

1 'Men thought they recognised Thorveig's eyes'. Icelandic courtesy of Netútgáfan (n.d.) http://www.snerpa.is/net/netut-e.htm, *Kormák's saga*, 18.

2 Price commented that the emphasis in Eirík's saga on the seeress' cushion, stuffed with hens' feathers, may bear further investigation.
3 Possible evidence for neolithic use of henbane comes from a beaker found in a Scottish excavation (Barfarg/Balbirnie) mentioned by Dronfield though he adds that 'Whether this hallucinogenic plant was present by design or accident is unclear' (Dronfield 1995: 265). Dronfield's own evidence comes from examination of components of rock-art in Irish passage-graves, drawing comparisons with elements of entoptics associated with migraine, epilepsy and entheogens including mescaline, cannabis, LSD and psilocybin. The study is complicated, but seems to suggest support for association of the art components with altered consciousness states, and at some locations specifically with psilocybin, thus giving some support for hypothesised use of *P. semilanceata* in achieving the state relating to the art.
4 It is worth noting at this point that some other *Amanitas*, notably *A. phalloides* and *A. virosa*, are indeed deadly poisonous: and that although from most illustrations there seems little likelihood of mistaking *A. muscaria* for either of those, mushrooms in the field do not always look quite like mushrooms in the book. There is a saying that 'There are old mushroom hunters, and there are bold mushroom hunters, but there are no old, bold mushroom hunters'. Bil Linzie and others point out that *A. muscaria* is not, either, the most pleasant of potions for most of its users. *P. semilanceata* is today well known to much of the 'alternative' community in Northern Europe. Legalities on these wild species vary from one jurisdiction to another: In Britain at present possession of *P. semilanceata* is not illegal, but preparation of it, or passing it to another person, is. In Canada, by contrast, possession is illegal in Nova Scotia, and people are required to report instances of its finding, to the authorities (though whether any do so I do not know).
5 This version translated from selections given in Gordon (1957: 37).
6 The booths (búðir) were the temporary dwellings at the Þing, or Assembly, the parliament.
7 Today's practitioners credit Þorgeirr's words with preventing the suppression of Heathen lore and practices, permitting the transmission of poems and stories until such time as they could be written down, and thus providing material for the revival of Heathenism in the present.
8 'Terms used loosely in a very non abrahamic manner,' Rauðhildr commented.

6 Re-evaluating the Witch-Queen

1 When her foster-son, Bard, arrives the saga says that 'Kerlingin æmtir við innar í húsinu en hún var í rekkju sinni.' (The old woman was muttering to herself in the inner part of the house where she was lying on her bed.) While she relates that she was sleeping because of being up during the night preparing provisions for her foster-son, the 'muttering to herself' together with the charm she places on him

(in part through a necklace) may connect with ways that people who wished to know things were said to mutter into their cloaks or under blankets: see discussion of útiseta, in chapter 4. (Netútgáfan, http://www.snerpa.is/net/isl/heidarv.htm, chapter 23.)

2 An alternative explanation, discussed but generally rejected within the Heathen community, comes from a nineteenth-century interpretation of the mythology as the remnants of a 'True' systematic account in which Gullveig/Heiðr is not Freyja but one of her servants, a giant-woman who is out from the start to cause trouble for deities and people. Discussions of Rydberg's highly systematised versions of the mythology periodically surface on Ásatrú mailing lists and other public fora for debate. They have a few adherents within the community: however, on the whole the community rejects them, as do academics today, as being attempts to create an artificial order based on flawed methodological principles and nineteenth-century definitions of deity. See Rydberg 1906 (Norroena Society translation, containing the first three volumes of Rydberg's six–volume Swedish work). I should perhaps add that I do not recommend this as an introduction to Norse mythology!

3 'Heiðr' may not be a personal name, but simply a word for 'magic worker' that refers here to Gullveig. Indeed, Boyer (1983) points out that 'We do not know whether Heiðr represents Gullveig, or the sybil herself who has been speaking since the beginning of the poem... or else the sorceress who invented seiðr (Freyja?)' (1983: 122). So even the equation of Heiðr and Freyja is complex and may be attained by more than one route.

4 Though claims regarding their numbers have been much exaggerated, charges, trials and at times executions, did none the less occur.

5 According to Christina Larner (1981) those who used their talents to heal were regarded by churchmen as *more* evil than those who did not do so.

7 *Ergi* seiðmen, queer transformations?

1 And indeed addressed also in the article (Blain and Wallis 1999) in *The Pomegranate*, to which she was responding.

2 *Nið* requires some explanation. It can be translated as total unworthiness, depravity. A *niðing* was despicable, cast out by the community. Calling someone *nið* was an actionable insult, as was *ergi*.

3 First three lines from the translation by Larrington (1996: 89), Larrington's final line to each of these two verses gives 'and that I thought the hallmark of a pervert' which keeps the spirit of 'insult' possibly denoted by the word *ergi*. Icelandic from Sigurðsson (1998: 124–5) is

'...átta vetur
vartu fyr jörð neðan,
kýr mjólkandi og kona,
og hefir þú þar börn of borið,
og hugða eg það args aðal.'

'En þig síga kváðu

Sámseyju í
og draptu á vétt sem völor;
vitka líki
fórtu verþjóð yfir,
og hugða ec það args aðal.'

4   Þú vart völva
í Varinseyja,
skollvís kona,
bartu skrök sman,
kvaðstu sngi mann
eiga vilja,
segg brynjaðan,
nema Sinfjötla.
(Sigurðsson1998: 172)

5   Solli suggests, speculatively, an 'Odinic' hanging as the initiatory journey of a new shaman – a journey which many would not survive. I do not share her speculation on this, but concur in seeing Óðinn as central to Norse 'shamanic' practice, ambiguous, feared, and in the sense used by her (1999a), again following Halperin (1995), 'queer'. However, Grundy does not regard Óðinn as a shaman, and suggests that (at least in the literature and in the interpretations of its writers) the hanging on Yggdrasill is not partial, and Óðinn should be seen as a god who died physically. Shamanistically these interpretations may not be in conflict.

6   The poem is given in the fourteenth-century manuscript *Flateyarbók*, and this verse quoted – differently – in Snorri's *Edda*.

Eru völvur allar
frá Víðólfi,
vitkar allir
frá Vilmeiði,
skilberendur [*seiðberendur* from Snorri's *Edda*]
frá Svarthöfða,
jötnar allir
frá Ymi komnir
(*Hyndluljóð* 32, Sigurðsson 1998: 402)

7   Though it must be remembered that, for some in today's multivocal community at least, *ergi* and seiðr do indicate transgression, according to the comments made to Jordsvin and others. Seiðr is contested practice.

8   This story indeed holds many meanings. It is cited by both academics and Heathens as indicating a 'cult of Freyr' in which the god's statue is taken around the country in a wagon, and parallels with the 'cult of Nerthus' (described in Tacitus' *Germania*) thereby drawn.

9   A number of these apparent staffs are metal. Price's work includes a re-evaluation of them, in a context of seiðr as shamanic practice in late Iron Age Scandinavia.

10 Also, Solli mentions white phallic stones (1999b) associated with iron-age burials – speculating these may have associations with sacredness,

alternate gendering, and shamanic practice, several centuries before the 'Viking age'.

11 It could be speculated that the openness associated with the seiðr trance in a community environment was still a problem – either that the insights afforded therein were given to all, regardless of their degree of kinship with the speaker, or that the seiðwoman was deliberately putting herself into a relation of reliance on the audience/participants who might not be kin to her (which could even be seen as a kind of promiscuity, thus linking to the common meaning of the term applied to women).

8 The dance of the ancestors

1 '. . . the shaman specialised in a trance during which his soul is believed to leave his body and ascend to the sky or descend to the underworld' (Eliade 1964: 4–5). Note the 'is believed to': Heinze (1991) points out that Eliade did not 'believe in' either the shaman's spirits or her/his journey.

2 Long-term shamanistic practitioners who have spoken with me quite emphatically do not view workshop attendees as 'shamans'. Some of the workshop attendees, however, do use the term of themselves. For some, learning to *not* define themselves as 'shamans' takes time.

Bibliography

In this book, works from mediaeval literature are often referred to by title only. For the convenience of interested readers, I list English translations of primary sources mentioned. Translations or editions specifically referenced in the book are also listed by the name of the translator or editor, in general references.

Primary sources

Icelandic editions of sagas and other Icelandic material are available online from *Netútgáfan* at http://www.snerpa.is/net/index.html.

Poetic Edda

Edda: Die Lieder des Codex Regius (VI. Text) H. Kuhn and G. Neckel, (eds) (1962) Heidelberg: Carl Winter.
Eddukvæði, Gisli Sigurðsson (ed.) (1998) Reykjavík: Mál og menning.
The Poetic Edda trans. C. Larrington (1996) World's Classics, Oxford: Oxford University Press.

Prose Edda of Snorri Sturlusson

Snorri Sturlusson *Edda*, trans. A. Faulkes (1995) London: Everyman.

Histories

Ágrip af Nóregskonugasögum: A twelfth-century synoptic history of the Kings of Norway. trans. M.J. Driscoll (1995) London: Viking Society of Northern Research. (Old Icelandic and English).
Ari Þorgilsson, *Íslendingabók*, trans. H. Hermansson (1930) New York: n.p.
The Book of Settlements: Landnámabók, trans. H. Pálsson and P.G.

Edwards (1972) Winnipeg: University of Manitoba Press.

Orkneyinga saga: the history of the Earls of Orkney, trans. H. Pálsson and P.G. Edwards (1978) London: Hogarth Press.

Saxo Grammaticus, *Gesta Danorum*. H.E. Davidson and P. Fisher (eds and trans.) (1998) *Saxo Grammaticus: The History of the Danes, Books I–IX*. Woodbridge: Brewer.

Snorri Sturluson, *The Heimskringla: A History of the Norse Kings*, trans. S. Laing (1906) London: Norroena Society. (This edition does not include Ynglingasaga. The original 1844 edition of this translation, reproduced on the web by OMACL, does.)

—— D.B. Killings (ed.) Online Mediaeval and Classical library release #15b. Online: Available: http://sunsite.berkeley.edu/OMACL/ Heimskringla/ (1 January 2001). In particular, 'Ynglingasaga', Online: Available: http://sunsite.berkeley.edu/OMACL/Heimskringla/ ynglinga.html; 'Harald Harfager's Saga' Online: Available: http:// sunsite.berkeley.edu/OMACL/Heimskringla/harfager.html; and 'Saga of King Harald Grafeld', Online: Available: http://sunsite.berkeley.edu/ OMACL/Heimskringla/grafeld.html.

—— *Heimskringla, or The Lives of the Norse Kings, by Snorre Sturlason*. trans. E. Monsen (1932) Cambridge: W. Heffer & Sons Ltd.

Sturla Þórðarson, *Sturlunga saga*, trans. J.H. McGrew, 2 vols. (1970, 1974) New York: Twayne Publishers and the American Scandinavian Foundation.

Tacitus *The Agricola and the Germania*, H. Mattingly (ed. and trans.) (1970) Harmondsworth: Penguin Classics.

—— *The Histories*, D.S. Levene (ed. and trans.) (1999) Oxford: Oxford Paperbacks.

Sagas and short stories

(For most recent translations of all sagas listed see *The Complete Sagas of Icelanders*, Reykjavík: Leifur Eiríksson Publishing, 1998.)

'Arrow-Odd's saga', trans. M. Magnusson and H. Pálsson (1980) in *Seven Viking Romances*, Harmondsworth: Penguin Books.

Arrow-Odd: a Medieval Novel, trans. P.G. Edwards and H. Pálsson (1970) New York: New York University Press.

Eirik the Red and Other Icelandic Sagas, trans. G. Jones (1961) Oxford: Oxford University Press.

Egils saga, trans. C. Fell (1975) London: J.M. Dent & Sons.

Egil's Saga, trans. H. Pálsson and P.G. Edwards (1976) Harmondsworth: Penguin.

Eyrbyggja Saga, trans. H. Pálsson and P.G. Edwards (1973) Toronto: University of Toronto Press.

The Story of the Ere-Dwellers, trans. W. Morris and E. Magnússon (1892)

London: Bernard Quaritch. Ed. D. B. Killings (1998) Online: Available: http://sunsite.berkeley.edu/OMACL/EreDwellers/. (1 January 2001).

The Saga of Gisli, trans. G. Johnson (1987) Toronto: University of Toronto Press.

The Saga of Grettir the Strong. trans. G.A. Hight (1987) London: Everyman (1914 edition). Ed. D.B Killings (1995) Online: Available: http://sunsite.berkeley.edu/OMACL/Grettir/. (1 January 2001).

Gold-Thorir's Saga (Gull-Þóris Saga), trans. A. Maxwell (1998) in *The Complete Sagas of Icelanders* Vol. III, Reykjavík: Leifur Eiríksson Publishing.

'The Saga of Gunnar, the Fool of Keldugnup (Gunnars Saga Keldugnúpsfífls)', trans. P. Acker (1998) in *The Complete Sagas of Icelanders* Vol. III, Reykjavík: Leifur Eiríksson Publishing.

'The Saga of the Slayings on the Heath (Heidarvíga Saga)', trans. K. Kunz (1998) in *The Complete Sagas of Icelanders* Vol. IV, Reykjavík: Leifur Eiríksson Publishing.

'The Story of the Heath-Slayings', trans. W. Morris and E. Magnússon (1892) London: Bernard Quaritch. Ed. D. B. Killings (1998) Online: Available: http://sunsite.berkeley.edu/OMACL/Heitharviga/ (1 January 2001).

'King Hrolf and His Companions' (*Hrólfs saga kraka*), in G. Jones (1961) *Eirik the Red and Other Icelandic Sagas*, Oxford: Oxford University Press.

The Saga of the Jomsvikings, trans. L.M. Hollander (1989) Austin: University of Texas Press.

The Story of Kormak the Son of Ogmund (*Kormáks saga*), trans. W. Morris and E. Magnússon (1970), London: William Morris Society.

The Life and Death of Cormak the Skald, trans. W.S. Collingwood and J. Stefansson (1901). D.B. Killings (ed.) (1995) Online: Available: http://sunsite.berkeley.edu/OMACL/.

Laxdaela Saga, trans. H. Pálsson and M. Magnusson (1969) Harmondsworth: Penguin.

The Laxdaela Saga, D.B. Killings (ed.) (1997) based on *Laxdale* Saga, trans. M. Press (1899) London: The Temple Classics. Online: Available: http://sunsite.berkeley.edu/OMACL/Laxdaela/ (1 January 2001).

Njal's Saga, trans. M. Magnusson and Hermann Pálsson (1960) Harmondsworth: Penguin.

'Tháttr of Nornagest' trans. N.K. Chadwick (1921) in *Stories and Ballads of the Far Past*, Cambridge: Cambridge University Press.

'Story of Ögmund Dytt' (Ögmundar þáttr dytts), trans. L.M. Hollander (1972) in *Víga-Glúms saga and the story of Ögmund Dytt*, New York: Twayne Publishers.

The Vatnsdalers' Saga, trans. G. Jones (1973) Princeton: Princeton University Press.

Viga-Glúms saga and the story of Ögmund Dytt, trans. L.M. Hollander
(1972) New York: Twayne Publishers.
The Saga of the Volsungs: the Norse Epic of Sigurd and the Dragon Slayer,
trans. J. Byock (1999) Harmondsworth: Penguin Books.

General references

Achterberg, J. (1985) *Imagery in Healing : Shamanism and Modern
Medicine*, Boston and London: Shambala.
Aðalsteinsson, J.H. (1978) *Under the Cloak*, Acta Universitatis Upsaliensis
4, Uppsala: Almqvist & Wiksell.
Anisimov, A.F. (1963) 'The Shaman's tent of the Evenks and the origin of
the shamanistic rite', in H.N. Michael (ed.) *Studies in Siberian Shamanism*,
Arctic Institute of North America: Anthropology of the North, 84–123.
Arnould, E.J., Price, L.L. and Otnes, C. (1999) 'Making consumption
magic: a study of white-water river rafting', *Journal of Contemporary
Ethnography* 28,1: 33–68.
Auden, W.H. and Taylor, P.B. (1981) *Norse Poems*, London: Athlone Press.
Basilov, V.N. (1997) 'Chosen by the spirits', in M.M. Balzer (ed.) *Shamanic
Worlds: Rituals and Lore of Siberia and Central Asia*, Armonk, NY, and
London: North Castle Books.
Bates, B. (1983) *The Way of Wyrd*, London: Century.
—— (1996) *The Wisdom of the Wyrd*, London: Rider.
Bauman, Z. (1997) *Postmodernity and Its Discontents*, New York: New
York University Press.
Bauschatz, P. (1982) *The Well and the Tree*, Amherst: University of
Massachusetts Press.
Blain, J. (1992) 'To be in control: Men and their families'. *CSAA meeting,
Learned Societies*, University of Prince Edward Island, Charlottetown
P.E.I., May 1992.
—— (1997) 'Constructing identity and divinity: Creating community in an
Elder religion within a postmodern world', *Interdisciplinary perspectives:
using qualitative methods to study social life*, Annual Qualitative
Methods conference, Toronto, August 1997.
—— (1998a) 'Presenting constructions of identity and divinity: Ásatrú and
oracular seidhr', in S. Grills (ed.) *Doing Ethnographic Research:
Fieldwork Methods*, Thousand Oaks: Sage, 203–27.
—— (1998b) 'Seidhr and seidhrworkers: recovering shamanic practice in
contemporary heathenism', *The Pomegranate* 6: 6–19.
—— (1999) 'Seidr as shamanistic practice: reconstituting a tradition of
ambiguity', *Shaman* 7, 2: 99–121.
—— (2000) 'Speaking Shamanistically: seidr, academia, and rationality', DISKUS. Online: Available: http://www.uni-marburg.de/
religionswissenschaft/journal/diskus/blain.html (1 January 2001).

—— (in press) "'Now many of those things are shown to me which I was denied before": Seidr, shamanism, and journeying, past and present', *Studies in Religion/Sciences Religieuses*, special issue on Shamanism, ed. R. Adlam.

—— (forthcoming, a) 'Magic, healing or death? Issues of seidr, "balance" and morality in past and present', in G. Carr and P. Baker (eds) *New Approaches to Medical Archaeology and Anthropology*, Oxford: Oxbow Books.

—— (forthcoming, b) 'Seidr, magic, and community: reinventing contested Northern shamanic practice', *Anthropology of Consciousness*.

Blain, J. and Wallis, R.J. (1999) 'Men and "women's magic": contested narratives of gender, seidr, and "ergi"', *The Pomegranate* 9: 4–16.

—— (2000) 'The "ergi" seidman: Contestations of gender, shamanism and sexuality in northern religion past and present', *Journal of Contemporary Religion* 15,3: 395–411.

—— (Forthcoming) 'Seiðr, gender and transformation: from the sagas to the new millennium', *Proceedings of the Viking Millennium Symposium, Newfoundland, September 2000*.

Bohannan, L. (1964) *Return to laughter*, Garden City, NY: Doubleday.

Borovsky, Z. (1999) 'Never in public: Women and performance in Old Norse Literature', *Journal of American Folklore* 112: 6–39.

Boyer, R. (1983) 'On the composition of Völuspá', in R. J. Glendinning and H. Bessason (eds) *Edda: A Collection of Essays*, Winnipeg: University of Manitoba Press.

Butler, J. (1990) *Gender Trouble: Feminism and the Subversion of Identity*, London: Routledge.

—— (1993) *Bodies That Matter: On the Discursive Limits of 'Sex'*, London: Routledge.

Byock, J. (1982) *Feud in the Icelandic Saga*, Berkeley: University of California Press.

Cohen, A.P. (1994) *Self Consciousness: An Alternative Anthropology of Identity*, London: Routledge.

Coles, B.J. (1990) 'Anthropomorphic figures from Britain and Ireland,' *Proceedings of the Prehistoric Society* 56: 315–33,

—— (1998) 'Wood species for wooden figures: A glimpse of a pattern', in A. Gibson and D. Simpson (eds) *Prehistoric Ritual and Religion: Essays in Honour of Aubrey Burl*, Stroud, Gloucestershire: Sutton Publishing, 163–173.

Cope, J. (1998) *The Modern Antiquarian*, London: Thorsons.

Cowan, T. (1995) *Fire in the Head*, San Francisco: HarperSanFrancisco.

Crawford, J.R. (1967)*Witchcraft and Sorcery in Rhodesia*, London: Oxford University Press.

Crossley-Holland, K. (1980) *The Norse Myths*, New York: Pantheon Books.

Csordas, T.J. (1996) 'Imaginal performance and memory in ritual healing', in C. Laderman and M. Roseman (eds) *The Performance of Healing*, London: Routledge, 91–114.

Czaplicka, M.A. (1914) *Aboriginal Siberia: A Study in Social Anthropology*, Oxford: Clarendon Press.

Davidson, H.R.E. (1964/1990) *Gods and Myths of Northern Europe*, Harmondsworth: Penguin.

Dowson, T.A, (1996) 'Review of Garlake, P, 1995, The Hunter's Vision: The Prehistoric Rock Art of Zimbabwe', *Antiquity* 70: 468– 69.

—— (1999) 'Rock Art and Shamanism: A Methodological Impasse', in: A. Rozwadowski, M.M. Kosko and T.A. Dowson (eds) *Rock Art, Shamanism and Central Asia: Discussions of Relations*, Warsaw: Wydawnictwo Academickie, 39–56.

Driscoll, M.J. (ed. and trans.) (1995) *Ágrip af Nóregskonugasögum: A twelfth-century synoptic history of the Kings of Norway*, London: Viking Society of Northern Research.

Dronfield, J. (1993) 'Ways of seeing, ways of telling: Irish passage tomb art, style and the universality of vision', in M. Lorblanchet and P.G. Bahn (eds) *Rock Art Studies: The Past Stylistic Era, or where do we go from here?* Oxford: Oxbow Monograph 35, 179–93.

—— (1995) 'Migraine, light and hallucinogens: the neurocognitive basis of Irish Megalithic art', *Oxford Journal of Archaeology* 14,3: 261–75.

Dubois, T. (1999) *Nordic Religions in the Viking Age*, Philadelphia: University of Pennsylvania Press.

Eliade, M. (1964) *Shamanism: Archaic Techniques of Ecstasy*, New York: Pantheon.

Elliott, R.W.V. (1989) *Runes*, Manchester: Manchester University Press.

Ellis, H.R. (1968) *The Road to Hel*, New York: Greenwood Press.

Epple, C. (1998) 'Coming to terms with Navajo nádleehí: a critique of berdache, "gay", "alternate gender", and "two-spirit"', *American Ethnologist* 25,2: 267–90.

Evans-Pritchard, E.E. (1937) *Witchcraft, Oracles and Magic among the Azande*, Oxford: Clarendon Press.

Favret-Saada, J. (1980) *Deadly Words: Witchcraft in the Bocage*, Cambridge: Cambridge University Press.

Fischer, C. (1999) 'Face to face with your past', in B. Coles, J. Coles and M.S. Jørgensen (eds) *Bog Bodies, Sacred Sites and Wetland Archaeology*, WARP (Wetland Archaeology Research Project) Occasional Paper 12, Exeter: WARP.

Flaherty, G. (1992) *Shamanism and the Eighteenth Century*, Princeton, NJ: Princeton University Press.

Foucault, M. (1980a) *The History of Sexuality*, trans. R. Hurley, New York: Vintage Books.

—— (1980b) *Herculine Barbin: Being the Recently Discovered Memoirs of a Nineteenth-Century French Hermaphrodite*, trans. R. McDougall, New York: Pantheon.

Fridman, E.J.N. (1999). 'Buryat shamanism: home and hearth – a territorialism of the spirit', *Anthopology of Consciousness* 10,4, 45–56.

Fries, J. (1996) *Seidways*, Oxford: Mandrake.

Glob, P.V. (1969) *The Bog People: Iron Age Man Preserved*, trans. R. Bruce-Mitford, London: Faber and Faber.

Glosecki, S.O. (1986) 'Wolf dancers and whispering beasts: shamanic motifs from Sutton Hoo?', *Mankind Quarterly* 26: 305–19.

Goodman, F.D. (1990) *Where the Spirits Ride the Wind: Trance Journeys and Other Ecstatic Experiences*, Bloomington: Indiana University Press.

——— (1999) 'Ritual body postures, channeling, and the ecstatic body trance', *Anthropology of Consciousness* 10: 54–9.

Gordon, E.V. (1957) *Introduction to Old Norse*, revised edition, by A.R. Taylor, Oxford: Clarendon Press.

Goulet, J.G. (1994) 'Dreams and visions in other life-worlds', in D.E. Young and J.G. Goulet (eds) *Being Changed by Cross-Cultural Encounters: the Anthropology of Extraordinary Experience*, Peterborough, Ontario: Broadview Press.

Goulet, J.G. and Young, D. (1994) 'Theoretical and methodological issues', in D.E. Young and J.G. Goulet (eds) *Being Changed by Cross-Cultural Encounters: The Anthropology of Extraordinary Experience*, Peterborough, Ontario: Broadview Press.

Green, M.J. (1996) *Celtic Art: Reading the Messages*, London: Weidenfield and Nicholson.

Greene, S. (1998) 'The shaman's needle: development, shamanic agency, and intermedicality in Aguarina Lands, Peru', *American Ethnologist* 25,4: 634–58.

Greenwood, S. (2000) *Magic, Witchcraft, and the Otherworld: an Anthropology*, Oxford: Berg.

Grundy, S.S. (1995) 'The Cult of Oðinn, God of Death', Ph.D. Thesis, University of Cambridge.

——— (1996) 'Freyja and Frigg', in S. Billington and M. Green (eds) *The Concept of the Goddess*, London: Routledge.

Guédon, M.F. (1994) 'Dene ways and the ethnographer's culture', in D.E. Young and J.G. Goulet (eds) *Being Changed by Cross-Cultural Encounters: the Anthropology of Extraordinary Experience*, Peterborough, Ontario: Broadview Press.

Gundarsson, K. (1994) 'Spae-Craft, seidhr and shamanism, part I – spae', *Idunna: a Journal of Northern Tradition* 25: 33–6.

——— (1995) 'Spae-Craft, seidhr and shamanism, part II – seidhr', *Idunna: a Journal of Northern Tradition* 26: 7–12.

Gyrus (n.d.) 'Aspects of Shamanism'. Online: Available: http://home.freeuk.net/rooted/aoshaman.html (1 January 2001).

Halperin, D.M. (1995) *Saint Foucault: Towards a Gay Hagiography*, Oxford: Oxford University Press.

Haraway, D. (1988) 'Situated knowledges: the science question in Feminism and the privilege of partial perspective', *Feminist Studies* 14,3: 575–99.

Harner, M. (1980) *The Way of the Shaman*, New York: Bantam Books.

Harvey, G. (1997) *Listening People, Speaking Earth: Contemporary Paganism*, London: C. Hurst & Co.

Harwood, A. (1970) *Witchcraft, Sorcery and Social Categories among the Safwa*, London: Oxford University Press for the International African Institute.

Hastrup, K. (1985) *Culture and History in Medieval Iceland : an Anthropological Analysis of Structure and Change*, Oxford and Toronto: Oxford University Press.

—— (1990) 'Iceland: sorcerers and Paganism,' in B. Ankarloo and G. Henningsen (eds) *Early Modern European Witchcraft: Centres and Peripheries*, Oxford: Clarendon Press.

—— (1996) *A Passage to Anthropology: Between Experience and Theory*, London: Routledge.

Heinze, R.I. (1991) *Shamans of the 20th Century*, New York: Irvington.

Herdt, G. (1996) 'Introduction', in G. Herdt (ed.) *Third Sex, Third Gender: Beyond Sexual Dimorphism in Culture and History*, New York: Zone Books..

Hjørungdal, T. (1989) 'Noen aspekter på tolkning av gravgods i eldre jernalder: kan gravgods belyse kult?' In L. Larsson, L. and B. Wyszomirska (eds) *Arkeologi och religion. Rapport från arkeologidagarna 16–18 januari 1989*, University of Lund, Institute of Archaeology, Report Series No. 34, 99–106.

Hollander, L. (trans.) (1972) *Víga-Glúms saga*, New York: Twayne Publishers.

—— (trans.) (1962) *The Poetic Edda*, Austin, Texas: University of Texas Press.

Hoppál, M. (1987) 'Shamanism: an archaic and/or recent belief system', in S. Nicholson (ed.) *Shamanism: An Expanded View of Reality*, Wheaton, IL.: Quest/The Theosophical Publishing House.

Horwitz, J. (n.d.) 'The Absence of "Performance" in the Shamanic Rite: Shamanic Rites Seen from a Shamanic Perspective II'. Online: Available: http://www.snail.dircon.co.uk/SCSS/Articles/Rites2.htm (1 January 2001).

Høst, A. (n.d.) 'Exploring seidhr: a practical study of the seidhr ritual', Scandinavian Center for Shamanic Studies: forthcoming in *Religious Practises and Beliefs in the North Atlantic Area*, Center for North Atlantic Studies, Århus University.

Hultkrantz, Å. (1992). 'Aspects of Saami (Lapp) shamanism', in M. Hoppál and J. Pentikäinen (eds) *Northern Religions and Shamanism*, Budapest: Akadémiai Kiadó, and Helsinki: Finnish Literary Society.

—— (1994) 'Religion and environment among the Saami: an ecological study', in T. Irimoto and T. Yamada (eds) *Circumpolar Religion and Ecology: An Anthropology of the North*, Tokyo: University of Tokyo Press, 347–74.

Jakobsen, M.D. (1999) *Shamanism: Traditional and Contemporary Approaches to the Mastery of Spirits and Healing*, New York and Oxford: Berghahn Books.

Jesch, J. (1991) *Women in the Viking Age*, Woodbridge: Boydell Press.

Jochens, J. (1989) 'Völuspá: Matrix of Norse Womanhood', *Journal of English and Germanic Philology* 88,3: 345–62.

——— (1995) *Women in Old Norse Society*, Ithaca: Cornell University Press, 1995.

——— (1996) *Old Norse Images of Women*, Philadelphia: University of Pennsylvania Press.

Jones, G. (trans.) (1961) *Eirik the Red and Other Icelandic Sagas*, Oxford: Oxford University Press.

——— (trans.) (1973) *The Vatnsdalers' Saga*, Princeton: Princeton University Press.

——— (1984) *A History of the Vikings*, revised edition, Oxford: Oxford University Press.

Kapferer, B. (1997) *The Feast of the Sorcerer: Practices of Consciousness and Power*, Chicago: Chicago University Press.

Kelly, K. (ed.) (1999a) *Spirit Talk*, 9. Summer 1999 issue on Seiðr.

——— (1999b) 'Close to Nature: an interview with Annette Høst', *Spirit Talk*, 9.

King, A.D. (1999) 'Soul suckers: vampiric shamans in Northern Kamchatka, Russia', *Anthropology of Consciousness* 10,4: 59–68.

Kodratoff, Y. (1998) *Nordic Magic Healing*, Paris: Kodratoff.

Kuhn, H. and Neckel, G. (eds) (1962) *Edda: Die Lieder des Codex Regius (VI. Text)*, Heidelberg: Carl Winter.

Laing, S. (trans.) (1906) *The Heimskringla: A History of the Norse Kings*, London: Norroena Society.

Larner, C. (1981) *Enemies of God: The Witch-hunt in Scotland*, Baltimore, MD: Johns Hopkins University Press.

Larrington, C. (trans.) (1996) *The Poetic Edda*, World's Classics, Oxford: Oxford University Press.

Leary, T. (1968) *The Politics of Ecstasy*, New York: Putnam's Sons.

Leary, T, Metzner, R. and Allpert, R. (1964/1983) *The Psychedelic Experience*, Secaucus, NJ: Citadel Press.

Leto, S. (2000) 'Magical potions: entheogenic themes in Scandinavian mythology', *Shaman's Drum* 54: 55–65.

Lewis, I.M. (1989) *Ecstatic Religion: A Study of Shamanism and Spirit Possession*, 2nd edn. London and New York: Routledge.

Lindquist, G. (1997) *Shamanic Performances on the Urban Scene: Neo-Shamanism in Contemporary Sweden*, Stockholm: Stockholm Studies in Social Anthropology.

Linzie, W. (1995) 'Interview with the shaman', *Idunna: a Journal of Northern Tradition* 26: 13–19.

—— (n.d.) 'The Seiðman Rants'. Online. Available HTTP: http://www.angelfire.com/nm/seidhman (1 January 2001).

Lönnroth, L. (1976) *Njáls saga: A Critical Introduction*, Berkeley: University of California Press.

MacLellan, G. (1999) *Shamanism*, London: Piatkus.

Magnusson, M. (1975) 'Introduction', in M. Magnusson and H. Pálsson, trans. *Njal's Saga*, Harmondsworth: Penguin.

Magnusson, M. and Pálsson, H. trans. (1960) *Njal's Saga*, Harmondsworth: Penguin.

Marcus, G. (1998) *Ethnography through Thick and Thin*, Princeton: Princeton University Press.

—— (1999) 'Critical anthropology now: an introduction', in G. Marcus (ed.) *Critical Anthropology Now: Unexpected Contexts, Shifting Constituencies, Changing Agendas*, Santa Fe, NM: School of American Research Press.

Markale, J. (1986) *Women of the Celts*, Rochester, Vermont: Inner Traditions International.

Matthews, C. (1995) *Singing the Soul Back Home*, Shaftesbury: Element.

Matthews, J. (1991) *The Celtic Shaman*, Shaftesbury: Element.

Merkur, D. (1992) *Becoming Half Hidden: Shamanism and Initiation among the Inuit*, New York and London: Garland.

Meulengracht Sørenson, P. (1983) *The Unmanly Man: Concepts of Sexual Defamation in Early Northern Society*, trans. J. Turville-Petre, Odense: Odense University Press.

Monsen, E. (trans.) (1932) *Heimskringla, or The Lives of the Norse Kings, by Snorre Sturlason*, Cambridge: W. Heffer & Sons Ltd.

Morris, K. (1991) *Sorceress or Witch? The Image of Gender in Medieval Iceland and Northern Europe*, Lanham, MD: University Press of America, Inc.

Näsström, B.M. (1996a) 'Freyja, a Goddess with many names', in S. Billington and M. Green (eds) *The Concept of the Goddess*, London: Routledge.

—— (1996b) *Freyja: Great Goddess of the North*, Lund Series in Studies of Religion, #5, Philadelphia: Coronet.

Netútgáfan (n.d.) Online: Available: http://www.snerpa.is/net/index.html (1 January 2001).

Noel, D.C. (1997) *The Soul of Shamanism: Western Fantasies, Imaginal Realities*, New York: Continuum.

Nordal, S. (1978) *Völuspá*, trans. B.S. Benedikz and J. McKinnell, Durham: Durham and St. Andrews Medieval Texts, number 1.

Oosten, J.G. (1984) 'The Diary of Therkel Mathiassen, 1922–1922', in M. Hoppál (ed.) *Shamanism in Eurasia*, Göttingen: Edition Herodot, vol. 2: 377–90.

Paxson, D. (n.d.) 'The return of the Völva', Online: Available: http://www.hrafnar.org/seidh/seidh.html (13 August 2001).

—— (in prep.) 'Trance journeying in the Norse tradition'. Training materials for Seidworkers.

Pentikäinen, J. (1984) 'The Sámi shaman – mediator between man and universe', in M. Hoppál (ed.) *Shamanism in Eurasia*, Göttingen: Edition Herodot, vol. 1: 125–48.

—— (1994) 'Shamanism as the expression of Northern identity' in T. Irimoto and T. Yamada (eds) *Circumpolar Religion and Ecology: An Anthropology of the North*, Tokyo: University of Tokyo Press, 375–401.

—— (1998) 'The Shamans and Shamanism', in J. Pentikäinen, T. Jaatinen, I. Lehtinen and M.R. Saloniemi (eds) *Shamans*, Tampere, Finland: Tampere Museums Publications 95, 29–49.

Price, N. S. (in press) *The Viking Way: Religion and War in the Later Iron Age of Scandinavia*, Uppsala: Uppsala University Press.

—— (2000 and forthcoming) 'The archaeology of Seiðr: Circumpolar traditions in Viking Pre-Christian religion', *Viking Millennium Symposium*, L'Anse aux Meadows, Newfoundland, September 2000. Forthcoming in *Proceedings of the Viking Millennium Symposium*.

Priest, P.O. (1999) Letter to the editor. *The Pomegranate* 10:3.

Quinn, J. (1998) '"Ok verðr henni ljóð á munni" – Eddic Prophecy in the fornaldarsögur', *Alvíssmál* 8: 29–50.

Ripinsky-Naxon, M. (1993) *The Nature of Shamanism. Substance and Function of a Religious Metaphor*, Albany, NY: State University of New York Press.

Rodriguez, L.J. (1993) *Anglo-Saxon Verse Charms, Maxims and Heroic Legends*, Pinner: Anglo-Saxon Books.

Roscoe, W. (1991) *The Zuni Man-Woman*, Albuquerque: University of New Mexico Press.

—— (1996) 'How to become a berdache', in G. Herdt (ed.) *Third Sex, Third Gender: Beyond Sexual Dimorphism in Culture & History*, New York: Zone Books, 329–72.

—— (1998) *Changing Ones: Third and Fourth Genders in Native North America*, New York: St. Martin's Press.

Rydberg, V. (1906) *Teutonic Mythology: Gods and Goddesses of the Northland*, vols 1–3, London and New York: Norroena Society.

Saladin d'Anglure, B. (1992) 'Rethinking Inuit Shamanism through the concept of "third gender"', in M. Hoppál and J. Pentikäinen (eds) *Northern Religions and Shamanism*, Budapest: Akadémiai Kiadó, and Helsinki: Finnish Literature Society.

Salmond, A. (2000) 'Maori and modernity: Ruatara's dying', in A.P. Cohen (ed.) *Signifying Identities*, London: Routledge.

Schach, P. (1983) 'Some thoughts on Völuspá', in R.J. Glendinning and H. Bessason (eds) *Edda: A Collection of Essays*, Winnipeg: University of Manitoba Press.

Schieffelin, E. (1996) 'On failure in performance: throwing the medium out of the séance', in C. Laderman and M. Roseman (eds) *The Performance of Healing*, London: Routledge, 59–90.

Schultes, R.E. and Hofmann, A. (1992) *Plants of the Gods: Their Sacred, Healing and Hallucinogenic Powers*, Rochester, Vermont: Healing Arts Press.

Shirokogorov, S.M. (1935) *Psychomental Complex of the Tungus*, London: Kegan Paul, Trench, Trubner & Co.

Sigurðsson, G. (ed.) (1998) *Eddukvæði*, Reykjavík: Mál og menning.

Siikala, A.L. (1992) 'Singing of incantations in Nordic tradition', in A.L. Siikala and M. Hoppál (eds) *Studies on Shamanism*, Helsinki: Finnish Anthropological Society, and Budapest: Akadémiai Kiadó, 68–78.

Smith, D.E. (1987) *The Everyday World as Problematic*, Toronto: University of Toronto Press.

Solli, B. (1999a) 'Odin the *queer*? On *ergi* and shamanism in Norse mythology', in A. Gustafsson and H. Karlsson (eds) *Gylfer och arkeologiska rum – en vänbok till Jarl Nordblach*, Gotarc Series A vol. 3, Göteborg: University of Göteborg, 341–49.

—— (1999b) '"Holy white stones". Remains of fertility cult in Norway', in U. von Freeden, U. Koch and A. Wieczorek (eds) *Volker an Nord- and Ostsee und die Franken,* Aktens des 48, Sachsensymposiums in Mannheim vom 7. bis 11. September 1997, 99–106.

Storms, G. (1948) *Anglo-Saxon Magic*, The Hague: Martinus Nijhoff (rpt. Folcroft Library Editions, 1975).

Strmiska, M. (2000) 'Ásatrú in Iceland: The Rebirth of Nordic Paganism?' *Nova Religio* 4,1: 106–32.

Ström, F. (1974) *Níð, Ergi and Old Norse Moral Attitudes*, London: Viking Society for Northern Research.

Strömbäck, D. (1935) *Sejd: Textstudier I nordisk religionshistorie*, Stockholm: Hugo Gebers Förlag.

Swatos, W. and Gissurarson, L.R. (1996) *Icelandic Spiritualism: Mediumship and Modernity in Iceland*, Piscataway, NJ: Transaction Publishers.

Tambiah, S. J. (1990) *Magic, Science, Religion, and the Scope of Rationality*, Cambridge: Cambridge University Press.

Taussig, M. (1987) *Shamanism, Colonialism and the Wild Man: A Study in Terror and Healing*, Chicago: University of Chicago Press.

Taylor, C. (1971) 'Interpretation and the Sciences of Man.' *Review of Metaphysics* 25. (Reprinted in E. Bredo and W. Feinberg (eds) (1982) *Knowledge and Values in Social and Educational Research*, Philadelphia, Temple University Press.

Thompson, B. (1998) '"Cliff Richard is a Pagan," an interview with Julian Cope', *The Independent Weekend Review*, 24 October, p. 12.

Turner, E. (1994) 'A visible spirit form in Zambia', in D.E. Young and

J.G. Goulet (eds) *Being Changed by Cross-Cultural Encounters: The Anthropology of Extraordinary Experience*, Peterborough, Ontario: Broadview Press.

Venn, C. (1984) 'The subject of psychology', in J. Henriques *et al.* (eds) *Changing the Subject*, London: Methuen.

Vitebsky, P. (1995a) 'From Cosmology to environmentalism: shamanism as local knowledge in a global setting', in: R. Fardon (ed.) *Counterworks: Managing the Diversity of Knowledge*, London: Routledge, 182–203.

—— (1995b) *The Shaman,* London: Macmillan.

Wallis, R.J. (1999a) 'Altered states, conflicting cultures: shamans, neo-shamans and Academics', *Anthropology of Consciousness* 10,2: 41–9.

—— (1999b) 'Autoarchaeology and neo-shamanism: the socio-politics of ecstasy', unpublished Ph.D. Thesis, University of Southampton.

—— (2000) 'Queer shamans: autoarchaeology and neo-shamanism', *World Archaeology* 32,2: 252–63.

—— (forthcoming, a) *Neo-shamanism: Wannabe Indians, Heathen Ecstasies and Druidic Archaeologies*, London: Routledge.

—— (forthcoming, b) 'Return to the source: neo-shamanism and shamanism in Central Asia and Siberia', in: T.A. Dowson, M.M. Kosko and A. Rozwadowski (eds) *Rock Art, Shamanism and Central Asia: Discussions of Relations*, International Rock Art Monographs 2. Series Editor: T.A. Dowson, Oxford: British Archaeological Reports.

Wasson, R.G. (1971) *Soma, Divine Mushroom of Immortality*, New York: Harcourt Brace Jovanovich.

Wilson, C.R. (1994) 'Seeing they see not', in D.E. Young and J.G. Goulet (eds) *Being Changed by Cross-Cultural Encounters: the Anthropology of Extraordinary Experience*, Peterborough, Ontario: Broadview Press.

Winch, P. (1958) *The Idea of a Social Science*, London: Routledge and Kegan Paul. Selected extracts reprinted in E. Bredo and W. Feinberg (eds) (1982) *Knowledge and Values in Social and Educational Research*, Philadelphia: Temple University Press.

Young, D.E. and J.G. Goulet (eds) (1994) *Being Changed by Cross-Cultural Encounters: The Anthropology of Extraordinary Experience*, Peterborough, Ontario: Broadview Press.

Zoëga, G.T. (1910) *A Concise Dictionary of Old Icelandic*, Oxford: Clarendon Press.

Index